you will be convinced, like I am, that the SBC must once again 'fuel the fire' and make evangelism a priority."

—*Fred Luter, senior pastor, Franklin Avenue Baptist Church, New Orleans, LA, and former president, Southern Baptist Convention*

"For decades, Dr. Chuck Kelley has been a leading scholar and practitioner of evangelism in both the academy and our churches. No one matches the quality and accuracy of his research and analysis regarding evangelism among Southern Baptists. In *Fuel the Fire,* Dr. Kelley assures Southern Baptists that the evangelistic successes of their past can be recovered. Any pastor, congregant, or student seeking an honest assessment of the history and current state of Southern Baptist evangelism must read this volume. As one who longs for the fires of evangelism to burn brightly and to spread quickly again, I sincerely believe God will use this book to *fuel those fires.*"

—*Matt Queen, L. R. Scarborough Chair of Evangelism, associate professor of evangelism, Southwestern Baptist Theological Seminary*

"We live in a day of instant everything, from oatmeal to information. In such a day, it's easy to focus on the immediate and the urgent while forgetting the lessons from the past. My friend, Chuck Kelley, offers Southern Baptists a remarkable survey and analysis of evangelism throughout our history. Lessons from history help us to avoid making the same mistakes over and over. History encourages us by reminding us of times when the gospel went forth with great impact. History convicts us the same way by showing us we can do better. Read this, learn from it, and pray to the Lord of the Harvest to bring a revival of evangelistic fervor and impact today!"

—*Alvin L. Reid, Bailey Smith Chair of Evangelism, senior professor of evangelism and student ministry, Southeastern Baptist Theological Seminary*

"This book is a critical read for all who are determined to reach our world for Christ. Every believer ought to revisit the biblical mandates for evangelism seen so clearly in yesterday's world but so desperately needed today. What a great re-read of a powerful reminder of the things that matter to all who see the fields which are ripe unto harvest!"

—*Don Wilton, senior pastor, First Baptist Church, Spartanburg, SC, and president, The Encouraging Word Television Ministry*

FUEL
THE FIRE

FUEL
THE FIRE

Lessons from the History of
Southern Baptist Evangelism

Charles S. Kelley Jr.

Series Editors
Paige Patterson & Jason G. Duesing

A TREASURY OF BAPTIST THEOLOGY

ACADEMIC

NASHVILLE, TENNESSEE

Fuel the Fire
Copyright © 2018 by Charles Kelley

Published by B&H Academic
Nashville, Tennessee

ISBN: 978-1-5359-0823-8

Dewey Decimal Classification: 286.132

Subject Heading: SOUTHERN BAPTIST CONVENTION \ SOUTHERN
BAPTISTS \ EVANGELISTIC WORK

Unless otherwise indicated, Scripture quotations are taken from the New King
James Version®. Copyright © 1982 by Thomas Nelson. Used by permission. All
rights reserved.

The web addresses referenced in this book were live and correct at the time of
the book's publication but may be subject to change.

Some material previously published in *How Did They Do It?*, ©1993, Insight
Press. Used by Permission.

Printed in the United States of America
1 2 3 4 5 6 7 8 9 10 VP 23 22 21 20 19 18

Contents

Dedication

To
Rhonda

For
the glory of God
and
the building up of the Church

From
a soul given life by God's illustration
of
godly parents

Acknowledgments

In life there are no solo acts. We are who we are, and we do what we do because of the people in our lives. Two men fueled the fire of evangelism in me. My brother-in-law, Dr. Paige Patterson, modeled personal evangelism for me and taught me how to share my faith as I was growing up. Passion for reaching the lost drives all that he has done in his extraordinary life. I am also grateful he gave me the opportunity to do this project. Rev. Bob Harrington, former Chaplain of Bourbon Street and my father-in-law, taught me that boldness as a witness comes from obedience, not the absence of fear. I have never known or studied a more effective communicator of the gospel and personal soul-winner.

My oldest sister, Dr. Dorothy Patterson, has this crazy idea that her brother can write and has something significant to say. Her confidence and her gentle encouragement are two of many reasons for which I am grateful to her.

Without the generosity of Insight Press, this volume would not have been possible. Thank you for your permission to revise my earlier work: *How Did They Do It?* Waylon Bailey and Fisher Humphreys gave me my first opportunity to write on Southern Baptist evangelism.

Many thanks to Dr. Bill Day, Professor of Evangelism and Church Health at New Orleans Baptist Theological Seminary (NOBTS), who is a phenomenal researcher with a passion for evangelism. I have learned so much in our many collaborative investigations. His chart on the total number of SBC churches and the total number of baptisms recorded by those churches is the most stunning, revealing snapshot of the SBC I have ever seen. At a crucial time, NOBTS doctoral student Tim Walker pulled together some important, awkwardly located source material, for which I am most appreciative.

Members of the President's Team at NOBTS make all things possible for me. Robbin Phelps does more than I ever know to keep my life organized, solve problems, and help me find writing time. A better executive assistant does not exist. Kathrin White did a great deal of typing, much of it as unglamorous as it gets, always in the midst of a sea of other projects. Thank you for making it look easy so that I don't feel as guilty as I should about all I expect. Chris Shaffer searches every day for details to manage on my behalf as Assistant to the President. You did a terrific job of making some things happen for me in the process of this project. Thank you so much. It is an honor to work with each of you!

Only an author can fully appreciate the essential contributions of a publisher and editorial team. To put it plainly, the professionals at B&H Academic made this a better book. My deepest thanks to Jim Baird for making this project happen on a tight timeline. The work of Audrey Greeson, Sarah Landers, and Tamra Hernandez was phenomenal. Any mistakes are mine alone. Thanks team for a terrific job!

For my Beloved, Dr. Rhonda H. Kelley, language completely fails me. Thank you for typing the final manuscript, nudging and encouraging, offering feedback and creative insight, knowing when to leave me lost in thought on this project and when to pull me into reality, and so much more. It is very humbling to have a woman of your intelligence and skill give yourself so completely to my projects while managing all of yours plus our household and family as well. When I say thank you, hear the ocean of gratitude crammed inside those two simple words.

Abbreviations

BF&M	*Baptist Faith and Message*
BWR	Building Witnessing Relationships
CP	Cooperative Program
CWT	Continuing Witness Training
EE	Evangelism Explosion
FMB	Foreign Mission Board
HMB	Home Mission Board
IMB	International Mission Board
LES	Lay Evangelism School
NAMB	North American Mission Board
NOBTS	New Orleans Baptist Theological Seminary
SBC	Southern Baptist Convention
TELL	Training for Evangelistic Lifestyle and Leadership
VBS	Vacation Bible School

A Treasury of Baptist Theology

B aptists have always been grateful for the contributions of great Christians from every era. Where would we be without Athanasius's *The Incarnation of the Son of God,* Augustine's *Confessions*, or the multiplied books of the Reformers who laid the foundations for the Reformation? And as much as we look forward to the return of Christ and a true ecumenism, adjudicated by none other than the Lord from heaven, we must until then be faithful in the expression of the truth as we know it.

The *Treasury of Baptist Theology* represents an effort to do exactly that. This series of more than 30 volumes written by notable Baptist theologians from a number of different institutions and churches reflects the understanding of holy Scripture as Baptists have grasped it. There is diversity among authors, including Asian, German, and French theologians, as well as several Baptist women. Each author is writing from a distinctively Baptist perspective.

As you begin to read these volumes, our prayer to God is that He will use them to encourage faithfulness from all in delivering the New Testament witness to our own era. The concept of a believer's church—that is, a church made up of only twice-born men and women who have witnessed their faith through the covenant of believer's baptism and who have committed themselves wholly to the fulfillment of the Great Commission as given by our Lord in Matt 28:18–20—will hopefully incline the hearts of all to the Savior and to His program of witness to the nations. Along the way, the plea for religious liberty will also be made apparent, together with the teachings on those doctrines where there is agreement across denominational lines, such as Christology, the Trinity, and other significant foundational doctrines. Volumes on evangelism, apologetics, and God's purposes for the home will also be among those coming from this series.

So begin your journey with us, and hear the significant witness of today's Baptist theologians. And may God help us to embrace these doctrines with the same thoroughness and commitment as those in the generations who have gone before.

Paige Patterson, President
Southwestern Baptist Theological Seminary
Fort Worth, Texas

PREFACE

Fuel the Fire

F*uel the Fire: Lessons from the History of Southern Baptist Evangelism* is a critical volume in the Treasury of Baptist Theology. Drawing on decades of research and experience as a Southern Baptist, the author identifies the greatest contributions of Southern Baptists to the evangelical world and beyond. Chuck Kelley has served as the president of New Orleans Baptist Theological Seminary for more than 20 years. As a popular preacher in churches of all sizes throughout the US, he is also a prolific witness to the lost. Through his research and evaluation of the fruit of Baptists' historic evangelistic efforts, namely in conversions and baptisms, he documents God's profound blessings on our denomination. Kelley goes even further, however, and in this priceless volume joins past and future, creating an outline for how Baptists can recover the blessings of God.

Paige Patterson
Fort Worth, Texas

Introduction

Building and Dismantling Greatness:
A Case Study in the Growth and
Decline of SBC Evangelism

In the twentieth century, the Southern Baptist Convention (SBC) became the largest Protestant denomination in the nation. From a rural, regional base in the South, the SBC moved into all 50 states, developed the greatest missions funding strategy in the history of American Christianity, fielded one of the largest missionary forces of the century, became the nation's largest publisher of Christian literature, grew six of the largest seminaries in the world, and in one decade doubled the number of baptisms recorded annually by its churches. In so doing, it set the bar for size, influence, and fruitfulness at an unprecedented level for Protestant churches in America.

Time passed, and with the passage of time came change. With change came a lessening of Southern Baptist statistical greatness. As I write these words, the SBC is in year 16 of the longest decline in baptisms in its history. For most of the last decade, the number of Southern Baptists, the number of Southern Baptists attending worship, and the number of Southern Baptists attending small groups (Sunday School classes, Bible studies, etc.) has steadily declined. For the first time in anyone's memory, the Convention's International Mission Board (IMB) reduced the number of missionaries on the field dramatically because their budget could not sustain the number of those commissioned and serving among the nations of the world. The focus is shifting from multiplying the number of career missionaries to multiplying the number of volunteers working with a smaller number of career missionaries.

These events are not unexpected, for the common story of American church families, especially those having a period of extensive growth, can be summed up in three words: growth, plateau, and decline. That is the Southern Baptist story in a nutshell. Southern Baptists experienced enormous growth. For a number of years, they were on a statistical plateau. Now for more than a decade, their numerical decline is clear. The depth and permanence of this emerging decline could be reversed, but the present growth of decline is real.

Why is this decline happening? Although not uncommon in American churches, what is driving these downward trends in Southern Baptist life? To acknowledge the beginning of decline is very difficult for those immersed in a denominational culture rooted in the inevitability of growth and expansion. The reality of Southern Baptist decline is too well documented to ignore, and it must be acknowledged before it can be addressed.

What This Study Is Not

Be aware of what this study is not! It is not exhaustive, identifying every factor contributing to the growth of decline in Southern Baptist life. It is not definitive, offering the only possible explanation for what is happening. It is not complete, providing all the necessary data to understand the issues. It is not critical, seeking to find out what Southern Baptists are doing wrong. In point of fact, there is no lack of wisdom or moral failure required for denominational decline. Churches and pastors can do all or many of the right things and still be unfruitful. For the record, I know this study is not inerrant. I could be wrong on some important points. Having described what this study is not, how do I describe what it is?

These are the personal observations of an informed Southern Baptist. I am a Southern Baptist through and through, with a very strong, positive sense of denominational identity. I may have blind spots of which I am unaware. But, I am not just any Southern Baptist. I am a professional scholar who has spent his adult life studying, writing about, and teaching evangelism in Southern Baptist life. I am a seminary president, itinerant preacher, and evangelist. I have been in nearly every size and kind of church Southern Baptists have, and I am continually moving among them, not often in the same church two weeks in a row. I am connected to overlapping networks representing many facets of the SBC, from the mainstream to the fringe and all points in between. Nevertheless, my experience is not complete. The Convention is far too diverse for any one person to have a complete experience of SBC churches. Although my experience is not complete, it is extensive. I was also a near witness to the "glory days" of Southern Baptist evangelism and growth as well as part of the scene during the years of plateau and early decline. Take all of my insights and generalizations with a grain of salt, but do consider them thoughtfully. They are from an informed observer with wide Southern Baptist experience.

The simplest possible description of my purpose is this: I intend this book to be a conversation starter. The style is popular, not formal or academic, because I want any interested Southern Baptist to be able to read it quickly and enter into a conversation on the issues. Because this is not a formal academic treatise, I have not collected here the data charts and footnotes to "prove" my points, but I hope what I say will stimulate serious research and discussion. There is much our students, scholars, and leaders need to do to extend and enhance the discussion. Clearly a new era has dawned in the Southern Baptist story. How our churches deal with the present circumstances will have profound implications for our Great Commission impact in the future. The puzzle to be solved is the future, but perhaps some clues on how to solve that puzzle can be found in understanding our past. Here, then, is the purpose of this project: Seek to understand the present by exploring our past in order to provide hope and counsel for our future.

How Did We Do It?

The SBC achieved its remarkable growth by doing what no other American church family had ever succeeded in doing on so large a scale—engaging completely autonomous congregations in a deeply rooted and broadly based strategic plan that combined intentional evangelism and comprehensive discipleship as the twin focal points of normal congregational life. This strategic plan was so deeply rooted and so broadly based that it was implemented in churches of every size and type in every region of the country. It continued functioning through generations of leadership changes, with or without a pastor in place, in happy churches and troubled churches, across every demographic setting. It was continually tweaked by churches at the congregational level and by denominational staff at the state and national levels, but for decades it remained remarkably consistent as a strategic plan widely embraced by the ministers and laity of nearly every type of SBC congregation. This strategic plan for evangelism and discipleship, implemented through voluntary cooperation on a massive scale, drove SBC growth. To put it another way: The SBC transformed thousands of diverse, independent, autonomous (and mostly small) churches into a fully functioning team of churches implementing a commonly understood game plan in accordance with a widely accepted playbook, without intruding on the independence or autonomy of those churches.

Go back to the preceding paragraph, read it again slowly, and think about it. There was a cooperative strategic plan for evangelism and discipleship fully and freely embraced and implemented by nearly all the denomination's completely autonomous churches. That plan was so well understood and so widely embraced by both pastoral and lay leadership that it continued to function through multiple generations of leadership in healthy churches, struggling churches, and churches in transition across all regions of the country and all demographic settings. This cooperative strategic plan could be adjusted at any time for any reason by any congregation without disrupting the core elements of the plan or interrupting the cooperative implementation of the plan by nearly all SBC churches. To quote an ancient Hebrew expression: "Wow!" The combination of the effectiveness of the plan and its near universal implementation across the nation through multiple generations of both lay and ministerial leaders drove the SBC's phenomenal growth into the nation's largest Protestant denomination.

Here is the recap so far. The story of the Southern Baptist Convention can be summarized in three words—*growth*, *plateau*, and *decline*. The driving force behind the growth was a widely embraced strategic plan combining intentional evangelism and comprehensive discipleship as the twin focal points of normal church life. The passage of time unraveled that strategic plan, opening the door for the growth of decline.

The Disclaimers

I must make four regrettable admissions. First, time and space do not allow me to tell the story of the growth and decline of the strategic plan for discipleship in Southern Baptist life. The discipleship story is every bit as remarkable as the story of SBC evangelism. If anything, the approach of the Convention to discipleship was even more aggressive than its approach to evangelism. The relationship between the two was rarely noted or appreciated, but the Convention's evangelistic decline was preceded by a decline in the level of engagement in discipleship. I will comment on the relationship between the two, but the full story of SBC discipleship will have to wait for another day.

Second, time and space do not allow an explanation of the role of the Cooperative Program (CP) in the story of Southern Baptist evangelism. I am unaware of any funding strategy among American church families that can match the impact CP has had on the work of Southern Baptists. CP is a funding strategy that relies upon SBC churches setting aside some portion of weekly tithes and offerings to fund the work of their respective state Baptist Conventions and the national and international ministries of the national Southern Baptist Convention. The amount given by each church is voluntary. It normally comes from a church's weekly offerings, not a special annual offering. The distribution process is so efficient that Convention entities normally receive their portion of CP income *every week*. CP made possible the development of an evangelism structure and culture in some very interesting ways. Changes in the present use of CP appear to be a factor in the emerging decline in some unexpected ways. However, that aspect of this story is too complex for the size and scope of this volume.

Third, the tragic defense of slavery was involved in the creation of the Southern Baptist Convention. That tragedy was compounded by a number of other sinful decisions on racial issues by the SBC and many of its churches, particularly regarding African-Americans. Thankfully, the SBC has issued a formal apology for this part of our story, and there are many positive indicators that the SBC and its churches are finally moving in the right direction, rejecting racism and taking specific steps to be more ethnically diverse. The unanimous election of Dr. Fred Luter Jr., in 2012, as the first African-American president of the Southern Baptist Convention was one of my most cherished Convention moments. These issues are important, but beyond the focus of this book. Southern Baptist evangelism will be the sole subject of this book.

One final disclaimer remains. From their earliest beginnings, Southern Baptists have given much attention to church planting. Reaching a community requires having a church to address the people and needs of that community. The focus of this book is the work of the SBC's existing churches to help reach the lost in their communities. There is a deep and wide recognition that the SBC needs and wants more churches. That said, church planting is not at a crisis point, as are the attempts by existing churches to reach the lost in their communities. The SBC is steadily growing in the number of churches, but the churches we have are baptizing fewer and fewer converts and engaging fewer and fewer people in worship and Bible study. Given the limitations of this volume, and given the relative health of the church planting efforts of the SBC as opposed to the congregational evangelism efforts of its churches, the story of church planting in and through the SBC will have to be added to the list of things to do another day.

With this explanation of purpose and these disclaimers in mind, the time has come to move into a story that has occupied me for most of my adult life. As I explored the remarkable story of Southern Baptist evangelism in depth, five lessons emerged:

***

Lesson 1   Without a gardener, there can be no garden.

Lesson 2   Old McBaptist needs a farm designed to sow the gospel and reap conversions.

Lesson 3   Theological focus enhances evangelistic engagement.

Lesson 4   When the winds of change are blowing, the adjustments you make will determine the direction you sail.

Lesson 5   The knock of opportunity is useless unless you answer the door.

If this case study intrigues you, read on and join the conversation about the present and the future of SBC churches!

LESSON 1

Without a gardener, there can be no garden.

I once read an interview with a landscape architect telling the story of a client who wanted a low-maintenance garden. As she discussed her proposal with him, he kept asking how much maintenance this feature or that feature would require. He was single, busy, and not very interested in yard work of any sort, but he liked the look of a beautiful garden. In exasperation she finally told him, "Sir, without a gardener, there can be no garden!"

Southern Baptists began with a deep passion for missions but without any assigned responsibility to help churches do evangelism in their communities. In a controversial discussion that involved three annual meetings of the Convention and two different study committees, Southern Baptists called for the creation of a Department of Evangelism in the Home Mission Board. Eventually that decision resulted in the creation of a structure for evangelism, assigning responsibility for it to receive attention at the national, state, association, and local church levels of SBC life. With the creation of that structure, the Convention exploded in growth. Over time, attention given to assisting local churches with their evangelistic responsibility slowly eroded. As the priority of helping churches with their evangelistic ministry faded, so did baptisms. SBC history suggests that at least two questions about evangelism are worth asking. For national and state conventions, who is encouraging and assisting the churches in reaching the lost in their communities? At the local church level, who is developing and driving a strategy for reaching the lost in this community? Here is what happened to teach this lesson.

CHAPTER 1

The Great SBC Evangelism War

A motion from the floor in the 1904 annual meeting of the Southern
Baptist Convention started the action. Perhaps that is not entirely
accurate. Throughout the previous 59 years of Convention history, there
had been several expressions of the evangelistic passion of Southern Baptists. Motions had been made and some actions taken in attempts to reach
the nation with the gospel. Always keen observers of what works, pastors
and other leaders saw evangelistic fruitfulness in other American church
families that they longed to see in their own churches. A slowly growing
feeling arose that there was a missing piece Southern Baptists needed for
greater evangelistic effectiveness. The simmering passions and ongoing
observations came to a head in the motion of a Georgia pastor during an
SBC business session. Convention processes turned that motion and the
controversy it sparked into a defining moment for how Southern Baptists
would go about the work of reaching the nation for Christ.

Early Approaches

In 1845, the first convention proceeded, and the following resolution was
soon adopted:

> "*Resolved*, That for peace and harmony, and in order to accomplish
> the greatest amount of good, and for the maintenance of those
> scriptural principles on which the General Missionary Convention
> of the Baptist denomination of the United States, was originally

formed, it is proper that this Convention at once proceed to organize a Society for the propagation of the Gospel."[1]

Those assembled believed that the unifying passion for Baptists had been
and should continue to be evangelism. They shared a common cultural
heritage; they shared common beliefs and practices; but most of all they
shared a common task—fulfilling the Great Commission of their Lord.

The first expression of that foundational evangelistic passion was
the creation of a Board for Foreign Missions and a Board for Domestic Missions, which became known, respectively, as the Foreign Mission
Board (FMB) and the Home Mission Board (HMB) and later still the
International Mission Board (IMB) and North American Mission Board
(NAMB). The work of the two boards in spreading the gospel to the nation
and world reinforced the identity of Southern Baptists as an evangelistic, mission-minded people. The pressures of financially supporting the
work of those boards continually strengthened the image of the churches
as co-laborers working *together* to share Jesus with the world. Evangelism
was thus a critical factor in encouraging an even stronger denominational
identity. The principle of local church autonomy that has always characterized Southern Baptists was balanced with the recognition that cooperative
ventures could also enhance the productivity of each congregation.

Initial resolutions regarding the Board for Domestic Missions (called
Home Mission Board or HMB) defined its task narrowly. The HMB was
to take measures for "the religious instruction of our colored population"
and to "direct its effective attention to aid the present effort, to establish
the Baptist cause in the city of New Orleans."[2] In addition to these specific charges, the HMB was understood to be responsible for guiding the
denomination in evangelizing the home territory. At this point, the field
of operations for Southern Baptists went from Maryland in the North to
Texas in the South, and from Missouri in the West to Florida in the East.

---

[1] *Proceedings of the Southern Baptist Convention*, Augusta, Georgia (May 8–12, 1845),
13. Digitized text of the Southern Baptist Convention Annuals (1845–2010) is available at
http://digitalcollections.baylor.edu/cdm/landingpage/collection/ml-sbcann.

[2] J. B. Lawrence, *History of the Home Mission Board* (Nashville: Broadman Press,
1958), 29.

In that area, J. B. Lawrence estimated there were only 350,000 Baptists, including 125,000 slaves.

Vast distances and small numbers were only two of the challenges facing the newly formed Board as it attempted to fulfill its purpose. Transportation and communication were slow, making it difficult to establish an identity and sense of kinship among Baptists. As a result, little financial support for the work had been developed. Three men were elected to lead the HMB within its first year. Each resigned soon after his election, adding to the atmosphere of instability. Previously, before the organization of the SBC, while Luther Rice traveled the country building support and raising money for foreign missions on behalf of the General Missionary Convention of the Baptist Denomination in the United States of America, no such voice had yet captivated the hearts of Southern Baptists about the need to evangelize the homeland.

Despite the obstacles, the HMB began by appointing six missionaries in 1846, including one for the city of New Orleans and two for the state of Texas. Most missionaries were appointed as pastors for mission churches or as church planters expected to start a church in an area without Baptist work. Evangelists were appointed as well, but generally the focus was on establishing new churches rather than engaging in evangelistic campaigns. The work grew slowly but steadily until the Civil War caused massive disruption.

Although the period of reconstruction following the Civil War was a difficult time for Southern Baptist work, the concern of Southern Baptists for evangelism was undiminished. In 1866, the Convention instructed the HMB to make evangelism its major work and to promote a comprehensive system of evangelism, including the appointment of evangelists. The resolution appeared to express a desire on the part of some for the Board to expand its methodology of evangelism as the great evangelist D. L. Moody was beginning to make his impact from the Midwest through the Northwest and across the ocean in Great Britain. Whereas many missionary appointees had been church planters, the call was raised for the appointment of some preaching evangelists. This move appears to be the earliest formal indication of the impact that mass evangelism in the form of revivalism would have on Southern Baptist life.

The response of the Board to the call for evangelists simply reaffirmed the emphasis on church planting. The challenge of surviving the aftermath of the Civil War was viewed as a more pressing need then shifting the strategy to enlarge an emphasis on evangelism. The crushing defeat of the South left the churches in desperate condition, and the ministries of the HMB were reduced drastically. The economy collapsed. Religious leaders in the North attempted to confiscate church property in the South. Gradually, however, Southern Baptists and their mission boards began to recover. The missionaries who served as chaplains and worked with the soldiers during the war began helping churches rebuild and planting new work. Debts were paid, budgets were raised, and ministries were expanded. And then it happened: the Great SBC Evangelism War.

The Unexpected Battle

In 1904, Len G. Broughton, a Georgia pastor, raised the issue of the Convention's approach to evangelism. He proposed the following resolution:

> That the Convention appoint a committee of twelve pastors, not members of any Convention Board, to be known as the Committee on Evangelism for the Needy Sections of our Convention Territory;
> That this Committee, in co-operation with the Secretaries of our Boards, shall employ a general evangelist, who shall also be Secretary of the Committee;
> That said evangelist shall, in addition to his evangelistic work, gather statistics, disseminate information and call to his aid such help and helpers as the Committee may approve;
> That the co-operation of the State Boards be secured as far as possible, where work is to be done in needy and destitute fields;
> That the salary of the general evangelist be paid by the three Boards of the Convention, and other expenses, including the salaries of special evangelists, be arranged for by the field or cooperating board;
> That collections be taken at every meeting held by the evangelists for the work of the Evangelistic Committee;

That the Committee also report annually to the Convention.[3]

The resolution marked a significant milestone in Southern Baptist life. The action proposed by Broughton was an attempt to have the denomination accept specific responsibility for the task of calling lost people to Christ, becoming involved in that task with the churches in clear, definite ways. It was also a call for the Convention to receive annual reports on evangelistic progress. As logical as that step may seem to Baptists today, a great storm of controversy erupted and lasted for two years.

After some discussion, the Convention decided not to act on the motion. Instead, a study committee of five persons was appointed to consider the matter and report to the next meeting of the SBC. Broughton was not included on the study committee. The members were Andrew Jackson, Spears Thomas, Milford Riggs, John E. White, T. B. Ray, and W. S. Ryland.

In 1905, the SBC met in Kansas City, Missouri. The report of the Evangelism Study Committee was not given until the afternoon of the fourth day. Committee members felt that the appointment of a permanent evangelism committee and the hiring of a secretary for that committee were inappropriate. Instead, they recommended the formation of another committee to study further the situation and suggest a course of action. Their recommendations were:

1. That this Convention appoint a special committee of five brethren whose duty it shall be to take this whole matter under advisement and into consideration, and to report at the next Convention on the "Work of Evangelism in the several States of the Convention."
2. That the committee be instructed to seek information as to the wisest methods in the work of evangelism consistent with our church polity and our denominational policy; to ascertain as far as practicable the special needs, and what is being done in the several States, as to the number of evangelists employed,

---

[3] *Annual of the Southern Baptist Convention, 1904*, Nashville, Tennessee (May 13–16, 1904), 7. See also "Appendix A" for the full text of Broughton's motion.

where, and how employed, and as to the general results obtained; to agitate the whole subject of evangelism, and to gather any statistics in connection with the work, and any other information or intelligence touching the spiritual condition of our people, and the work of the denomination in reaching the unsaved masses at the very doors of our churches.

3. That in the prosecution of this work the committee shall solicit the co-operation of our religious newspapers, the State mission secretaries, and the secretaries of our general boards, and that these brethren be requested to render any aid they can to this committee in seeking the desired information.

4. That this committee, after a careful study of men and methods, shall feel it their privilege to discreetly recommend to inquiring pastors and churches such brethren as in their view possess the evangelistic gifts, and who can acceptably do the work of an evangelist.

5. That it is understood that the committee in their work shall not entail any expense upon the Convention, or its boards, but that the committee is at liberty to receive any contributions that may be furnished by the friends of this cause for any necessary expenses that may be incurred in the successful prosecution of its work.[4]

Although Broughton's motion was not fully rejected, the report of this committee did reshape his motion in significant ways. The creation of a temporary committee, small in size with no employees, was advocated as opposed to a large, permanent committee employing at least one evangelist. The cooperation of Baptist agencies was suggested but not required, and no definite source of funding for the work of the committee was recommended. The SBC was to be made aware of evangelistic statistics, needs, and methods, but the Convention was to assume no new responsibilities for helping churches with evangelism.

---

[4] *Annual of the Southern Baptist Convention, 1905*, Kansas City, Missouri (May 12–15, 1905), 40. See also "Appendix B" for the full text of the committee's report.

The report of the committee was accepted by the Convention in Kansas City in 1905. A second committee of five was appointed, this time including Broughton, along with George W. Truett of Texas, W. W. Hamilton of Kentucky, W. M. Vines of Virginia, and A. J. S. Thomas of South Carolina. The stage was set for what proved to be a "battle royal" over what Southern Baptists should do about evangelism.

The new committee gave its initial report during the first evening session of the 1906 Convention. Further discussion of their recommendations was postponed until Sunday afternoon. This schedule was a parliamentary move intended to make it impossible for the messengers to act on a motion, for business could not be conducted during a Sunday session. Later, an attempt was made to move the discussion to a time period when action could be taken. After much debate and in a close vote, the time shift was denied. The failed motion to shift the time was followed by a motion to give the evangelism committee a third opportunity to address the body at a time when the messengers could take action. That motion carried. Vociferous debate and parliamentary maneuvering had not been unknown in Southern Baptist life, but what kind of evangelism report could create this kind of controversy?

Len Broughton presented the report. He began by telling of great evangelistic harvests that other denominations were experiencing across the United States. Two factors seemed to be present where these harvests were taking place. First, the methodology of revivalism was widely used, especially campaigns involving groups of churches in a joint crusade:

> The large central meeting, or a number of simultaneous meetings in the same general movement, has usually been the order of the evangelistic work of the past year so far as the cities are concerned. Great halls, theaters, skating rinks, and other large central meeting places have been utilized by evangelists, and thousands of non-churchgoers have been reached in this way.[5]

---

[5] *Annual of the Southern Baptist Convention, 1906*, Chattanooga, Tennessee (May 11–14, 1906), 40. See also "Appendix C" for the full text of Broughton's report.

Revival meetings were proving to be a very productive approach to urban evangelism in the United States.

The second common factor was the presence of denominational evangelists. Other denominations were appointing evangelists to organize and preach these revival campaigns. The committee felt that Southern Baptists were not capitalizing on the ready harvest of souls because they lacked evangelists to mobilize their churches for evangelistic crusades. Broughton noted, "But with all our opportunities as Southern Baptists there is a serious weakness. We have the evangelistic soil; we have the evangelistic spirit; but we need better evangelistic organization."[6]

The committee believed that the time had come to institute a more intentional approach to evangelism. Their recommendations were as follows:

> **First**, That the Convention instruct its Home Mission Board to create the Department of Evangelism, and that a general evangelist, with as many associates as practicable, be employed.
>
> **Second**, That the Home Mission Board be requested to adopt such measures and methods as may be found necessary to give effectiveness to this department of the work.
>
> **Third**, That in view of this advanced work our people be requested to increase their contributions by at least $25,000 for its support, and that the Home Mission Board be instructed to take the necessary steps to raise this amount in addition to the amount needed for other work.[7]

From these recommendations the controversy arose. What was the issue provoking such strong feelings?

For many of the messengers, the real issue was a matter of Baptist polity—that is, the role of the local church versus the role of the denomination—for evangelism is ultimately the responsibility of the local church. Why should the denomination get involved in doing what every local church should be doing on its own? The concern over this question reflects

---

[6] Ibid., 41.
[7] Ibid., 42–43.

the lingering influences of Landmarkism within the Southern Baptist Convention. *Landmarkism* can be described as what many today would call an extreme emphasis on the autonomy of the local church. In the late nineteenth century, proponents such as J. R. Graves embroiled the Convention in bitter controversy over the appropriate roles for the church and denomination. This debate was not over the importance or priority of evangelism. The issue was the role of the denomination in a ministry belonging to the local church.

Broughton and his committee attempted to address this issue in the report. He explained, "To be sure, this work [of evangelism] is, and ought to be, under the direction of the churches, just as every other agency of the denomination is. It is our profound conviction that the supreme centers of evangelism are the churches."[8] Concern remained, however, over the propriety of forming an Evangelism Department.

From the committee's perspective, their recommendations were an attempt to strengthen and assist the evangelistic efforts of Southern Baptist churches. Even though evangelism was a local church responsibility, not all churches were engaged effectively in the work. The committee felt that a Department of Evangelism would stimulate uninvolved churches to become involved and would enhance the work of those churches already reaching out to the lost. Acceptance of these recommendations would also make evangelism possible on a larger scale than a local church could attempt on its own. This, after all, was one of the reasons for forming a convention in the first place.

A second point of the controversy concerned the legitimacy of evangelists. Did the New Testament teach the calling and ministry of evangelists? Some questioned whether or not an "outsider" should help a local church do evangelism. Were local church members the only ones with the responsibility or authority to lead a church in evangelism? It appeared the SBC would not vote for a Department of Evangelism unless evangelists were understood to be fulfilling the New Testament office or function as servants of the local church.

---

[8] Ibid., 41.

The turning point of the debate came in a plea to the messengers from B. H. Carroll, later the founder and president of Southwestern Baptist Theological Seminary. Making frequent reference to the New Testament, Carroll demonstrated that the evangelist was an appointee of God for a permanent kind of work in the kingdom of God; that the evangelist's ministry was to be in the context of the local church; that the New Testament clearly stated his unique functions and qualifications; and that the Bible offered several illustrations of the work of evangelists in first-century churches. He concluded with magnificent flair:

> Let us give the report a rousing, unanimous endorsement. The bedrock of Scripture underlies it. Experience demonstrates its wisdom and feasibility. If the Home Mission Board may employ any man, it may employ evangelists. Altogether, then, with a ring, let us support this measure. If I were the secretary of this board I would come before this body in humility and tears and say: "Brethren, give me evangelists. Deny not fins to things that must swim against the tide, nor wings to things that must fly against the wind."[9]

The fervor of his speech carried the day. The motion passed easily, and Southern Baptists instructed the HMB to form a Department of Evangelism.

Institutionalized Methodology

The acceptance of the recommendations of the evangelism committee was a decision that would affect Southern Baptists for years to come. The messengers made a denominational response to the Great Commission, incorporating evangelism into the structure of the SBC. Now, an entity would have the specific responsibility of leading Southern Baptists to call the lost to Christ. There would be a gardener to tend the evangelism garden of SBC

---

[9] B. H. Carroll, "Shall the Atlanta Board Be Instructed to Employ Evangelists and to Call for an Extra $25,000 for Their Support?" (speech, Southern Baptist Convention, Chattanooga, TN, May 14, 1906), *Baptist Standard*, May 31, 1906, 1–2. See "Appendix D" for the full text of Carroll's address.

churches. The decision also strengthened the denominational identity of Southern Baptists. Faced with the lingering influences of Landmarkism, Southern Baptists affirmed a commitment both to the autonomy of the local church and to the importance, even necessity, of cooperative fellowship and labor for kingdom purposes. When autonomous churches voluntarily choose to cooperate through the work of a Board they have created to work on their behalf, they surrender neither their autonomy nor their local missional responsibility. Evangelism is the responsibility of the local church, but a cooperative approach to the task can enhance the impact of each local church. The decision of the messengers to use denominational resources to support a local church task was an important milestone in the development of the self-identity of Southern Baptists.

The formation of the Department also institutionalized a method of evangelism within Southern Baptist life. The Evangelism Department was designed for one purpose—to plan, promote, and lead revival meetings. The secretary or head of the Department was identified as a general evangelist. His staff consisted of other evangelists, preachers, and musicians who traveled from place to place leading revivals. This approach was taken because other denominations and churches were finding revival meetings to be the most effective strategy available for winning lost people in the cities of the nation. Clearly, Southern Baptists were increasing their focus on the emerging urban future.

CHAPTER 2

Foundation for the Future

O nce the decision was made, the Home Mission Board immediately moved ahead in response to the action of the Convention. A Department of Evangelism was organized. The task of the Department was simple: function as an evangelistic arm working with and through SBC churches, assisting them in evangelism. The Convention determined that Southern Baptist polity, incorporating both cooperation and autonomy, would be applied to the task of evangelism. The approach taken by the founding director of the Department quickly won the support of the churches and became the model for many years to come. As the story unfolded, however, the creation of the Department of Evangelism proved to be a first step toward the gardener principle but not the only step.

The Stable of Evangelists

W. W. Hamilton was the first Secretary of Evangelism for Southern Baptists. Born in Kentucky in 1868, Hamilton came from evangelistic stock. His maternal grandfather was a schoolteacher and pastor who baptized 5,000 people during the 98 years of his life. Hamilton was saved at the age of 10 during a revival campaign. His background included both Baptist and Presbyterian influences. An evangelist who preached at the Presbyterian church in his community used a chalkboard to illustrate his biblical message. Hamilton liked the idea and developed the habit of using a chalkboard on Sunday evenings to jot down outlines and Scripture references as he preached.

Two factors influenced Hamilton's call to the ministry. Home prayer meetings for youth aroused his interest in spiritual matters, and the tragic death of a young friend who was going to attend law school with him settled the issue. In a passage that appears to be autobiographical, Hamilton revealed the life-changing impact trauma can make:

> ". . . Won't you win some souls for you and me?" This was the dying request of a young man, who in his heart felt the desire to be a harvest hand for the Master, but now the end was near. He looked up into the face of his friend, and spoke the words which helped him to decide and which through the years have helped him in his greatest soul-winning work.[1]

Hamilton loved to attend Bible conferences at Winona Lake, the retreat center in Indiana made famous by Billy Sunday. While he was there one year, Hamilton heard about the "Pittsburgh Plan" developed by J. Wilbur Chapman, a founder of Winona Lake and the General Secretary of Evangelism for the Presbyterian denomination. A simultaneous revival strategy for cities, this plan called for the churches to divide a city into sections. In each section, one church would be designated as the host church where nightly services were held during the crusade. The other churches would join in promoting attendance and supporting the meetings. The goal was to get the attention of the city, arousing interest in the evangelistic services.

Hamilton led the churches of Louisville, Kentucky, to plan such a crusade using three host churches. The Pittsburgh pastor who was to lead the meeting became ill at the last minute, and Hamilton was asked to do the preaching. The campaign was a great success and may have been a factor in the selection of Hamilton as the first Secretary of Evangelism.

As Secretary of Evangelism, W. W. Hamilton adapted the Pittsburgh Plan to the needs of Southern Baptists. Crusades were organized to involve Baptist churches only. Every Baptist church in the community was used for night services, and one central church hosted united day services. The campaigns concluded with a praise service held in the largest meeting

---

[1] William Wistar Hamilton, *Bible Evangelism* (Atlanta: Home Mission Board, 1921), 144.

place in the city on the last Sunday afternoon. The approach proved to be very successful for the denomination and its churches.

To implement the plan on a denominational scale, Hamilton recruited a staff of evangelists and singers to plan and lead the crusades. When B. H. Carroll pled with the Convention on behalf of the Evangelism Department, he emphasized the need for trained and qualified evangelists to help churches plan and carry out these larger, more complex meetings. Southern Baptists hoped that this type of revival meeting would help them reach more people in their communities with the gospel, especially in the cities. Hamilton called the approach denominational evangelism, and he described his staff and their work in this way:

> It is composed of white and Negro evangelists and singers, who are paid a regular salary, and who go to mission fields, to weak and strong churches in country and town and city. They hold individual or group meetings, and as occasion offers, the staff of workers is brought together for an associational or city or state campaign, conducting meetings as far as possible in every Baptist church at the same time, and having a great central service daily in which instruction in personal work is given and where special music, definite prayer, reports of meetings, and inspirational preaching are features.[2]

Acutely aware of the negative image associated with evangelists, even in his day, Hamilton addressed what he thought were two of the biggest problems in his approach to staff selection and departmental organization. Many complained about evangelists who were more interested in their own needs and ministries than they were in the needs of the churches who used them. Various forms of financial impropriety were also a major concern. In response, Hamilton recruited evangelists who had a pastor's perspective and paid them a salary rather than all or part of the love offerings they raised. With this approach, the Evangelism Secretary believed:

---

[2] Ibid., 37–38.

More men who are apt to teach and who have the shepherd heart will be willing to give themselves to evangelism. The churches which these men help will have their interest in denominational affairs quickened and intensified and broadened. Such evangelists are in a position to leave the best impression for good on the whole community, being less tempted to self-seeking and self-exaltation. This plan should encourage a kind of giving which is not done out of pity, or to the individual, but to the cause of Christ. Strong and capable men are available for places which could not otherwise secure them, and there is no reason why the evangelist should hold back any truth which needs to be preached.[3]

By finding the right kind of men to be evangelists, giving them financial stability, and making them available to all churches on the basis of need rather than ability to pay, Hamilton felt the contributions of evangelists to Southern Baptist life could be maximized and the problems they created could be minimized. The result of his plan was a Department of Evangelism that functioned as a "stable of evangelists." When a church needed a team for a revival, the Department was contacted to secure the services of men in whom they could have confidence. When a group of churches wanted to have a large and complex campaign to reach a city or area, the Department of Evangelism could supply someone to help with the planning and promotion as well as with the preaching and singing. The purpose of the Department was to perform a function—helping Southern Baptist churches *do* the work of evangelism.

Several significant aspects of Hamilton's approach should be noted. First, he implemented an innovative financial plan suggested in Len Broughton's original proposal for the Department. The evangelists he employed were paid a salary by the Board. Love offerings were still taken at their meetings, but these love offerings went to the Home Mission Board. In this way, the Department could recover much of its operating expenses and enlarge its staff. At one point as many as 50 evangelists were employed. Churches could have confidence in the financial integrity of the evangelists from the HMB, and the Department could operate and expand

---

[3] Ibid., 94.

without draining funds from other aspects of the HMB. This approach was especially important for a new department assigned by the SBC but not sought by the leadership of the Board. Many years later, international evangelist Billy Graham would take a similar approach to address concerns about financial integrity. Hamilton's positioning the Department to grow in proportion to its success was an important accomplishment in a day of uncertain finances.

Another significant component of Hamilton's approach was the linking of evangelistic crusades with evangelistic instruction. When several churches came together for a revival effort, the central meeting held daily in the host church included training and instruction in evangelism. At this time, Southern Baptists had only one seminary. The majority of pastors had little or no theological training. By incorporating various aspects of evangelistic training with the meetings, the Evangelism Department could provide basic training or continuing education for the pastors and laymen who attended. To use contemporary terminology, Hamilton's approach was a study in contextualized education. The field of ministry became the classroom, and the lessons taught could be implemented immediately.

Finally, this first evangelism leader recognized the contributions of music to evangelism. From the beginning, Hamilton included on his staff musicians to handle the singing and other musical needs of the evangelistic crusades. Hamilton had strong opinions about the significance of music. In his work titled *Bible Evangelism*, he noted:

> *Every great revival has been accompanied by great singing* [emphasis his], and the Bible has as much to say about praise as it has about prayer or about preaching. All the great evangelists have felt as did Mr. Moody, that there must be a Mr. Sankey if the meetings were to be at their best. There is need for the sermon in song as well as for the spoken message, and in going with Jesus after the lost, it will always be helpful if we will go with songs on our lips. The great value of gospel singing in the quest for souls should be so emphasized that those who are thus gifted will feel the obligation to dedicate their best to Christ, rather than to the devil.[4]

---

[4] Ibid., 167.

Because the revival setting required what he called "soulful singing," the secretary believed that many churches needed to incorporate a different type of music than what they used in regular worship services. Musicians with experience and expertise in evangelistic music were kept on the staff as a resource for churches that wanted their help.

W. W. Hamilton earned an important place in the story of Southern Baptists. He was the first Secretary of Evangelism, but more than that, he did his job well. Although the birth of the Department took place in an atmosphere of controversy, the approaches he took won quick approval. There is no trace of criticism in Convention records after he began the work. By emphasizing the popular methodology of revivalism and implementing a creative financial plan, Hamilton made the Evangelism Department productive from the beginning. Under his leadership, the Department fulfilled its assigned function of helping churches do evangelism. A stable of evangelists and musicians were on call to assist local churches with revival meetings and evangelistic crusades as needed. Traces of his influence continue to this day, and the model he developed lasted many years.

The Hamilton approach remained in place through a succession of other leaders. One of those other leaders was Hamilton himself, who to this day remains the only person to have served twice as the Convention's evangelism leader. Refinements were added over time. Among the most notable was that of Weston Bruner, who served from 1910 to 1917. His staff of evangelists included an evangelist for colleges, an evangelist for the mountain schools of Appalachia, and an African-American evangelist to work with African-American churches. No record remains of how they approached those special assignments, but they provide an early illustration of Southern Baptists aggressively seeking to reach specific people groups. All went well until a scandalous criminal act changed everything.

CHAPTER 3

Crime and Consequences

H aving decided that the Convention should help churches in their evangelistic task and having found a popular model that worked, Southern Baptists seemed poised for an era of strong evangelistic growth. It was not to be. The stultifying impact of the Great Depression on the nation deeply affected SBC churches as well, but that problem was compounded by the shocking action of a Home Mission Board employee. The damage was severe, taking years to overcome, but eventually it prepared the way for a crucial milestone in the story of Southern Baptist evangelism.

The C. S. Carnes Legacy

Have you ever wondered why many Baptist churches require two signatures on a check or have two or more people count the offering? C. S. Carnes was a man well respected in Southern Baptist life, serving as Treasurer of the Home Mission Board. For convenience, HMB directors (trustees) authorized him to borrow money on his signature alone. In 1928, Carnes embezzled $909,461 from the Board.[1] He did not take money they had. He borrowed money and directed it to personal accounts. The HMB was already in debt, and this huge amount, added as the Great Depression unfolded, was a crushing blow.

In 1920, Southern Baptists had begun the most ambitious financial campaign in their history. The Seventy-Five Million Campaign intended to

---

[1] Lawrence, *History of the Home Mission Board*, 110.

raise 75 million dollars for SBC ministries. Much of the money raised was in the form of pledges. With the coming of the Depression, actual receipts fell short. Unfortunately, the HMB spent the money it anticipated receiving from the pledges that never materialized. To the great debt resulting from the shortfall was added the loss from the Carnes embezzlement. Available cash was severely limited, the debt load was far, far greater than anyone ever imagined it would be, and the ability of Southern Baptists to cover the loss was dramatically hindered by the economy. Filing bankruptcy was encouraged, but Southern Baptists insisted on paying the debts in full. The work went on, but deep cuts were made to keep the Board afloat.

Carnes was finally caught and sent to prison, but nearly all the money had been wasted and could not be recovered. The damage to the missions and evangelism work of Southern Baptists was enormous. Some HMB church planters and missionaries were left in Texas, but all in California were recalled. What would Baptist work in California be like today if the workers had been left in place during the lost decade as they were in Texas? We will never know. The Evangelism Department was another casualty. Even though it recovered much of its operating expenses through love offerings given to HMB evangelists, the Board decided to completely defund the program. At the 1930 Convention, messengers called upon the Board leaders to employ an evangelism commissioner as soon as possible, but the response was an insistence that sufficient funds were still unavailable for such a move.

The crimes of C. S. Carnes prompted permanent and widespread changes in Southern Baptist financial practices that made theft and embezzlement much more difficult and unlikely. More importantly, however, Carnes did more damage to Southern Baptist efforts in missions and evangelism than any other individual in Convention history.

Finally, in his report to the 1936 Convention, HMB Executive Secretary J. B. Lawrence announced that the Department of Evangelism could be reinstituted if desired. A motion to that effect was immediately forthcoming, and it passed without opposition. However, financial constraints on the Board remained. The Department of Evangelism was given new life, but it had to have a fresh vision.

New Life, New Focus

When Lawrence made his announcement, M. E. Dodd, pastor of First Baptist Church, Shreveport, Louisiana, immediately moved that the messengers act upon his suggestion. On this vote about the reestablishment of an Evangelism Department, there was no controversy:

> Dr. Dodd's motion to recommend and approve this action was passed enthusiastically and was followed by prolonged applause. Leading pastors from every section in personal conversations spoke favorably of the action of the Convention and rejoiced that emphasis was again to be given to evangelism.[2]

Southern Baptists desired a denominational expression of their commitment to evangelism. While the local church was the center of the actual work, the people wanted evangelism to have a clear identity within the denominational structure. The churches wanted help.

The Department that emerged following the financial crisis was quite different from the original design of W. W. Hamilton. The Home Mission Board felt it could support only one man in the Department. There was no interest in building a staff of evangelists and singers to go out and do revivals. The only reason given for this change in philosophy was the lack of financial resources. J. B. Lawrence wanted someone who could work with the state conventions to develop "a distinctive Southern Baptist type of church-centered evangelism."[3] The man selected to fill the new position in 1936 was Roland Q. Leavell, who came to the Board from the pastorate of First Baptist Church of Gainesville, Georgia.

The task facing Leavell was difficult. Southern Baptists were accustomed to having a Secretary of Evangelism whose primary role was to function as an evangelist. Specifically prohibited from building a staff of evangelists to plan and promote revivals, the new secretary had to work within the limitations of what one person could do. With brilliant insight,

---

[2] Arthur B. Rutledge and William G. Tanner, *Mission to America: A History of Southern Baptist Home Missions* (Nashville: Broadman Press, 1969), 218.
[3] Lawrence, *History of the Home Mission Board*, 142–43.

Leavell changed the nature of the Department. In a report to the 1937 Convention, Leavell described his role in the following words:

> One of the primary purposes of the Department of Evangelism is to keep aflame the spirit of evangelism. Someone must assume the supreme task of re-creating and fostering the spirit of evangelism in the South. The Department's superintendent should think evangelism, pray evangelism, practice evangelism, and promote evangelism in every way possible.[4]

Leavell saw himself as the voice for evangelism within Southern Baptist life. His job was to keep evangelism in front of the agencies and churches of the Denomination. He did whatever he could to mobilize Southern Baptists for the work of bringing the lost to Christ. Pastors of local churches had a multitude of responsibilities, but his job was simple and clearly defined—evangelism. Leavell believed he was to become the evangelism specialist for the SBC.

This approach was a major shift from a functional role to a strategic role. While Leavell remained very active in doing evangelism, he was something more than the general evangelist his predecessors had been. The Secretary of Evangelism became one to whom Southern Baptists looked for strategy and programming in the area of evangelism, as well as one who could preach revivals and lead evangelism clinics. This change remained a permanent part of the philosophy of the HMB. Never again would the Evangelism Department be a stable of evangelists assembled to help churches plan and implement evangelistic crusades. The Secretary of Evangelism was expected not only to be personally involved in doing evangelism but also to mobilize the whole SBC for evangelism. His work did not start when a church called for help. His work began with stimulating churches to seek help to be more productive in their evangelism efforts.

One of the reasons why Leavell's changes were so significant is that they separated the Evangelism Department from a single evangelistic methodology. Although his predecessors had employed various forms of

---

[4] *Annual of the Southern Baptist Convention, 1937,* New Orleans, Louisiana (May 13–16, 1937), 274.

evangelism, the Department had been organized to implement one approach—evangelism through revivalism. Although revivalism proved to be popular and effective in Southern Baptist life, no one method is ever sufficient, especially for a denomination steadily increasing in diversity and complexity. Leavell built the identity of the Department around the task rather than the method. The Department became more of a true Evangelism Department than a *de facto* department of revival meetings. With this change, Leavell gave the Department the flexibility to adapt to the changes time inevitably brings.

As Secretary of Evangelism, Roland Q. Leavell emphasized three aspects of evangelism. First, he remained deeply involved in planning, promoting, and participating in simultaneous and other forms of revival campaigns in cities, associations, and states. Although Leavell did not lead a staff of evangelists and singers, he still recognized the effectiveness of revivalism in Southern Baptist life. When he was asked to develop a soul-winning campaign for Southern Baptists in 1938 and for the Baptists of America in 1940, revival meetings were a major part of the strategy.

Another major contribution of Leavell's leadership was an emphasis on training the "rank and file" church member to witness. He recognized that the church could never accomplish its Great Commission mandate without the witness of all believers to the saving work of Christ. During the first 100 years of the SBC, personal evangelism received its greatest emphasis from Roland Q. Leavell. He wrote books, developed training programs, and led evangelism clinics to motivate Southern Baptists to share their faith.

The development of evangelistic resources was the third aspect of evangelism to which Leavell gave constant attention. He wrote extensively himself, and he encouraged others to write. His works included articles for the many Southern Baptist periodicals, study courses, tracts, pamphlets, and books. He dealt with a variety of evangelistic methods, including preaching, personal witnessing, revival meetings, family evangelism, and others. Leavell believed that if Southern Baptists were to be an evangelistic people, they would need a constant supply of evangelistic literature.

Perhaps what Roland Q. Leavell made possible is more important than what he accomplished. Len Broughton and B. H. Carroll were important for helping Southern Baptists to see the importance of engaging in evangelism as a denomination. The SBC evangelism garden needed a gardener. W. W. Hamilton was significant for making the Department of Evangelism, born in controversy, a popular and effective entity in Southern Baptist life. Under Roland Q. Leavell, the SBC began to look to the Department for evangelistic strategies and plans, in addition to resources and guidance for implementing the strategies. That someone needed to be assigned to help SBC churches do evangelism was undisputed. With this role and identity in place, the stage was set for the man who would lead Southern Baptists during the greatest time of harvest in their history. By redefining the role of the Evangelism Department, Leavell prepared Southern Baptists to respond to a plan one man believed was a vision from God.

CHAPTER 4

The Energizing Key

After completing his five-year commitment to serve the Department of Evangelism, Roland Q. Leavell returned to the pastorate. With the outbreak of World War II, SBC baptisms began to decline. The Convention was averaging fewer than one baptism per 25 members, a baptismal ratio that would be a cause of wild celebration to today's leaders. Then, it was a deep disappointment.

A replacement for Leavell had not been found, but Convention leaders felt something had to be done to reignite evangelistic growth. To celebrate its hundredth anniversary, plans were made for a Centennial Crusade, calling upon all SBC churches to work together doing evangelistic crusades in a geographic wave across the country in 1945. It was the most ambitious evangelistic effort ever attempted by the SBC. Although the Centennial Crusade succeeded in statistical growth in nearly every category, it fell well short of expectations.

Crusade Chairman M. E. Dodd was deeply disappointed, and Convention leaders were left with a hunger for answers about how to reach the nation for Christ. When Fred Eastham served only briefly as Leavell's replacement in the Evangelism Department, many were discouraged about its future. However, brighter days were ahead. In 1936, a Texas pastor felt that he was given a vision from God for an evangelism strategy that could mobilize Southern Baptists as never before. Ten years later, God began moving together the Convention's hunger for change and that pastor's visionary strategy for evangelism. A mighty work of God was about to unfold.

A Vision Received

C. E. Matthews always dreamed of making a name for himself as a major league baseball player. He did make a mark in history but in an entirely different field. When an injury dashed his dream of athletic success, Matthews focused on success as an accountant. He was a rising star in his company when he was born again, a convert of the visitation program of a Baptist church near his home. He immediately became involved in church and was soon a leader in the Sunday School program.

Matthews taught a class for boys in the youth department. On his way to work one morning, he noticed the headline story in the paper about the death of a boy struck by lightning. When he looked at the picture, Matthews saw that the boy was Grady, a member of his Sunday School class. He met the boy's father for the first time at the funeral. As they talked, the teacher realized that neither one of them knew whether or not Grady was a Christian. Matthews realized that he had been more concerned with teaching the class than leading his boys to Jesus. The tragedy marked a turning point for the future Evangelism Secretary. By the end of the day, Matthews spoke to each boy on his roll about salvation. The urgency and passion for evangelism awakened by his inattention to the salvation of the boy he taught in Sunday School never left him.

Another unexpected death reinforced his lifetime commitment to evangelism. A tragic illness took the life of his oldest daughter before she reached her teenage years. For the next several days, person after person came to Matthews and told him of his daughter's witness. She had led many of her Sunday School class members to Christ, one at a time. She also witnessed to many adults. Matthews realized again the supreme importance of evangelism. He renewed his commitment to put evangelism first and to be the kind of soul-winner his daughter had been during her brief life.

The commitment of Matthews to be a witness eventually led him to enter the Christian ministry. He left the security of his company to enter Southwestern Baptist Theological Seminary and prepare for the pastorate. While a student, Matthews began working in a church Sunday School program under Arthur Flake, the man who taught Southern Baptists to make Sunday School the outreach arm of the church. The organizational genius later displayed by Matthews reflected Flake's influence. The pastor who had both Arthur Flake, the denomination's most influential Sunday School leader, and C. E. Matthews, the denomination's most effective evangelism leader, working in his church at the same time was J. Frank Norris, the fiery fundamentalist. He later turned against Matthews and bitterly contested his ordination to the ministry.

When Roland Q. Leavell became the Secretary of Evangelism in 1936, C. E. Matthews was the pastor of Travis Avenue Baptist Church in Fort Worth, Texas. One day during that year, Matthews and evangelist Hyman Appleman were having a discussion about evangelism. Matthews suggested that mass evangelism, using the simultaneous associational crusade, was the method of evangelism closest to the New Testament approach. Appleman agreed, but he said the approach would never work today because of the jealousy among pastors and churches. That comment deeply disturbed Matthews, and he kept the topic of evangelistic methods alive in his thoughts.

Not long afterward, Matthews had what he believed was a divine revelation. Here is the experience as described by Matthews:

> Exactly on the morning of September 28, 1936, I was in my study preparing a funeral message for a sainted Mother, Mrs. E. J. Tarlton. All of a sudden, I found my mind centered on Evangelism and completely lost my thoughts in meditation on the subject. Suddenly there came to me a complete program of evangelism as though I had read it all in a flash from a book. It was so visibly indelible in my mind that not a semblance of it has ever left me.[1]

The program that was impressed upon Matthews's mind was to become the first Southern Baptist program of evangelism. C. E. Wilbanks, his biographer, summarized the program as visualized by Matthews in relationship to the Baptist General Convention of Texas.

---

[1] C. E. Wilbanks, *What God Hath Wrought through C. E. Matthews* (Atlanta: Home Mission Board and Southern Baptist Convention, 1957), 110.

    I. Organizational
        1. An employed secretary of evangelism in the state to su-
            pervise the program. [Remember this was a Texas pro-
            gram.]
        2. An associational chairman in every association to super-
            vise the work of evangelism on an associational level.
        3. An evangelism church council in every church to plan and
            direct evangelism on a church level.
    II. Promotional
        1. A state-wide evangelistic conference each year.
        2. An annual simultaneous revival crusade in every associa-
            tion.[2]

Matthews later acknowledged that others added suggestions and refinements to the program. However, this plan is the only written description of
his original vision available.

Matthews began thinking of the program in terms of his state convention, but he soon recognized its application to the whole denomination.
Having seen Southern Baptists adopt a unified program of giving (the Cooperative Program) to strengthen their financial resources, Matthews saw
the potential of a master plan of evangelism involving all the churches,
boards, and agencies. A strategy comprehensive enough to give every element of the SBC a specific role in winning the nation to Christ was needed.
He felt that God had given him that strategy.

Matthews also longed to see permanent stability brought to the Department of Evangelism. Following the C. S. Carnes embezzlement, the
Secretary of Evangelism position was unfilled for eight years. After the
resignation of Roland Q. Leavell, the position remained vacant for two
years. Matthews believed Southern Baptists could not reach their evangelistic potential without the continuity of a stable, dependable approach to
evangelism. He wanted to establish a program so rooted in Southern Baptist life that both the Department and the program would be perpetuated.

As a result of his vision of an evangelism program, his love and identification with the denomination, and his passionate convictions about

---

[2] Ibid., 111–12.

evangelism, C. E. Matthews became a man possessed with a great sense of destiny. He believed God had given him the responsibility to mobilize Southern Baptists for a great harvest. Ten years after his vision, events moved rapidly toward the fulfillment of that destiny.

A Harvest Reaped

In 1946, Texas Baptists hired Matthews as their Secretary of Evangelism. Immediately he began to implement his program of evangelism. Later that year, Fred Eastham resigned from the SBC Department of Evangelism after a very brief tenure. J. B. Lawrence, still head of the Home Mission Board, contacted C. E. Matthews about the vacancy. In the first sentence of his response to Lawrence, Matthews said, "I was looking for your letter."[3] What he had long believed would happen began to unfold.

Matthews accepted the position with the provision that he be allowed to keep his office in Texas and complete some responsibilities for Texas Baptists. The Evangelism Department of the HMB remained in Dallas until the mid-1960s. By 1947, the new Evangelism Secretary was ready to present his program to the SBC. In May of that year, the Southern Baptist Convention met in St. Louis, Missouri, and approved the following resolution:

1. That a unified program of evangelism be recommended to our states and churches;
2. That each state in the Convention create a Department of Evangelism;
3. That all associations be organized with two officers namely, an organizer and a general chairman; and
4. That all types of evangelism that God sees fit to bless be emphasized, but the stress be on mass evangelism, chiefly the associational simultaneous method.[4]

---

[3] Ibid., 117.
[4] *Annual of the Southern Baptist Convention, 1947*, St. Louis, Missouri (May 7–11, 1947), 161.

For the first time in its history, the Convention adopted a specific program of evangelism. That program included giving an assigned responsibility to focus on evangelism at every level of SBC life. There was a gardener clearly assigned to tend the evangelism garden at every level of SBC life. What began in 1906 was refined in 1936 and finally reached its ultimate fulfillment in 1947.

The plan of Matthews was further refined and presented to the SBC in 1948. Again it was approved. In 1949, Matthews put his plan in book form and published *The Southern Baptist Program of Evangelism*. Free copies were given to all the ordained Southern Baptist ministers in active service. Other additions with minor revisions were published in 1952, 1956, and 1958. The entire Convention was saturated repeatedly with a relatively simple plan, assigning each component of Southern Baptist life a role to play in reaching the lost. The result was the greatest period of growth in the history of the SBC.

Virtually every statistical category measured by Southern Baptists increased during the decade 1945–1955. A great time of growth for the United States followed the end of World War II, but the progress of the SBC was even greater. The size of the Southern Baptist Convention grew five times faster than the population of the United States at a time when the nation's population was exploding.[5] C. E. Wilbanks compared the baptisms of that period with the previous decade:

> In the nine years preceding the adoption of the Southern Baptist Program of Evangelism, 1938-1946, total baptisms were 2,120,773. The first nine years of the Program of Evangelism, 1947-1955, baptisms totaled 3,211,823, a total gain of 1,091,050 baptisms in the second nine-year period. That is an average gain of 121,228 baptisms per year for the nine years of the Program of Evangelism.[6]

Annual baptisms topped 400,000 a year by the end of the Matthews era and remained at or near that level for the next six years.

---

[5] John Havlik, "Back to the Bible?" *Missions USA*, March–April 1982, 53.
[6] Wilbanks, *What God Hath Wrought*, 123.

Several factors were involved in the success of the program proposed by Matthews. His greatest stroke of genius was the organizational structure he proposed and implemented. His recommendations included the formation of a Department of Evangelism in every state convention, the election of two officers for every evangelism association, and the appointment of an evangelism church council in every local church. A gardener was in place to tend the evangelism garden at every level of the SBC: national, state, regional, and local.

The task that is everybody's job often becomes nobody's job. With this structure, Matthews ensured that Southern Baptists would be consistently reminded to make definite plans for evangelism. The staff of the Evangelism Department remained small, yet through the network he created, Matthews actually had more than 40 evangelists and musicians. Massive coordination efforts in evangelism were easier to implement by working with evangelism workers in each state convention and evangelism committees in each association. By motivating, training, and involving this network in evangelistic campaigns, Matthews was able to mobilize the Convention for evangelism.

The use of a popular, easily understood methodology was another key factor in Matthews's program. As stated previously, revivalism had been the basic strategy for evangelism among Southern Baptists from the beginning. Matthews believed that there were only two forms of evangelism: personal evangelism and mass evangelism. His research and experience convinced him that mass evangelism in the form of simultaneous crusades was the most productive form of evangelism for his day. He encouraged the use of other methods, even writing a book on personal evangelism, but he focused his attention on the simultaneous revival meetings. The Evangelism Secretary wanted every church to have two revival meetings each year. He suggested that one be a meeting for the church alone, perhaps with the pastor doing the preaching. The other was to be some form of a simultaneous crusade.

By simultaneous crusade, Matthews meant the two-week period when all the churches of a given area conducted revival meetings at the same time. The meetings were to start on the same date and end on the same date. A daily meeting was held for all the pastors, evangelists, singers, and interested others to inspire them and to train them in effective ways to reach the lost. During the first week, attention was given to church members and the status of their relationship with God. The prayer was that revival would break out among the Christians by the end of the week, preparing the way for a harvest of the lost. The second week focused on evangelism with messages on salvation and strong evangelistic appeals. Most churches would see the largest number of conversions during the second week.

Because he built his program around revivalism, Matthews did not have to convince Southern Baptists that his basic method was sound nor train them to do something unfamiliar. Instead he was able to focus on motivating them and training them to implement a familiar approach to revivalism. The concept was not new. Every feature of his simultaneous crusades had been done in days past. He simply did it more thoroughly, more extensively, and more frequently than his predecessors.

Another significant feature of his program was training. Matthews left nothing to chance. He stressed continually the importance of thorough preparation. In this regard, he stands in the line of Charles Finney, Dwight Moody, Billy Sunday, and Billy Graham. Although God is the one who sends a revival and an evangelistic harvest, Christians are responsible to prepare for it. All of Matthews's books were training manuals. In great detail, he described exactly what to do in preparation for a crusade (even down to the amount of money to charge for the morning fellowship meal for pastors and evangelists). Over and over and over again, Matthews told Southern Baptists how to do the program of evangelism. As a result, the effectiveness of the crusades increased. Three national simultaneous crusades were conducted during his tenure. Each one set a new record for baptisms.

A final factor in the success of the program appears to be the visibility that Matthews gave evangelism in Southern Baptist life. He suggested that each state conduct an evangelism conference every year. These conferences were to be times of inspiration and training, reminding participants of the importance of evangelism and preparing them to do evangelism effectively. The statewide conferences became very popular and remained a fixture in Southern Baptist life for decades. In some states, the evangelism conference was attended by more people than the state convention. Each year Matthews also wrote articles for Southern Baptist periodicals. A person reading any of the magazines and journals produced by the boards and agencies of the SBC would encounter some articles about evangelism. By keeping evangelism before the people, Matthews believed that he could keep people and churches involved in bringing the lost to Christ. The gardener tended his garden constantly.

In many ways, the Matthews era could be called "the golden age of Southern Baptist evangelism." The harvest was enormous, and the momentum Matthews created for evangelism within the Convention remained for years. It was not a perfect time, however. Matthews himself recognized the weakness of follow-up procedures for new Christians. By emphasizing so strongly the simultaneous approach to revivalism, pastors eventually grew tired, and the method was ignored for many years. His program was both simple to understand and easy to communicate. In a largely homogeneous denomination, the strengths of building a program around a single method overshadowed the weaknesses. As a much more complex and pluralistic body today, Southern Baptists would probably not respond again to such a focused attention on one method.

However, Matthews was not trying to reach people in our day; he was trying to reach the people of his time. He understood well the dynamics at work and was able to mobilize Southern Baptists for evangelism on an unprecedented scale and with incredible results. Matthews should be remembered for the organizational structure that he brought to the Convention's evangelism program, for his philosophy of assigning specific responsibility for evangelism at each level of the SBC, and for his determination to keep evangelism a visible and exciting aspect of Southern Baptist life. If the 1906 vote of the SBC to create a Department of Evangelism in the Home Mission Board was a first step toward assigning responsibility to help the churches with evangelism, the Matthews era was the ultimate step. There was not an assumption that Southern Baptist churches would be evangelistic. There was an assignment to make it so.

CHAPTER 5

Return to Yesterday

For more than 50 years, the structure put in place by C. E. Matthews remained. Growth in baptisms continued for many years, reaching a peak in 1972 as the Jesus Movement swept the nation. The methodology for evangelism became more balanced, emphasizing various forms of mass and personal evangelism. The Department of Evangelism assumed a larger and larger role in the Home Mission Board, eventually becoming a section headed by a vice president involved at the heart of the strategic planning and budget process for the whole Board. But eventually things changed.

Consolidating the Gains

Matthews resigned his position in 1955 due to poor health, and he died as the result of heart problems shortly thereafter. His game-changing innovation was an administrative one—the creation of a structure for continually giving attention to evangelism throughout the SBC. Most of that structure remained in place in some form into the twenty-first century. The notable exception was the Church Evangelism Council of local churches. Over time, it became a church council that focused on church programs in general rather than on evangelism in particular. That was a significant change, gradually reducing the continual attention to evangelism in many congregations. Among today's SBC churches, few set a specific evangelistic goal or target for baptisms or other evangelistic markers. Few have a strategy for evangelism in the community that is as clearly defined as their strategy for stewardship, mission trips, or other aspects of congregational life. Without doubt, the movement from Church Evangelism Council to church council had an effect on evangelistic fruitfulness, but the other elements of Matthews's administrative vision kept a clear focus on evangelism in the ongoing life of the SBC as a whole.

Of particular importance has been the ability of Southern Baptists to mobilize churches for participation in evangelistic emphases on a massive scale. In the past, coordinated, simultaneous evangelistic activities were generally popular and nearly always produced increased numbers of baptisms. Evangelistic programs and materials were produced with confidence on a large scale due to a certainty that they would be used. There were occasional misfires in that regard. The effort to enlist SBC churches to use a technology-based personal evangelism training program called *TELL* (*Training for Evangelistic Lifestyle and Leadership*) failed to achieve widespread results. It was an attempt to replace the most popular witness training program in SBC history. The churches were not ready for or interested in a replacement for the existing Lay Evangelism School, which had been extremely productive and well received during the Jesus Movement years when high numbers of baptisms were recorded. The churches believed that program was still quite effective, and so most simply ignored the new process. Despite such occasional misfires, the system in place worked smoothly overall. Whatever Southern Baptists did in evangelism was closely watched by others because it was usually fruitful and well executed.

Refinements Were Added

While the Matthews organizational model remained operative, his successors did continually seek to enhance the work of the Department. Some of the adjustments included methodological diversity, incorporating personal evangelism strategies and media-based strategies for a balanced focus on personal and mass evangelism. The production of materials and resources for evangelism training and events significantly increased and became a major component of the Department's work. Other added components included prayer for spiritual awakening, interfaith witness, and work with Southern Baptist vocational evangelists. Several attempts were made to incorporate the use of media within the SBC evangelism strategy, but with mixed results. Evangelism leader Ken Chafin attempted a weekly TV program (*Spring Street USA*), but it did not prove to be viable. Thirty- and 60-second TV spots were produced occasionally, but they were most affordable and effective when connected to a national emphasis such as simultaneous revivals. Radio, print, and social media were all part of the media mix; but thus far in the SBC story, no media-based platform has ever captured the hearts of Southern Baptists or generated compelling interest in evangelism.

With these developments came the growth of the evangelism staff and the role of evangelism in the total work of the HMB. After starting as a Department, it became a Division, and later on a Section with a HMB Vice President as its leader, who was involved at the highest levels of strategic planning.

This growth in size and influence appeared to be popular with the SBC at large. Those attending both state and national conventions were eager to hear reports of the evangelistic progress of the churches. The leader of the evangelism group was always widely known across the SBC and the evangelical world. The annual evangelism conference in some states was better attended than the state convention. Partnership with the HMB often made these programs possible.

At one point, there was concern that the work of evangelism might not be receiving enough attention within the HMB. The Convention appointed a study committee to consider forming a separate Evangelism Commission, much like today's Ethics and Religious Liberty Commission. The study committee concluded that an Evangelism Commission was not necessary, but it recommended that evangelism be given every consideration in the planning and operations of the Board. After this study, evangelism became a Section with a vice president.

Convention-Wide Coordination

The structure that C. E. Matthews put in place made coordination possible on a large scale. His successors continued this practice and extended it.

Working with state convention and associational leaders, the evangelism group was able to secure levels of participation in cooperative evangelistic ventures that were remarkable in light of Baptist polity and the complete autonomy of SBC churches. The periodic misfire (see the TELL experience above) reinforced the necessity of a cooperative approach. Such efforts were most often the result of task forces composed of representatives of church leaders, state convention evangelism workers, denominational leaders, and Board evangelism personnel. As SBC seminaries added evangelism professors, those professors were also included in the annual meetings of state and national evangelism personnel and were represented on evangelism task forces.

Processes were put in place to coordinate with other entities whose work included some connection with evangelism, such as the Sunday School Board (later renamed LifeWay), and with groups such as vocational evangelists. The various groups within the SBC, particularly the state conventions, were generally included in both the earliest stages of planning and the evaluation process that would follow an initiative. These efforts at inclusion were stronger under some leaders than others, but more often than not they were present.

As an occasional member of an HMB evangelism task force, I experienced a sense of true participation in the creation and design process for SBC evangelism events, processes, and materials. These were not meetings for the staff to give an early announcement of what was coming. They were collaborative efforts to build something or do something that reflected a shared understanding of Southern Baptist needs, opportunities, and identity. This collaborative approach may be the clearest indicator of the distinctively Southern Baptist approach to a denomination's evangelistic task. It does not take much time in any SBC church to realize its complete autonomy. No outside authority assigns leaders, tasks, or anything else to a Southern Baptist church of any size. Yet through the years, SBC churches have operated both cooperatively and independently with great effect in part because all involved realized cooperation was the key to significant impact.

The Sea Change

Every SBC entity files an annual written report on its activities. This report is typically incorporated into a formal report at the meeting of the Southern Baptist Convention each year and is published in the SBC *Book of Reports*, available to all messengers attending the annual meeting. Prior to the 1906 Convention, the Home Mission Board would report its emphasis on Church Planting and Missions (Ministry). Since the creation of the Department of Evangelism following the 1906 Convention, it became common for the HMB executive to note each year some version of this statement: "We have three focal points for our ministry: Evangelism, Church Planting, and Ministry." Particularly after the restoration of the Department of Evangelism in 1936, after the lost years following the Carnes embezzlement, the emphasis on HMB priorities clearly included evangelism as one of three priorities. This practice carried through combining the Home Mission Board, the Brotherhood Commission, and the Radio and Television Commission to create the North American Mission Board (NAMB) in 1996. The three priorities reported to the SBC after this change was made were Evangelism, Church Planting, and Ministry.

In recent years, the shift in NAMB's priorities has been reflected in a dramatic increase in the strategic planning and funding for church planting. Southern Baptists clearly need more churches. Churches are essential for getting the gospel to unreached communities. This era may have the greatest emphasis and support for church planting in SBC history, and that is a good and necessary priority. The ministry efforts of NAMB are also important. Disaster relief and other ministry efforts do much to open the door for a gospel witness. The response of Southern Baptists to New Orleans after Hurricane Katrina literally changed the image of Southern Baptists in a very non-Baptist place, opening the door for a great many gospel conversations. Ministry in the name of Jesus is a good and important priority. Surprisingly, however, for the first time in many years, evangelism is no longer included as a primary focal point for the entity charged with reaching North America with the gospel.

The report of the North American Mission Board to the 2016 Southern Baptist Convention states:

Our Send North America strategy is designed to help churches push back lostness in North America through two primary points of emphasis:

First, with the Send Network we want to help Southern Baptists plant more churches. . . .

Our other area of focus at NAMB is called Send Relief. It includes the types of ministries that the Church has been involved with (or at least should be involved with) for centuries.[1]

The following year, NAMB again reiterated its strategic priorities in its report to the 2017 meeting of the annual Southern Baptist Convention:

Pastors are NAMB's number one customer. We are here to serve them and help them succeed as they minister on the front lines. We serve pastors and churches in two primary ways: Send Relief [ministry] and Send Network [church planting].[2]

In 1906, after a discussion involving three annual meetings, two study committees, and prolonged discussions in business sessions, the Convention clearly and decisively assigned to the HMB the responsibility to help SBC churches with evangelism. Very few issues involving the ministry assignment and structure of an entity have ever consumed that much time during the Convention.

The HMB immediately complied with the assignment, and the Evangelism Department quickly became widely respected by the churches. Periodically, efforts to increase attention to evangelism have been made at the annual meeting. There is no indication that the Convention ever included motions or resolutions to decrease attention to evangelism. The evangelism office is still present at NAMB, but as of this writing it is not listed as a primary focal point in the strategic plan of the Board. NAMB is following its stated strategy by reducing the size of the evangelism staff, by limiting its internal role in planning and operations, and by avoiding

---

[1] *Annual of the 2016 Southern Baptist Convention*, St. Louis, Missouri (June 14–15, 2016), 188–89; http://www.sbcec.org/bor/2016/2016sbcannual.pdf.

[2] *Annual of the 2017 Southern Baptist Convention*, Phoenix, Arizona (June 13–14, 2017), 190; http://www.sbcec.org/bor/2017/2017SBCAnnual.pdf.

straightforward emphasis on winning people to Christ. Clearly, things are different now. Time will tell how these internal changes to the gardener affect the evangelistic health of SBC churches. The goal is not to reproduce the past. The goal is to help SBC churches evangelize their communities. The question is: How important is the public emphasis on evangelism at the national level?

How are the churches of the Convention doing now in their efforts to reach the lost in their communities? For the first time in its history, the SBC has recorded declining numbers of baptisms for 16 years in a row. Our churches are back to reaching about the same number of people as they did before C. E. Matthews implemented his plan for evangelism, even though the SBC has many more churches today. Attention to evangelism has been significantly reduced during this decline, and that reduction does not appear to be improving evangelistic results. More attention to the present state of evangelism in the SBC will be given in Part 4.

A great Baptist battle was necessary to create an assigned responsibility for someone to help SBC churches with evangelism. The fading of attention on that assignment in Baptist life today is best seen in the relatively little attention given to the deepest, longest decline in baptisms in the history of the SBC. As I write this chapter, there are some indications that new initiatives in evangelism are developing. However, they are coming in the sixteenth year of the decline, not the tenth year. The absence of tension over this decline for many years is more telling than any statistical snapshot.

***

Lesson 1

Without a gardener, there can be no garden.

The difference between a yard and a garden is not the number of plants in the ground but the level of attention given to the grass and plants. Historically, when SBC churches became more and more concerned about reaching the lost and unchurched in their communities, they created a Department of Evangelism with the responsibility of helping churches with evangelism. There was a gardener for the evangelism garden. Evangelistic results grew. In recent years, the level of attention to evangelism has been reduced, and evangelistic results have declined. Giving specific attention to an activity can make a significant difference.

*** *** ***

Questions for Conversation

1. Who is tending the evangelism garden in the SBC today, or who should be doing so?
2. Who is tending the evangelism garden in your church or ministry?
3. What specific steps are you taking to engage the lost in your community with the gospel?

LESSON 2

Old McBaptist needs a farm designed to sow the gospel and reap conversions.

T hrough the years, Southern Baptists developed a distinctive, characteristic approach to church life that embodied the New Testament principle of sowing and reaping. Four basic methods for evangelism defined the rhythm of how churches functioned, week in and week out. This evangelistic rhythm was found in SBC churches of all sizes, in all demographic settings, in every geographic region. Every church had its own personality, and variations from the standard were not unusual. However, evident in almost every SBC congregation were the four basic notes in the rhythm of congregational life that made the typical SBC church, at least to some extent, an evangelistic church.

CHAPTER 6

Decisional Preaching

T he focal point of the typical worship center of an SBC church is the pulpit. The centrality of preaching is unmistakable. This is not unusual in evangelical churches, but the distinct emphasis of the Southern Baptist pastor is decisional preaching. The sermon, intended to do more than make the gospel known, makes the demands of the gospel known (repentance and faith) and calls for an immediate and public response as a part of the worship experience. For Southern Baptists, the purpose of preaching is to persuade the will as well as to inform the mind. One effect of the practice of decisional preaching is the creation of an evangelistic climate within the congregation. Every person every week is reminded that no one is right with God until they "call upon the name of the Lord."

The Architecture of Evangelism

The design of a church facility offers some hints about how that church engages in evangelism. For many years, the typical Southern Baptist church placed the pulpit in the center of the platform. In front of the platform and at ground level was the communion or Lord's Supper table. When the Lord's Supper was observed, the table held the elements of the Supper. At most other times, an open Bible was placed on this centrally located table. Variations occurred, but the basic design of most Southern Baptist churches—small, medium, large, and mega—was similar.

The prominence of the pulpit and Bible in the design of the worship center were intended to suggest the centrality of the preaching ministry in

Southern Baptist life. Indeed, throughout history, the significance of the Bible and of the minister as preacher have been at the core of what Southern Baptists understand about the church. Doctrinally, the church would be described as a gathering of believers on mission as the people of God. However, the people in the pew usually thought of the church as the place where the Bible is preached and taught, even though a great many other activities occur in most congregations. In fact, one preacher described the denomination this way: "Mary had a little lamb. It should have been a sheep. It joined a local Baptist church one day and died for lack of sleep!" Nevertheless, the basic activity of the church has always been the ministry of proclamation.

In this environment, no one is surprised that preaching is the fundamental approach to evangelism by Southern Baptists, but more is involved than the centrality of preaching. Other denominations also focus on biblical proclamation as the core of the church's mission in the world. The *type* of preaching, even more than the *act* of preaching, makes proclamation an important evangelistic tool for Southern Baptists, whose distinctive perspective is decisional preaching. The sermon does more than make the gospel known; the demands of the gospel are made known and a response is expected. For Southern Baptists, the purpose of preaching is to persuade the will as well as to inform the mind. The expectations of both the preacher and the congregation are for an immediate response made publicly as a part of the worship experience.

The assumption behind this expectation is the Holy Spirit's work through decisional preaching. The invitation is a method, and the Holy Spirit is the One who empowers the method. He alone brings conviction of sin and stirs the human heart to respond. The use of sermon illustrations is a homiletical method. Preachers find and incorporate these specific tools in their sermons, but the Holy Spirit must use an illustration if it is to have maximum effect. The invitation, too, is a method of evangelism the Spirit can use in the preaching event. The Spirit's power, not the preacher's personality or technique, drives the effectiveness of the invitation. For the Holy Spirit to use this method, however, it must be deployed. The following discussion of decisional preaching and the use of the invitation assumes the work of the Holy Spirit through the method. Greater attention to the role of the Holy Spirit follows in Lesson 3.

The Biblical Precedent

Why do Southern Baptists emphasize decisional preaching? Biblical, historical, and practical reasons are apparent. The Bible, in both the Old and New Testaments, is filled with the imagery of public choice concerning one's spiritual convictions. In his farewell address to the children of Israel, Joshua reviewed the history of Israel and then called on the people to make a specific choice about whom they would serve:

> "[C]hoose for yourselves this day whom you will serve, whether the gods which your fathers served that were on the other side of the River, or the gods of the Amorites, in whose land you dwell. But as for me and my house, we will serve the LORD" (Josh 24:15).

In his dramatic encounter with the priests of Baal on Mount Carmel, Elijah wanted an immediate and public response from the people regarding whom they would worship: "How long will you falter between two opinions? If the LORD is God, follow Him; but if Baal, follow him" (1 Kgs 18:21).

When King Josiah heard the Word of the Lord, he made a public response and called for a response on the part of his people as well (2 Kgs 23:1–3). As Ezra reminded the people of their covenant responsibility to obey God's law, he called them to immediate and public repentance (Ezra 10:1–5, 7–12). Nehemiah, Joel, and Haggai are among other Old Testament figures who called their hearers to a public response of repentance. Although the portion of Jonah's message recorded in Scripture does not indicate a specific invitation, the response of the people of Nineveh suggests that his message included the demand for a public response expressing their repentance (Jonah 3:5).

John the Baptist insisted on a response that was public enough to be evaluated (Luke 3:7–14). He wanted the people who heard him to respond with public baptism and with lives illustrating the fruit of repentance. Jesus called for an immediate and public response from His disciples. They were to walk away from their old lives and follow Him (Matt 4:19; Luke 5:27–28). Peter, in his sermon at Pentecost, called his hearers to repent and be baptized (Acts 2:38). In his defense before Agrippa, Paul evidently spoke in a way that made Agrippa think a public response of belief was the prisoner's true goal as he presented his case to the king (Acts 26:1–29).

Although these biblical examples cannot be cited as illustrations of a modern approach to the invitation used by Southern Baptists, a public response does seem to be indicated in Scripture. That precedent forms an important part of the foundation for the Southern Baptist philosophy of preaching. Preaching is more than proclamation; it demands a response to the message of God through His Word.

Influence of Rhetoric

Historical aspects of this philosophy of preaching are noted as well. John Broadus and E. C. Dargan were Southern Baptists who made significant contributions to the field of preaching. Broadus was on the founding faculty of The Southern Baptist Theological Seminary, the oldest of the denomination's six seminaries. Dargan was one of his students and later taught preaching for many years at Southern Seminary. Broadus wrote a popular textbook on preaching titled *On the Preparation and Delivery of Sermons*.[1] For more than a century, this textbook has been used in schools of all denominations. The material in the book was originally presented in a preaching class consisting of a single student who was blind! Dargan's *History of Preaching*[2] is the most comprehensive history of preaching ever published.

Both men saw the same three roots in the development of Christian preaching: Old Testament preaching, the New Testament gospel, and Greek rhetoric. Rhetoric is the use of all available means of persuasion. The democratic tradition of the ancient Greeks led them to be among the first to study and analyze persuasive speech. Individuals who could

---

[1] John A. Broadus, *A Treatise on the Preparation and Delivery of Sermons*, ed. Edwin Charles Dargan, rev. ed. (New York: A. C. Armstrong and Son, 1898).

[2] Edwin Charles Dargan, *A History of Preaching*, 2 vols. (New York: Hodder & Stoughton, 1905, 1912).

persuade others to act or believe soon gained power and prominence, making rhetorical ability greatly prized in the Greco-Roman world. In a book
titled *Rhetoric*, written more than 300 years before the birth of Christ,
Aristotle produced a classic study that remains a seminal work in the art
of persuasion even today.

Rhetoric was an important component of a classical Greek and Roman
education. The disciples and first-century Christians did not have such formal training because of their cultural background. The educational concern of the Jews was the development of a thorough knowledge of the law.
However, as the church became more Gentile than Jewish, its leaders began to be trained in the Greek tradition. By the fourth century, consciously
or unconsciously, the canons (rules) of rhetoric were being applied to the
task of preaching. Chrysostom and Augustine were the first two men to
write about the task of preaching. Each scholar was highly educated in the
Greek tradition; in the case of Augustine, rhetoric was his primary field of
scholarship.

Over the years, the natural relationship between rhetoric and preaching was recognized and developed. Broadus and Dargan built their
instructions about preaching around the canons of rhetoric.[3] Invention, ar-
rangement, style, delivery, and memory became the organizational framework for teaching students how to preach. From the beginning, Southern
Baptists were taught to link biblical proclamation with rhetorical intent.
Preachers must proclaim the Word of God with a view to persuading men
and women to respond to God's call for repentance, faith, and obedience.
Giving hearers the immediate opportunity to respond, which is the purpose
of the invitation, is a logical consequence of the historic emphasis on persuasion found in Southern Baptist homiletical theory.

As Southern Baptist preachers were being trained in the art of persuasive preaching, the modern invitation system was developing. Some
biblical precedents for preaching with a view to an immediate and public

---

[3] See John A. Broadus, *On the Preparation and Delivery of Sermons*, rev. by Vernon L.
Stanfield, 4th ed. (New York: HarperOne, 1979); and Edwin Charles Dargan, *The Art of
Preaching in Light of Its History*, "The Holland Lectures Given at the Southwestern Baptist
Theological Seminary in Texas, October, 1921" (New York: George H. Doran Company,
1922); and Dargan, *The History of Preaching, ibid.*

response have been seen, but clearly these precedents were not illustrations of the contemporary approach to the invitation. The question remains: How did the modern invitation develop?

Historical Influences

In biblical times, preachers appear to have called for an immediate and public response. The early church continued the plea for repentance, faith, and obedience. However, an event in the fourth century dramatically impacted evangelism. With the conversion of Emperor Constantine, Christianity became the official religion of the Roman Empire. A great victory was won, but a deadening effect on evangelism also occurred. Mass "conversions" of people to Christianity were a form of allegiance to the state. To be Roman was to be a Christian. People were responding to the power and authority of their government more than to the conviction of the Holy Spirit.

A case in point was the conversion of Clovis, the king of the Franks. Because he wanted his troops to be Christians, Clovis had them march by priests who used palm branches dipped in water to sprinkle them, constituting their conversion to Christianity. Coupled with a movement away from believer's baptism to infant baptism, conversion became more an act of birth than rebirth. An individual was assumed to be a Christian by virtue of family and citizenship. Little need existed to call people to a public and immediate response to the gospel.

As the centuries passed, a gradual movement to a call for a personal response to the gospel message began to develop. In the twelfth century, Bernard of Clairvaux reportedly asked people to raise their hands if they wanted to restore their fellowship with God or with the church.[4] The Reformers of the sixteenth century emphasized the need for personal repentance and conversion, though apparently no call for hearers to make a public response in the worship service was extended. By the eighteenth century, aspects of today's public invitation began to develop. Roy Fish noted that Separate Baptists and Methodists would exhort people to indicate a desire

---

[4] Lloyd M. Perry and John R. Strubhar, *Evangelistic Preaching* (Eugene, OR: Wipf and Stock, 2000), 44.

for conversion or for prayer after the sermon, and the preacher would go to them and provide counsel and prayer.[5]

From the nineteenth century forward, the development of the public invitation is clearly seen in the ministries of the great evangelists. Calvinistic evangelist Asahel Nettelton invited those "anxious" over their salvation to come to a designated room for prayer and counsel. Charles Finney designated a front pew as the "anxious seat" for people in need of salvation. In the latter half of the nineteenth century, as Southern Baptists began formal homiletical instruction. D. L. Moody, a layman and evangelist, invited those concerned about their souls to join him in an "inquirer's room" to find out more about how to be a Christian. In the early part of the twentieth century, Billy Sunday made famous the expression "hit the sawdust trail" as he invited those who wanted to become Christians or make other commitments to come forward and shake his hand. With Billy Graham, the invitation received its most popular and familiar form. Persons seeking spiritual help were encouraged to come forward. A counselor met them, shared the gospel with them, and recorded information for follow-up.[6]

As the invitation was being developed and popularized by the great evangelists, the time of response gradually became a characteristic feature of Southern Baptist preaching and worship. Every proclamation of the Bible was recognized as an evangelistic event and a prophetic challenge. The use of an invitation was the logical consequence of preaching for a denomination that always emphasized evangelism.

The Function of the Invitation

Several practical factors also affected Southern Baptist invitation practices. To become members of a Southern Baptist church, individuals come forward to profess what has happened in their hearts; and then, as believers, they are baptized in public confession of that faith. Birth, marriage, or attendance "do not a Baptist make." The weekly use of the invitation met a practical need of regularly making the path to membership obvious to

---

[5] Roy J. Fish, *Giving a Good Invitation* (Nashville: Broadman Press, 1974), 15.

[6] For a comprehensive look at the development of the invitation, see Alan Streett, *The Effective Invitation: A Practical Guide for the Pastor* (Grand Rapids: Kregel, 2004).

those in attendance. In other words, the use of the invitation incorporates a church membership drive in each worship service.

The invitation also serves a valuable function for the pastor as counselor. The congregation has a weekly appointment time with the pastor. During the invitation, he is available for those members with spiritual needs to come to him for counsel and prayer. At times those needs can be met by a conversation during the invitation. When more time is needed, the invitation becomes the beginning point for help. A reinforcement of the pastor's role as spiritual advisor takes place each time the pastor stands before his congregation, inviting them to hear his message from the Lord. Most important, the invitation brings hearers to a point of decision.

In response to the Iraqi invasion of Kuwait in August 1990, President George H. W. Bush said that he was drawing a "line in the sand." This line included economic sanctions, a prominent display of military might, and warnings that force would be unleashed if Iraq failed to meet a deadline for leaving Kuwait. The president said he drew the "line in the sand" to prevent Saddam Hussein from prolonging his occupation of Kuwait indefinitely. Bush wanted a decision to be made and the matter to be resolved as soon as possible.

Decisional preaching is preaching that draws a "line in the sand" about a person's relationship with God. Its purpose is to bring the hearer to a point of decision about how to respond to God's dealing with his or her soul. Some ministers suggest that preaching is decisional when the hearer is prompted to think about what God would have him do. Others would say that preaching is decisional when the hearer is moved to implement responsive changes at some point after the worship service is concluded. For most Southern Baptists, decisional preaching calls for an immediate and public response to the message proclaimed. The invitation is not a special approach reserved for evangelistic campaigns but an organic part of the sermon and characteristic of a worship service. As such, decisional preaching has been the fundamental way in which Southern Baptists have engaged in evangelism.

Types of Invitation

Southern Baptist pastors and evangelists have drawn this spiritual line in the sand in a variety of ways. The most basic approach is to ask the hearers to acknowledge that they are on the threshold of decision. The preacher asks those who recognize a spiritual decision may be needed in their lives to raise their hands, stand up, fill out a card, or take some other action. This response is not a call to come forward, and it does not necessarily indicate a decision is being made. The action is merely an affirmation that God is dealing with one's heart and that a decision is being considered.

Much is to be commended in this form of invitation. Because little is demanded of the hearer, this approach is one of the easiest invitations to which a person can respond. By so identifying those who are considering decisive responses to the message, the preacher can quickly determine if the call for a more overt response is appropriate at this time. If no one present recognizes the need for a decision to be made, response to a more demanding invitation is less likely. When the hearer acknowledges that he is considering a specific response to the message preached, he is preparing himself to make that response.

This form of invitation can be especially helpful with a congregation that is largely or completely Christian. Often such groups feel less inclined to respond to an invitation to come forward. Perhaps they recognize a personal need or application of the message shared, but they do not feel a need for counsel or prayer with the pastor or other counselors. The request for prayer or the acknowledgment that God is dealing with them offers at least some form of public response to the proclamation of God's Word.

A second form of invitation is related to the first. The *invitation to come forward* for counseling and prayer or to acknowledge publicly a private commitment is the most common form of invitation used in Southern Baptist life. Several purposes for this type of invitation are significant. The hearers have an opportunity for spiritual counsel and prayer at the time when they are most aware of their need. A vivid witness to God's work in the lives of contemporary people is provided for those who are present in worship. Some who wonder if God could possibly be dealing with them are reminded in the public response of others that God still moves in the hearts and lives of men and women today.

In his book *Stand Up and Be Counted*, R. T. Kendall, longtime pastor of Westminster Chapel in London, defends calling people to come forward because the response is a public declaration of what God has done and is doing in a person's life.[7] No saving value is part of the act of coming forward, but there is a witness value. Coming forward identifies the respondent as someone who belongs or wants to belong to Jesus. The idea that a person's religion is between the individual and God is certainly not a New Testament idea. Jesus Himself insisted on the unashamed identification of the disciple with his master (Mark 8:38). Coming forward during an invitation could be considered practice in witnessing, giving a witness that God is doing something in the respondent's life. Of course, that witness should be continued through the act of baptism as well as the words and deeds of one whose soul is right with God long after the worship service is over.

A *progressive invitation* consists of the call to indicate a need for prayer followed by a call to come forward. Initially the hearer acknowledges the need to make a commitment then he is urged to progress to the point of acting on that commitment before the service concludes. Southern Baptist evangelists often use a progressive invitation in revival meetings and evangelistic crusades. Properly used, this type of invitation follows a natural psychological process. The hearer recognizes a decision that needs to be made or a change that needs to take place and then acts on it. However, care must be taken not to abuse the process.

The use of a progressive invitation should not leave the hearer feeling coerced or manipulated into an accelerated decision process. One should know that he or she can make the first response without having to make a second. To rush people into expressing an insincere commitment is to deny them an opportunity to make a genuine commitment to the Lord. If proper care is taken to safeguard the integrity of the initial respondents, the progressive invitation can help the hearers work through the process of getting their souls right with God.

A related but distinct form of invitation is the *altar call* invitation. With this approach, the preacher invites hearers to come to the altar or front of

---

[7] R. T. Kendall, *Stand Up and Be Counted: Call for Public Confession of Faith* (Grand Rapids: Zondervan, 1985).

the church for a time of personal prayer. A public response of personal prayer, not a request for counsel or the registration of a commitment, is the purpose of this type of invitation. The target group is usually the believers who are present. The call for prayer may concern a person's relationship with God; a problem or need within the congregation, the community, the larger world; or any other pressing issue. The unique aspect of this invitation is that it is both public and private. The one who comes forward is doing so in front of the assembled congregation, but he is coming forward to engage in a private act of prayer. A public witness is given, and an internal response is made.

The altar call can be a very meaningful invitation for the mature believer and can deeply stir a congregation when a significant number of people respond. The critical factor is the motivation of the response. When people come in response to instructions that give them little alternative but coming to the altar, the lasting response will be minimal. When they come in response to an inner compulsion to do some business with God, the results can be profound.

Asking for a *delayed response* is another way to invite response from hearers. In this approach, the hearers are asked to make some definite response to the message after the worship service is concluded. That response can take any number of forms: witnessing to a friend, seeking forgiveness from someone who has been wronged, spending time alone with God, and so forth. The distinctive note in the invitation is a call for specific action in the world rather than in the church. When this approach is used, provision should be made for those who respond to report their actions or the responses to their action. To suggest an action and not be interested in what happens or who responds is to indicate that the suggested action has little importance. This type of invitation has not been commonly used in Southern Baptist life.

Another spin on the invitation in Southern Baptist churches is the *invitation by card*. Some form of registration card is distributed to all of those who gathered for worship. At the close of the services, the hearers are asked to complete the card. One section of the card outlines various responses to the message, allowing the people to indicate if they have given their lives to Christ, are interested in joining the church, or would like to talk to someone about a spiritual concern. The cards are collected or left in the seats, and the staff or volunteers contact those who responded. This type of invitation is not new, but it is receiving new attention, especially from those churches that have identified unchurched young adults as the target for their outreach.

Invitation Guidelines

Preachers who use some form of invitation system should keep in mind a few simple guidelines. The invitation should always flow from the sermon. The preacher should invite hearers to respond to what they heard, not to a standard appeal repeated at the end of each worship service. An evangelistic message should use an invitation that emphasizes becoming a Christian and making a public profession of faith. A sermon dealing with the spiritual life of Christians should incorporate a call to a deeper walk with the Lord. Sermon preparation is not complete without careful prayer and thought about how the congregation should be asked to respond to the message. The object of the sermon should relate clearly to the appeal of the invitation.

Variety in the types of decisional response to sermons is both possible and desirable. This practice is especially important for pastors, who deal with the same crowd week after week. Faris Whitesell has written a book titled *65 Ways to Give Evangelistic Invitations*, indicating the great potential for variety in types of invitations.[8] The use of varied forms of response will keep the minds of listeners engaged as the end of the sermon nears. Regular hearers who know exactly what will happen at the end of each sermon also know exactly how they will respond: they will get ready to go home.

Above all, the invitation should be clear. The hearers should be told clearly what to do in response to the sermon. Explain what will happen when they respond. Will they be met by a counselor? Will they be taken to another room? Never assume the hearers know what to do or what will happen if they respond. Even in congregations that regularly use the

---

[8] Faris D. Whitesell, *65 Ways to Give Evangelistic Invitations* (Grand Rapids: Zondervan, 1945; repr. Grand Rapids, Kregel, 1984).

invitation, many hearers do not understand the process. They may assume the invitation is not for them and not notice what happens. When they find themselves under conviction and ready to respond, clear instructions will make the response easier. Invitations are not for the whole congregation. They are for those with whom the Holy Spirit is dealing in that particular message. The worshipers who want to make a response *this time* need to know exactly what to do.

The use of an invitation system does require the provision of adequate counseling. A typical invitation lasts from five to fifteen minutes in most SBC churches. If the preacher is the only counselor, that is not very much time to help people with spiritual problems. Work with the assumption that not enough help was given during the invitation itself. Personal visits should follow all invitation responses. Clarify the decision that was made by asking the person to explain it in his or her own words outside the time-sensitive environment of a worship service. Pastors should train and use counselors to help them deal with persons who come forward. If a church has an evangelism training program, members with training and experience in talking with people about their relationship with God can be used as counselors. Be especially sensitive to children and those who come from an unchurched background. They are the ones most likely to need more help than the brief time of the invitation allows.

Finally, the invitation should be extended long enough, but not too long. The preacher who extends an invitation must be in tune with the Holy Spirit. To give hard and fast guidelines about how long the invitation should last would be unwise, for there will be exceptions to every rule. The invitation should be long enough to give people an opportunity to recognize the conviction of the Holy Spirit and realize that now is the time to respond. However, the invitation should not be so long that people feel bored or that they are being coerced to respond. Sensitivity to the leadership of the Holy Spirit and the body language of the congregation is required. The length of the sermon may affect how long people will remain open to the invitation appeal.

The Climate of Response

Pastors interested in leading an evangelistic, growing church face the question, Why are some churches evangelistic and others not? A church must have the air of an evangelistic atmosphere before it can or will support evangelistic programming and objectives. The problem comes in discerning how to help a church accept evangelism as a priority.

Southern Baptists are recognized as a denomination whose churches, on the whole, have emphasized evangelism more than those of many other denominations. While other factors are involved, decisional preaching has played a pivotal role in the development and maintenance of an evangelistic atmosphere in Southern Baptist churches. Each time the typical SBC church gathers, people are called to make an immediate and public response to the gospel. When a person makes a profession of faith, the entire congregation witnesses the declaration both when the public commitment is made and again when baptism takes place. The consistent appeal underscores the importance of a person's being right with God. The immediate and public nature of the appeal emphasizes its urgency. Perhaps without realizing it, the church comes to accept the importance of the evangelistic task and the necessity of conversion. Decisional preaching creates a climate of expectancy for evangelistic response. The church becomes a place where people are born again as well as a place where believers gather.

While not always the case in Southern Baptist life, more people tend to gather for the worship services than for any other aspect of church life. Decisional preaching provides a tool for doing evangelism week by week among the largest block of people involved in church activities. This reality makes the worship service a potential harvest vehicle for cultivation in the smaller units of church activity. Sunday School, ministry projects, the music program, athletic events, and other activities may attract and nurture more outsiders, but when people become involved in the worship services, they are brought into an atmosphere in which commitment to Christ is sought, illustrated, and affirmed. Decisional preaching often provides the occasion for a person's last step in the pilgrimage toward faith in Jesus Christ.

Decisional preaching and its emphasis on an immediate and public response to the gospel through the use of the invitation gives every Baptist church, large or small, liberal or conservative, at least one means of engaging regularly in evangelism. New budget money and specialized training are not required. Every time an invitation is extended, the pastor is reminding his hearers that a personal relationship with Christ is necessary for one to be right with God. For Southern Baptists, an evangelistic appeal is not reserved for a special campaign. The invitation is a weekly reminder that evangelism matters. This attitude and philosophy, when applied to the soul of a church—its weekly worship service—creates an evangelistic atmosphere within the congregation.

CHAPTER 7

Personal Evangelism

S outhern Baptists are pulpit-oriented but also understand that most people who need salvation are not in the worship service of a church.
The gospel must be proclaimed in the pulpit, but it must also be shared in
conversations outside the walls of the church. Early approaches to evangelism by the SBC emphasized evangelistic crusades, but as time passed,
more and more emphasis was given to personal evangelism and the need
to mobilize church members to share their faith as they lived their lives.

Historically, Southern Baptists have focused on preaching. The most
common image associated with evangelism for many Southern Baptists is
a preacher proclaiming the gospel and extending an invitation for persons
to be born again. What many members have not recognized is the critical
role that personal evangelism plays as a complement to decisional preaching. The earliest form of personal evangelism was a weekly visitation program as a standard procedure in most Southern Baptist churches. Over the
years, the emphasis shifted to witness training programs and appeared to
lessen the reliance of churches upon revivalism as the source of most conversions. To put it another way, there was a growing recognition that the
gospel needed to be heard outside of the church as well as inside.

A steady shift among the congregations from a base program of revivalism to a base program of personal evangelism gradually unfolded. In
terms of expectations, this shift is expressed in the anticipation of weekly
conversions as opposed to an annual "harvest time" with most conversions
being registered during a revival meeting. This shift has not de-emphasized

revivalism as much as it has focused on mobilizing the church for evangelism as a way of life.

Every Christian's Job

Personal evangelism is not a new emphasis for Southern Baptists. From W. W. Hamilton until today, the leaders of the Evangelism Department have used their publications, their preaching, and their programming to encourage believers to share their faith. The heritage of decisional preaching and revivalism (discussed in chapter 9) in Southern Baptist life appears to magnify the role of professional clergy in evangelism, suggesting that the laity have little sense of responsibility for evangelism and witness. While this assumption is true to some extent, the focus on evangelism from the pulpit has been offset by a consistent emphasis upon personal evangelism through the years.

Several indications of the importance of personal evangelism in Southern Baptist life are apparent. The first indicator is the role of visitation programs in Southern Baptist churches. As noted earlier, a visitation program of some sort was a standard feature in the majority of SBC churches, especially during the years when Southern Baptists were having their greatest period of growth. The typical church visitation program attempted to mobilize the congregation for outreach on a weekly basis. The format for the program included a brief devotional thought and prayer, instructions and assignments, visitation (usually in pairs), and a time to regather for reports of results and closing prayer.

In most churches, the prospects and visitation assignments were organized according to Sunday School departments. The prospects were assigned to a Sunday School department based upon the age or school grade of the person who was a potential member. Members of the appropriate Sunday School department visited the prospects, actually engaging in relational evangelism. Visits were to be made by the people with whom the prospect would have the most contact if he or she began attending church, making the formation of relationships easier and more natural.

One requirement for an effective visitation program is a steady flow of prospects for the people to visit. This pressure led SBC churches to look actively for specific people in the community who were not Christians or who did not have membership in a local church. Sources for prospects included new people in the community, visitors to the church, the unsaved or unchurched family and friends of church members, and people identified in a periodic census of the community. Prospect information was usually organized into a prospect file, which became a tool to help the church systematically identify and cultivate the unsaved people of the community.

The constant search for prospects made necessary by a weekly visitation program was thus an important factor in maintaining the evangelistic atmosphere of a church. Visitation located and cultivated new people to come under the influence of decisional preaching and evangelistic Bible study in Sunday School. A means to follow-up was also provided, exposing prospects, who had heard a public proclamation of the gospel, to a personal explanation of how to be saved. Even with the time constraints felt by today's believers and the barriers to visitation found in urban areas (i.e., apartment buildings, travel distance, and safety), a visitation program of some sort remains a strategy of many evangelistic Southern Baptist churches.

The materials for evangelism training from LifeWay Christian Resources are another indication of the importance of personal evangelism. Although data has not been compiled formally, any cursory examination reveals a tremendous amount of evangelism materials produced by Life-Way. The Evangelism Department was assigned to NAMB, but LifeWay has produced more evangelism materials over the years as the Convention's publisher and has the assignment of discipleship training.

Called by a variety of names over the years, since the early twentieth century Discipleship Training for SBC churches was the Sunday night program, which began as the Southern Baptist expression of a revival movement among young people in the United States. The focus became training for Christian service as opposed to the Bible study emphasis of Sunday School. To supply materials for Discipleship Training and the training of Sunday School workers, the Sunday School Board annually produced one or more study programs related to evangelism for much of the twentieth century. Virtually all the material has been designed to mobilize the laity, rather than the clergy, for involvement in personal evangelism.

The Role of Theological Education

Theological education was another source of emphasis on personal evangelism in Southern Baptist life. Evangelism was not included in normal theological education until B. H. Carroll established Southwestern Baptist Theological Seminary in Fort Worth, Texas. Carroll, a great Southern Baptist theologian and educator, was a key figure in the struggle to create a national Department of Evangelism. He founded Southwestern, shortly after that denominational battle, and decided that evangelism needed to be included in the regular course of theological studies. Carroll apparently established the first Chair of Evangelism for any seminary in the world. In the academic world, a "chair" is a faculty position guaranteed permanent funding through gifts placed in a restricted endowment fund; it establishes a professor in a position of prestige on a faculty. Inclusion in theological training assured evangelism not only a place but a prominent role in the curriculum of Southwestern Seminary. Over the years, all Southern Baptist seminaries have followed the lead of Southwestern, and now each of the six SBC seminaries has one or more evangelism professors, many of whom occupy "chairs" of evangelism.

Carroll called the evangelism chair the "Chair of Fire" and considered evangelism training essential in the preparation of people for ministry. L. R. Scarborough was chosen as the first evangelism professor. Scarborough emphasized personal evangelism in his classes, teaching his students the importance of visitation and how to lead a person to Christ in a one-on-one encounter. Class assignments always included the memorization of Scripture passages to be used in leading others to Christ. Attention was given to the personal witnessing practices of Jesus, Paul, and other people in the Bible. Scarborough also wrote several textbooks, the best known of which is *With Christ After the Lost*.[1] Sharing Christ personally was an emphasis in all his evangelistic writings. As the first evangelism professor, he created a model that made the value and importance of personal evangelism for productivity in ministry an unmistakable emphasis in seminary education.

---

[1] L. R. Scarborough, *With Christ After the Lost: A Search for Souls* (New York: George H. Doran Company, 1919; rev. ed., Nashville: Broadman Press, 1990).

Scarborough became a well-known denominational leader, following Carroll as president of Southwestern Seminary. As his profile rose within the SBC, so did the profile of evangelism, for he remained a professor of evangelism the rest of his life. His success and the growth of Southwestern into the largest seminary in the world helped to ensure the place of evangelism in Southern Baptist theological education. Thus, a strong emphasis upon personal evangelism was also secured.

Contributions to the educational emphasis undergirding personal evangelism were made by others as well. Gaines Dobbins was another highly respected Southern Baptist leader who served on the faculty of The Southern Baptist Theological Seminary in Louisville, Kentucky. His field was education, but he also taught evangelism. He wrote a textbook titled *Evangelism According to Christ*[2] and gave much attention to the personal work of Jesus. E. Y. Mullins, one of the most significant Southern Baptist theologians and a professor and president of Southern Seminary, wrote a book on personal soul-winning that appears to have been the earliest such book published by a Southern Baptist. W. W. Hamilton, the first Secretary of Evangelism for the Convention, was later selected as the president of New Orleans Baptist Theological Seminary and served as its first professor of evangelism. Roland Q. Leavell, another Secretary of Evangelism for NAMB, also served as president of the New Orleans seminary and taught classes in evangelism during his presidency. The effectiveness of Southern Baptists in evangelism cannot be separated from their decision to include specific instruction in evangelism in the theological training of ministerial students.

Denominational recognition tends to encourage imitation in the churches. Many people in the denominational spotlight for one reason or another were associated with evangelism. The prominence of SBC leaders associated with evangelism encouraged the evangelistic atmosphere of the Convention. Leaders committed to personal evangelism produce followers who were committed to personal evangelism as well. Gradually, Southern Baptists came to value person-to-person evangelism almost as much as they valued pulpit evangelism.

---

[2] Gaines S. Dobbins, *Evangelism according to Christ* (New York: Harper & Brothers Publishers, 1949).

Where There Is a Will, There Is a Way

Within the realm of personal evangelism, three basic approaches exist: proactive, reactive, and passive. The *proactive approach* emphasizes the initiative of the Christian witness. A believer creates a situation in which he or she will be able to share the gospel. Home visitation, for example, is a proactive approach. Believers go to the home of unbelievers in order to share the gospel. Starting a conversation in order to witness with someone in a public place, an office, or some other setting is proactive. The evangelistic encounter happens because the Christian starts the interaction in order to witness.

Reactive approaches emphasize turning an existing situation into a witnessing situation. The conversation of Jesus with the woman at the well illustrates this approach (John 4:7–30). He turned a conversation about water into a discussion of how to find true satisfaction. Relational and lifestyle evangelism programs emphasize this reactive approach. The goal for the witness is to take advantage, in life and relationships, of those moments that offer opportunities to explain the gospel. When a person approaches a Christian about a personal crisis, the Christian can share what Jesus has done to help in times of his or her personal crisis. When acts of kindness lead someone to ask why a believer has been so caring, an explanation of the impact Jesus has made can be given.

Passive programs of personal evangelism are those programs that make the gospel available to individuals without dialogue or personal interaction. Leaving a tract with the tip for a waiter or waitress is a passive way to share the gospel. Making an evangelistic television commercial, posting a billboard with the plan of salvation, sharing the plan of salvation through a social media post, or sending a direct mail piece that includes an explanation of how to become a Christian are all ways to share the gospel without immediate interaction with people. The prospect may see or hear the gospel presentation, but no one is there to follow up, clarify, or discuss the content of the Christian witness. The passive approach to personal evangelism has some obvious drawbacks, but it is more than a coward's way to do evangelism. At times, a passive witness may be the only means to give people at least some exposure to the gospel.

Southern Baptists have encouraged all three approaches, but their strongest emphasis is on proactive approaches. Most of the training processes developed by NAMB focus on how to initiate evangelistic encounters. Some training resources are available for reactive or relational evangelism. One of the biggest needs is training and strategy for legitimate approaches to passive evangelism, particularly strategies involving social media and websites.

Rhetoric versus Reality

As Southern Baptists began to talk more and more about personal evangelism, a dilemma surfaced about how to match the rhetoric with the reality of mobilizing congregations to share Christ with others. Training for personal evangelism was done in seminary classes and in church workshops often held in conjunction with revival crusades. For church members, personal evangelism training was done through the Discipleship Training program and related study course programs. The Discipleship Training program has been discussed briefly. Now attention will be given to the study course program.

Each year LifeWay produced several small, simple books on a variety of topics to be used for leadership training through a study course program. The books were taught at designated times by the pastor or other church leader. At the conclusion of the "course," an examination was given. Those members who attended the study course, read the book, and passed the test received a certificate. Many churches set aside one or more weeks a year as study course weeks. The church would gather in the evenings, often by age group, to study the designated book. Many of these books were on personal evangelism. For years these study courses constituted Southern Baptists' basic approach to evangelism training. The methodology was lecture, supplemented by reading, and evaluated by testing. The approach advocated was usually proactive, encouraging participants to take the initiative in telling friends, neighbors, and others about Jesus. This approach was especially popular during the 1940s and 1950s.

In the second half of the century, more attention was given to personal evangelism in the denominational evangelism program. Most of the evangelism directors sought to balance personal and mass evangelism programs. During his brief tenure, Ken Chafin made personal evangelism the primary emphasis of the evangelism office. The nearly exclusive emphasis on witnessing did not last beyond Chafin's time with NAMB, but the goal of shaping the evangelism program to reflect a more balanced emphasis on revivalism and soul-winning became a permanent part of philosophy of NAMB. Perhaps more important, the process for enlisting and equipping church members for personal evangelism significantly improved. The lecture/study approach was largely replaced by hands-on training. Some examples of Southern Baptist evangelism training programs will be discussed briefly.

The *Lay Evangelism School* (LES) was introduced in the early 1970s and quickly became the most popular evangelism training program in Southern Baptist history. The process involved 10 hours of training and included brief lectures, individual and small group activities, and at least one evening of actual evangelistic visitation. Participants were taught to share their personal testimonies and explain how to become a Christian by reading through a witnessing booklet (tract) with a prospect. The school itself was followed by a weekly visitation program lasting 10 weeks and including brief witness training each week. The program has also been called *Witness Involvement Now* (WIN).

The strength of the program was its simplicity. Very little spiritual knowledge or maturity was assumed. Little preparation or effort was required other than attendance. The program was appropriate for a large or small group, and the expense was minimal. By focusing only on the basic skills of sharing your testimony and reading a tract, some degree of competency and confidence was established in the brief training time. The group dynamic materials were excellent, helping people feel comfortable talking about their faith with others.

The greatest weakness appeared to be in the visitation strategy. Many churches found that attendance dropped significantly on the night for visitation. People were more willing to be trained than to engage in implementing the practices for which they were being trained. Not all churches implemented the visitation program, which was supposed to be conducted after the training; some considered the process to be complete after the 10 hours of initial training. However, training without sufficient experience seldom produces permanent changes in attitudes or behavior. The LES provided an excellent way to train a large number of people to witness, but the training did not always result in lasting commitments to and involvement in personal evangelism.

As mentioned earlier, the LES program was popular and successful in many ways. Introduced on a large scale in 1972, LES helped Southern Baptists set a new record in baptisms for the first time in a decade. The numbers dropped significantly the following year, however, indicating that many people were reached by the evangelistic efforts during and shortly after the schools but that the pattern of witnessing did not become permanent.

Another personal evangelism program developed by the denomination was Training for Evangelistic Lifestyle and Leadership (TELL). This program attempted to incorporate modern technology and to allow for the diverse needs of Southern Baptist churches. An audio-visual machine was used by an individual or a group and played special tapes combining film strips with a soundtrack. The tapes covered a variety of topics and could be played in any order, according to interest or need. Some suggestions for use were included. Participants were taught to witness by sharing their testimonies, reading a witnessing booklet, or marking a New Testament with the plan of salvation. In the latter stages of training, going out to witness after the sessions was recommended. The strength of the program was its flexibility. Users could arrange the audio-visual tapes to be used in any order desired. Groups as small as one or larger than 100 could be trained. Witnessing skills, motivation, problems, and examples were included in the materials.

Unfortunately, this highly adaptable program was one of the least used evangelism programs NAMB ever produced. The cost of machine and tapes, about $500, may have been a negative factor as most Southern Baptist churches had fewer than 300 members and a limited budget. The flexibility may have been as much a weakness as a strength. Many people like packaged products that give exact instructions. Having to design an individualized program might be liberating for some but intimidating for others. The audio-visual package may also have met resistance from leaders who were not confident with the technology. The delivery system was an uncomfortable fit for many Southern Baptist churches.

One of the greatest contributions to personal evangelism training in the last century appears to have been the *Evangelism Explosion* (EE) training program developed by D. James Kennedy, a Presbyterian minister. After completing seminary training, Kennedy became pastor of a promising congregation in Florida. Soon the church began dying under his leadership. He realized that he did not know how to lead a person to Christ. Kennedy was invited to lead a revival meeting for a church in another state. While he was there, the host pastor taught him how to witness by taking him out for evangelistic visitation every day. Kennedy returned to his church with a renewed vision and a determination to teach his people how to share their faith.

Kennedy's first effort was a lecture-based program that made little impact. His next effort was a longer, more thorough lecture-based program. Again, there was little impact. Finally, he decided to train his people the way he was trained, by taking them out for actual experience in sharing their faith while they were being taught what to say and do. He applied the ancient concept of apprenticeship to personal evangelism training, and the result was an "evangelism explosion." Kennedy put his training program together in a format that other churches could use, and he began to train pastors to equip their congregations to witness. Evangelism Explosion became a popular and productive program used by churches from many denominations all over the United States and the world.

Many Southern Baptists used Evangelism Explosion in their congregations. Over the years, pastors asked NAMB to develop a Southern Baptist version of EE. The Evangelism Division negotiated with the EE organization, asking them to develop a format of EE designed for Southern Baptist churches and more closely reflecting Southern Baptist doctrine and practices. When the request was denied, Southern Baptist leaders asked the Board to develop a Southern Baptist evangelism training program incorporating the apprenticeship approach pioneered in EE. The *Continuing Witness Training* (CWT) program was the result of that request.

In comparison with EE, Baptists' CWT program had similarities and differences. Like EE, CWT taught participants to memorize a presentation of the gospel and required "on-the-job" experience in witnessing during the training process. Both programs taught people to train others to witness. Participants were then expected to train others. Unlike EE, CWT dealt with the issue of believer's baptism for those making professions of faith. CWT was also a shorter training process (13 weeks as opposed to 17), had a stronger emphasis on the lordship of Christ, and was significantly less expensive. The cost difference was due in part to the denominational backing of CWT versus the independent status of EE. A crossover process for churches wanting to switch from EE to CWT was developed.

CWT became a cornerstone in the evangelism program of many Southern Baptist churches. Strengths of the evangelism training included thoroughness of training and actual witnessing experience. Sending people out to share their faith several times with someone who knows how to witness was a greater help in developing confidence than a classroom experience. Weaknesses included the extensive requirements of memorizing a plan of salvation and spending at least two and a half hours in training each week for 13 weeks. Not everyone in a church would attend CWT training, but those who did were better trained and more likely to continue sharing their faith than those who completed a less involved process.

As the lives of church members became more complex, they became increasingly more protective of their time. In response, NAMB developed a format allowing churches to do witness training in one day. The *One-Day Soul-Winning Workshop* was designed to be completed in a few hours on a Saturday. The schedule began with some basic training on the role of the Holy Spirit in witnessing and guidelines on how to share a personal testimony and present the gospel with a witnessing booklet. After lunch, participants practiced what they had learned, made witnessing visits, and then returned to the church for reports and a brief closing session.

First introduced in the 1989–1990 church year, the one-day workshop became very popular. Strengths included the potential to train groups of any size and the brief amount of time required for the training. This program could also be used easily in conjunction with other evangelism events, such as a revival, prospect dinner, etc. The primary weakness was the brevity of the training. Generally, the shorter the training process, the less impactful the results. The workshop was used to introduce church members to evangelism training in hopes of enlisting them for more extensive training at a later time. A "change of pace" was also provided to continue evangelism training while taking a brief break from a more demanding process.

Another process for personal evangelism training from NAMB was called *Building Witnessing Relationships* (BWR). This program was designed to train people for relational evangelism—sharing the gospel with family, friends, neighbors, etc. Southern Baptists had been involved in this approach to personal evangelism for years. C. E. Autrey's program, called *Cultivative Witnessing*, sought to involve people in making multiple visits to share Christ with people as the witness formed a relationship with the prospect. C. B. Hogue emphasized *lifestyle evangelism* during his tenure, asking believers to focus on sharing Christ with the people they encountered in the daily routines of life. As the culmination of these and other programs, BWR was the most comprehensive approach to relational evangelism training yet attempted by Southern Baptists.

The goals of BWR included teaching people how to evaluate where people are in their spiritual development, how to develop a strategy for sharing the gospel based upon an individual's openness to the gospel, and how to bring people to the point of decision about Christ. The seminar was designed for those who had already received some form of evangelism training. The purpose of BWR was to improve the witness of those who were sharing their faith, not to teach people who are uncommitted to personal evangelism how to witness.

The material was excellent and included a process for determining a person's spiritual condition as well as specific suggestions for developing witnessing strategies. Those who were looking for a program to motivate and equip nonwitnessing church members found BWR to be weak in basic training for soul-winning.

Mass Encounters of the Personal Kind

Newer forms of personal evangelism involved the use of mass media. Considering the audience for most forms of mass media as a crowd of people is a common mistake. The total audience may be large, but the presentation is usually received by one person at a time. The various forms of mass media are more than vehicles for reaching large numbers of people. Use of the various forms of mass media for evangelistic purposes necessitates planning the use and content according to the dynamics of personal evangelism. In most cases, attempts to use mass media for evangelism are passive approaches. The gospel may be shared, but rarely will there be a Christian witness present to supplement or interpret the mass media presentation.

Even effective *crusade evangelism* is built upon principles of personal evangelism. A staff member of the Billy Graham organization described Graham's crusades as "personal evangelism on a mass scale." The emphasis placed upon personal evangelism was a significant factor in the evangelistic impact of Graham's crusades. Preparation for each crusade included a plan to train and mobilize Christians in the area for personal outreach to the people they knew. Counselor training included training in how to lead people to Christ and encouragement for a lifestyle of witnessing. Graham and his team attempted to do mass evangelism by mobilizing as many people as possible for personal evangelism. Successful crusade evangelism is more likely where there is successful personal evangelism.

Telemarketing principles have been adapted for evangelism and church growth as alternatives for home visitation. The business world developed telemarketing as a sales strategy capitalizing on the fact that most homes had telephones. Many homes, especially those in apartment complexes, cannot be visited door-to-door. Use of the telephone gives access to more people in less time and for less expense than can be reached through personal visits. In evangelism, the telephone can be used for surveys, for gospel presentations, for invitations to evangelistic events, and for follow-up on other approaches.

The most common use of telemarketing in evangelism has been in survey work. In many places, especially urban areas, a door-to-door survey of every home may be difficult or impossible. A telephone survey is an alternative. The survey can be designed as a census (information gathering to locate possible prospects) or as an evangelistic tool (asking questions that lead to sharing the gospel with a respondent). To use telephones for surveying or for sharing the gospel, witnesses usually need some form of script to guide their presentations.

When a church is planning an evangelistic event, telephones can be used to issue personal invitations to large numbers of people. Many church planters use the telephone to find and invite prospects to the start of a new church. The most efficient use of the telephone approach is as a follow-up tool for other forms of evangelism. A church with televised worship services can put its telephone number on the screen during a broadcast and invite viewers to call the number for help. Visitors can be given a follow-up phone call soon after a visit or expression of interest in knowing more about the gospel or the church. The advantage of using the telephone in a follow-up process is the increased interest of the persons being contacted. Today a growing number of churches and ministries are using an internet address for viewers to contact, which offers greater flexibility and, in some way, fewer personal requirements.

The telephone is not as personal as a face-to-face visit, but it is more personal than most other forms of contact. Many church members feel less intimidated about sharing Christ over the telephone than they do in person. Creative use of the telephone offers an alternative for persons who would not otherwise become involved in personal evangelism. Commercial services, such as Criss Cross Directories, provide all available telephone numbers in a given geographical area. Other than knowledge of the numbers, the greatest requirements are telephone lines (unless callers work from their homes), callers, and a script for callers to follow. Churches using this method tend to write their own scripts.

However, there is a major problem with many of the uses that made the role of telephones in evangelism effective. The cultural shift from landlines to cell phones changed the rules and the possibilities. Many people today only use cell phones. Getting cell phone numbers can be significantly more difficult than getting landline numbers. Cell phones are often most effective for follow-up contacts and further sharing after a personal relationship with a prospect begins. They also open up possibilities to use text messages and social media to share the gospel and build relationships with growing numbers of people who use their cell phones as the foundation for most of their social interactions with others. So far there is no widely popular SBC resource or process to help churches incorporate cell phones into their evangelistic outreach.

Direct mail was another form of personal, passive evangelism on a mass scale used by local churches. Direct mail involves sending letters or other forms of correspondence to reach people. As in the case of tele-marketing, this methodology has been used effectively by the business community. Independent Christian ministries such as evangelists and para-church organizations were the first ones to employ direct mail on a signif-icant scale. More and more churches discovered direct mail to be a useful tool for local congregations as well.

Direct mail was often not very efficient when measured in terms of responses per piece sent. For many types of mailing, a response of 2–5 per-cent of those who received the piece was considered excellent. However, the impact could be significant. Direct mail requires a mailing list of the target group, a match between one or more needs of those persons and the services or products provided, and a budget to allow multiple mailings. A direct mail piece should highlight a need of the recipient that can be met by the church or its message. Each piece should contain some way for the recipients to respond or indicate interest (return card, telephone response, etc.). Multiple mailings can increase the likelihood of a response. Timing also affects the response ratio. Research has indicated that Christmas, Eas-ter, and back-to-school seasons appear to be times when people are the most open to messages from churches.

Direct mail had some advantages over the telephone in the task of con-tacting people. The mail could go where church visitors could not go. The mail even reached places the telephone does not go, for people without a telephone or a listed telephone number still receive mail. Many telephone calls may be required to reach some busy people, but letters will be deliv-ered to their residences. The disadvantages were that direct mail was less personal, more expensive, and, to a large extent, imprecise. A telephone caller knew when the telephone was answered and what kind of response resulted. One could not know if the mail received was actually read unless the recipient responded. As a method of outreach, direct mail is passive.

Television and *radio* are the two best known forms of mass media and are also the most expensive. Churches who choose to use them must be aware of their limitations apart from a scale of massive repetition. Research indicates that mass media is not very effective in changing opinions. Most often radio and television are perceived as reinforcements of views already held by the one listening or watching. The overwhelming majority of listeners and viewers of Christian radio and television are other Christians, especially older women. For evangelism, radio and television can best be used to inform, to create a positive climate for the Christian message, and to plant seeds about the gospel that can be cultivated in the lives of hearers and viewers at a more personal level. Most research indicates that the broadcast of Christian programming will not, in and of itself, produce a significant number of changed lives. The people most affected by gospel broadcasts will be those who are already in the midst of change.[3]

Christian radio and television broadcasts are another form of passive evangelism. Programs are received by hearers without the opportunity for dialogue with a believer who can "customize" the message for the particular concerns of the hearers on the basis of immediate feedback. This weakness exists in all forms of passive evangelism. Such methods do make contributions to the process of evangelization, but they do not eliminate the need for person-to-person evangelism. A comprehensive program of personal evangelism will include proactive, reactive, and passive forms of bearing witness to the gospel. Historically, Southern Baptists have found their greatest success in emphasizing proactive programs that seek to motivate and equip believers to initiate conversations about the gospel.

Personal Evangelism Today

Although other witness training processes have been introduced in recent decades, none has reached the level of penetration in actual practice as that achieved by the *Lay Evangelism School* or, to a lesser extent, *Continuing Witness Training*. Nevertheless, something of much greater significance is growing among SBC churches.

In its early years, NAMB continued a clear emphasis on evangelism and the development of personal evangelism strategies. However, the

---

[3] For a full discussion of mass media and evangelism, including research data and interpretation, see James F. Engel, *Contemporary Christian Communications: Its Theory and Practice* (Nashville: Thomas Nelson, 1979); and Razelle Frankl, *Televangelism: The Marketing of Popular Religion* (Carbondale: Southern Illinois University Press, 1987).

reduction of evangelism personnel gradually reduced attention to and conversation about personal evangelism. A movement away from training as a key component of NAMB's approach to evangelism clearly took place. Today's focus is on inspirational events and some instruction designed for pastors rather than churches. Providing a tool to use is a higher priority than providing a training process to use the tool. The personal evangelism tool currently promoted is the *3 Circles* gospel presentation. It is available as a printed piece and as a smartphone download. Some training is available, such as a kit for pastors, but engaging churches in using the tool and training pastors to use the kit is not as widely promoted as such tools would have been in earlier days. Not as much attention is given to how to get people in the habit of using the tool. The presentation itself unfolds smoothly and clearly. It should be in use for years to come.

The biggest change in mass media is the advent of social media and the distribution system made possible by the internet. No significant effort has been made to equip Southern Baptist churches with specific strategies for using social media for outreach. Perhaps one reason is the history of Southern Baptists with technology. To date, Southern Baptists have been late adapters to technology. No media or technology-based delivery system has ever had wide popularity in the SBC. The development of strategies, tools, and training in the use of social media for evangelism is an untested opportunity.

Perhaps it would be more accurate to say that the more profound change among Southern Baptist churches is the steadily growing apathy toward personal evangelism tools and processes. How to mobilize a congregation to share the gospel with their families, their neighbors, and their friends is less of a conversation in SBC circles than it used to be. The *3 Circles* gospel presentation is a useful tool. Social media and the internet do make available possibilities for sharing the gospel that never existed before. The burning question for NAMB and SBC churches is this: Is the mobilization of every believer to bear witness to the gospel—to those whom they know and those whom they encounter—still a major priority for today's Southern Baptists?

CHAPTER 8

Sunday School

The most pervasive organization found in the largest number of Southern Baptist churches is some form of Sunday School or small group Bible study. The typical SBC goal is for every church member and prospect to be enrolled in a weekly Bible study. The purpose of these groups is ordinarily to teach participants more and more of the Bible, to build positive relationships, and to multiply opportunities for the church to address the needs of the participants. In terms of evangelism, it provides the lost with an opportunity to hear and understand the gospel and to form friendships with Christians interested in their spiritual condition. Both issues are important in the path toward conversion.

By the 1980s, about 97 percent of Southern Baptist churches had a Sunday School program, making it far and away the most popular program in Southern Baptist life.[1] Virtually all Protestant denominations have implemented some form of Sunday School, but few others have seen Sunday School become as productive an evangelistic tool as have Southern Baptists. The purpose of this chapter is to examine how Sunday School became a major component in the evangelistic strategy of Southern Baptists.

---

[1] William P. Clemmons, "The Contributions of the Sunday School to Southern Baptist Churches," in *Baptist History and Heritage: Sunday Schools in Southern Baptist History* 18, no. 1 (January 1983), 39.

An Orphan Was Adopted

To imagine church without Sunday School would be difficult for many contemporary Christians. However, in the beginning, Sunday School had no connection with the church. Most historians agree that the Sunday School movement began in England in the late eighteenth century. Robert Raikes was an Anglican who felt a burden for the poor children receiving no education. He began a school that offered basic training in reading, writing, and arithmetic. Since classes met on Sunday, the only day many of the children were not working, the name Sunday School was fitting. Two sessions were held each Sunday for the purpose of literacy training for the disadvantaged. The meetings were in homes, and the teachers were paid for their labors.

William Fox was a wealthy Baptist layman who wanted to start a school using the Bible as its textbook. He, too, started classes in private homes using paid teachers, but his school met on weekdays. His primary goal was teaching the Bible. As Fox learned about the strategy of Raikes, he liked the idea of meeting on Sunday. Fox shifted the meeting day to Sundays and continued to build the curriculum around studying the Bible. The Sunday School movement appears to have begun from these two British sources. Interestingly, the two men were born in the same year, on the same day of the month, and in the same county. Their dreams were different, but both helped launch what eventually became a powerful international movement.

Sunday School appeared in America in the last decade of the eighteenth century. Most were schools meeting on Sunday and took the same form as the early English Sunday schools, with the purpose of providing some form of education to children who had no access to schools. In the nineteenth century, the purpose for Sunday School in America began to change. Evangelicals saw Sunday School as a way to reach people who were not being reached in church services. The attempts to provide basic literacy through the schools diminished in favor of a focus on the Bible and conversion. Because the schools were especially effective in reaching children, they were appreciated as excellent pre-conversion training. The measure of Sunday School's effectiveness became both the number of people attending and the number of conversions resulting from the classes.

By the middle of the nineteenth century, the Sunday School movement was a hotbed of evangelism.

D. L. Moody, the great evangelist, began his ministry in the Sunday School movement. When Moody arrived in Chicago, he intended to become a wealthy merchant or salesman. He became involved in Sunday School work and eventually decided to start a Sunday School in a poor section of town. The street kids fell in love with "crazy Moody," as they called him, and the school experienced enormous growth. His success with Sunday School opened doors for him to speak, and this "millionaire in the making" became an evangelist instead. He spoke for Sunday School conventions and YMCA[2] functions, becoming widely known in the process. The Sunday School movement helped to make Moody an internationally known evangelist.

As Sunday schools grew in popularity, churches gave them greater attention. For many years, the Sunday School movement was viewed with suspicion by local churches. Often Sunday schools were started without a connection to a local church. Conceived as a mission project for concerned laity, the schools tended to be nondenominational in background and practice. The greatest promoters of Sunday School were the religious publishers who produced the materials used and various independent organizations created for Sunday School promotion. The independent and nondenominational character of the movement did not lend itself to support from SBC churches with their strong sense of identity and focus on the local church.

By the turn of the twentieth century, the attitude about Sunday School was changing. The great success of many Sunday schools was an indication that they met real needs. Denominational publishing houses were established to produce materials and provide training. Under the leadership of a man named Benjamin F. Jacobs, a uniform course of study was developed. A uniform text was suggested each week for study by all schools, though each group was free to develop its own materials to interpret the text. The real turning point came in the recognition of the importance of incorporating the Bible study in Sunday School for church members and

---

[2] The Young Men's Christian Association (YMCA) was also founded in mid-nineteenth-century England.

their children as well as for the unchurched. Sunday School became more than a mission project for the disadvantaged or the unreached.

Southern Baptists struggled over accepting Sunday School due to suspicion over its northern heritage and interdenominational roots. The use of women teachers and the lack of a specific New Testament precedent for the Sunday School were serious difficulties for many Southern Baptists. Landmarkism, so influential in the last half of the nineteenth century, put an extreme emphasis on the local church, creating skepticism about the legitimacy of any institution with a life apart from the local church. Perhaps the most difficult barrier of all was the aftermath of the Civil War. Devastation and poverty resulting from the war caused difficulty in the promotion and training necessary to enlist churches in a new program. How difficult was it to enlist Southern Baptist churches? By 1857, only 25 percent of the congregations had a Sunday School. By 1900, the number was still only 50 percent.[3]

Two attempts were made to start a Sunday School Board. In 1863, the Convention voted to create a Sunday School Board to be led by Basil Manly Jr. The Board lasted only 10 years despite herculean efforts by Manly, John Broadus, and others. In 1873, the SBC voted to merge that board into the Home Mission Board. In 1890, J. M. Frost mounted a major campaign to establish a new Sunday School Board. A committee was appointed to study the issue and make a recommendation. That committee included both proponents and opponents.

J. B. Gambrell opposed establishing a Sunday School Board because he feared that buying denominational literature would become a test of denominational loyalty. He and Frost were made a subcommittee of two and told to resolve the conflict. After several hours of discussion, both men agreed to recommend the creation of the Sunday School Board, provided the recommendation included a warning not to make the use of the Board's literature a test of loyalty and a plea for all SBC churches to give the literature fair consideration. The recommendation was overwhelmingly approved by the SBC in 1891, and J. M. Frost was elected the first secretary. The battle was not over, for the churches of the SBC still had to

---

[3] Clemmons, "The Contributions of the Sunday School," 38.

be convinced of the value of Sunday schools. Bernard W. Spilman played a key role in that aspect of the battle. Today's language would identify him as a Sunday School consultant for Southern Baptists. Spilman traveled across the South, helping churches organize Sunday schools for their churches. When told that opposition would make the success of Sunday School impossible, he took his dictionary and crossed out the word "failure." That dictionary is still housed at the Sunday School Board—now LifeWay Christian Resources.

By the end of Frost's tenure in 1916, an important corner had been turned. Sunday School began as an orphan, often unattached to any local church. As the second decade of the twentieth century unfolded, Sunday School was adopted and made part of the Southern Baptist family. Frost worked diligently to keep Southern Baptist Sunday schools and churches closely connected, emphasizing Sunday School as a church program rather than as an independent, international, interdenominational movement. He encouraged teacher training and developed standards for evaluating the efficiency of a Sunday School. LifeWay became a resource of books and general materials as well as Sunday School literature, giving churches choices of denominational products to support. Frost also emphasized an age-graded Sunday School model, which would become a key factor in using Sunday School for evangelism and church growth. Under the leadership of J. M. Frost and those who served with him, Southern Baptists began to think of Sunday School as a normal feature of the way churches did evangelism.

Flake Was No Fluke

A danger arises in ascribing too much credit to any one man. With great accomplishments, a variety of influences will emerge. Nevertheless, some individuals do make outstanding contributions that overshadow the other factors in great deeds or great events. The philosophy of Sunday School work, which has made that institution so productive in evangelism for Southern Baptists, can be understood only by considering the impact of Arthur Flake. Perhaps more than any other denomination, Southern Baptists have used Sunday School for evangelism and church growth. "Flake's Formula" has been a major factor in that success for nearly 100 years.

Arthur Flake was born in Texas in 1862. He was not converted until the age of 31. By that time, he was firmly rooted in the business world, having worked as a traveling salesman and a department store manager. After his conversion, Flake became active in Sunday School and the Baptist Young People's Union. He made significant contributions to the work of those organizations in his local church and state convention. In 1909, he was hired by the Sunday School Board as a field worker.

Flake's early work was to promote Sunday School and the Baptist Young People's Union. When the Sunday School Board created a Department of Church Administration, Flake became its leader. He wrote seven books, the most popular of which was *Building a Standard Sunday School*.[4] Along with others, Flake helped Southern Baptists accept Sunday School as a program for all ages, not just children. A major factor in the evangelistic results of the Southern Baptist Convention was Sunday School work, for it made Sunday School the overarching program of the church, touching all other aspects of a church's programs. Flake also helped to convince the Convention about the value of Sunday School as a tool for evangelism. When the Sunday School movement in general began to emphasize nurture more than witness, Southern Baptists continued to perceive Sunday School as the outreach arm of the church.

Without question, Flake's greatest impact came in the development of "Flake's Formula," a simple method of how to grow a Sunday School. With his formula, Flake was able to standardize and popularize an approach to Sunday School work that made it the outreach arm of the church. The principles have proven to be flexible enough to apply to the broad spectrum of Southern Baptist churches and clear enough to be easily transferable. Those five principles are discover the prospects, expand the organization, train the workers, provide the space, and go get the people.[5]

(1) *Discover the prospects.* Many churches base their Sunday School plans on their current programs. Arthur Flake was an advocate of basing

---

[4] Arthur Flake, *Building a Standard Sunday School* (Nashville: The Sunday School Board, 1934).
[5] Derived from Flake, *Building a Standard Sunday School*, 29–55.

your plans on the *potential* of your church field or community. A census of the field to determine the number of legitimate prospects the church can reach is necessary before the church is ready to plan. A census should be done regularly because contemporary society is so mobile. As many people as possible should be involved in as short a time as possible. One day for the census is preferred. Careful attention should be given to the accuracy of the information and the comprehensiveness of the survey. The census will be useless unless the information is collected, interpreted, and applied to the Sunday School soon after it is gathered.

(2) *Expand the organization.* Once the number of prospects is known, the size of the Sunday School organization can be planned. The size of the organization should be based upon the size of the present Sunday School plus the number of prospects. If the prospects come, how many Sunday School classes and departments will be needed? How many teachers and officers would be required to staff those units? To experience growth, plan for growth to happen. The Sunday School organization should reflect potential size, not just actual size.

(3) *Train the workers.* If people are going to lead well, training is necessary. To create confidence and enthusiasm among workers, motivate and train them for their respective roles. Growing churches should have an ongoing leadership and teacher training program. Rarely will churches be able to train more people than they can use. A weekly training process for current and future workers is ideal, as well as special events and workshops.

(4) *Provide the space.* Contemporary church growth experts agree with Flake. Space is necessary for growth. The church that is using 100 percent of its facilities will not grow and cannot sustain present numbers indefinitely. Providing the space may mean adding an additional building or remodeling an existing building. There are other options. Multiple services or Sunday School times allow more people to be put in the same amount of space. Spaces outside the church, such as homes or offices, can be space multipliers. Other creative options may be available to you. However, the space available significantly affects the growth potential of a church.

(5) *Go get the people*. The first four steps are the necessary prepara-
tions for growth. Actual growth is the result of going after the people who
are the prospects. One method of identification is some form of visitation
program. Special programs designed to appeal to the people you want to
reach are another means of going after people. Phone calls and letters are
also helpful ways to identify your prospects. Special events and social
activities can attract prospects as well. Growing churches are aggressive in
going after the people they want to reach.

"Flake's Formula" is simple and has proven to be effective for more
than 50 years in a wide variety of churches. Several key elements of Southern Baptist Sunday School thought flow out of this philosophy but are
not clearly stated. Sunday School is not primarily for children or only for
children. As a comprehensive Bible study program, Sunday School gives
every age group an opportunity to be exposed to the gospel through the
study of Scripture. People should be enrolled in Sunday School whenever
and wherever possible. Sunday School is a vehicle for reaching unsaved
and unchurched people, not primarily a means to nurture believers. Easily
applied throughout the church, age grading is the method of choice for creating units, although it is less desirable for adults as they grow older. Small
classes are better than large classes because they are more likely to grow.

The success of Arthur Flake was no fluke. Nearly all Southern Baptist
Sunday School strategies are variations or elaborations of his philosophy
of Sunday School. Southern Baptists found that, with Flake's principles,
Sunday School can be an extremely effective vehicle for evangelism and
church growth. What made Sunday School such an important part of the
evangelism process? If lost and unchurched prospects could get connected
to a Sunday School class, two important things would happen over time.
First, they would hear more and more of the Bible explained. The gospel
would become more familiar and be better understood. Second, the lost
and unchurched would have natural opportunities to form relationships
with Christians in the class and church. Such relationships often proved
crucial in nurturing faith. "Bible-lationships" is my term for the power of
combining teaching the Bible and building relationships. Both goals must
be addressed in any Sunday School or small group strategy.

Rules Were Made to Be Bent

The principles underlying the Southern Baptist philosophy of Sunday School soon crystallized into rules on how to do Sunday School. These basic rules for Sunday School have not often been broken in SBC churches, though they have been bent. The churches of the Convention share many similarities, but they are not homogeneous. The observer will always find variations on the basic strategies promoted by the Convention agencies. What follows are a few examples of the ways in which the rules of Sunday School have been bent. Some versions have become part of the denominational strategy. Others are local church adaptations.

The great struggle involved in getting Sunday School into the churches was noted earlier. The first leaders in the Sunday School movement among Southern Baptists insisted that the Sunday School should not be independent of the church; instead, it should be organically related to the church, operated by the church, and meeting in the church. Church architecture went through a reformation of sorts as the design of churches was changed to include space for Sunday School. Some churches are experimenting with ways to bend this rule by exploring options for Sunday School to meet away from the church in homes, offices, etc. Other churches that are faced with space limitations organize worship services on a different schedule than Bible study classes. Sunday School classes may meet during the week while worship services remain on Sunday. A newer innovation is home cell groups.

The largest church in the world is the Yoido Full Gospel Church in Seoul, South Korea, founded by David Yonggi Cho. Current membership is more than 800,000 and climbing. That kind of success has attracted the attention of pastors from all over the world, including Southern Baptists. *Home cell groups* are the center of Cho's strategy. Small groups of no more than 15 families meet in homes or other nonchurch locations for Bible study, fellowship, and evangelism. According to Cho, the home cell groups were the most important human factor in the incredible growth of his congregation.

After studying Cho's philosophies and methods, some pastors attempted to adapt his strategy to SBC churches. Problems developed concerning the relationship between home cell groups and the Sunday School within the typical Southern Baptist church. The function of the cell groups is similar to that of Sunday School—the promotion of Bible study, fellowship, and evangelism, but there was a distinct difference. Several churches have discovered that their leaders perceived the introduction of home cell groups as a threat to traditional Sunday School and thus resisted the new program. Other churches, usually new congregations, have attempted to use home cell groups in place of Sunday School. No Southern Baptist church to date has achieved success on the scale of Cho's church with a foundation of home cell groups.

Experience now indicates that the relationship between traditional Sunday School and innovative home cell groups must be clarified and communicated carefully in the typical Southern Baptist church. Interested readers will find an excellent discussion of the issues and problems involved for churches with a strong traditional Sunday School program in *Home Cell Groups and House Churches* by Hadaway, DuBose, and Wright.[6] There appears to be less interest in home cell groups among today's churches.

Traditional Southern Baptist Sunday School theory emphasizes the importance of small classes. Classes that grow beyond an attendance of 10 to 12 people should be divided to form new units. The composition of classes is to be changed each year through age grading or some other process. These practices are designed to stimulate continuing growth, because small classes have a natural desire to grow larger. The teacher and class are motivated to work at growth. Today, several churches, especially the very large churches, are bending this rule and using a "master teacher" concept.

The *"master teacher" concept* suggests identifying truly excellent teachers and letting them grow a large class without size limitation. First Baptist Church of Dallas, Texas; First Baptist Church of Jacksonville, Florida; and Second Baptist Church of Houston, Texas, are examples of churches allowing teachers to have a class with more than 100 in attendance. The conviction underlying this approach is that the unique dynamic of a large group and the excellent quality of teaching will be attractive to some people who would not be attracted to a small group. On the positive

---

[6] C. Kirk Hadaway, Francis M. DuBose, and Stuart A. Wright, *Home Cell Groups and House Churches* (Nashville: Broadman Press, 1987).

side, a larger class allows the full utilization of the gifts of a skilled teacher. On the negative side, a diminishing sense of ownership and responsibility for making growth happen in a larger class may develop. Members feel more anonymous and less responsible to help the class grow.

Historically, Southern Baptist Sunday Schools have emphasized enrollment. Every effort should be made to involve every person possible in Bible study. Sunday School was one of the only programs a person could join without joining the church. Traditionally, enrollment has taken place in the Sunday School itself. Individuals who indicated enough interest to come one or more times were encouraged to join a class. That rule was bent with the development of the *Action* program by Andy Anderson. His thesis was that persons can be enrolled in Sunday School at any place or time—at home, on the job, or shopping—as easily as they can be enrolled within a church building; people should not be forced to come to church to be enrolled. Enrollment should be taken to them.

Anderson believed that greater enrollment would result in greater attendance and more conversions, regardless of where enrollment took place. A person who is willing to enroll in a Sunday School class, even when he is not in church, is indicating at least some interest in spiritual things. As a member of a Sunday School class, the person will not be surprised by efforts to visit and cultivate him. His enrollment is an indication of his willingness to accept follow-up. This approach is also another way to move Sunday School out of the church building and into the community.

Use of the Action plan and its derivatives brought Southern Baptists significant increases in Sunday School enrollment. However, those gains have not resulted in comparable gains in conversions and baptisms. The emphasis on the task of enrolling people may have obscured the continuing task of witnessing and calling people to Christ, especially in churches not emphasizing evangelism. Enrollment in a Sunday School class does not automatically lead to conversion. To enroll prospects in an evangelistically oriented Sunday School will produce different results than enrollment in a Sunday School oriented toward nurture. Training for open-enrollment programs should include or be followed by witness training as well.

Southern Baptists usually assign one teacher to one class. Strong personal relationships can be formed when there is one teacher and a small class. The intimacy and the weekly contact between the teacher and the class members can enhance the potential for ministry. More and more churches are experimenting with team teaching—two teachers taking turns teaching a class. The coteachers may rotate every week, every month, or at whatever interval is best for the two of them and the class.

The pace and mobility of modern life are probably the biggest influences on the bending of this rule. Some people are interested in teaching but do not feel that their schedules allow time for proper preparation every week. Others may want to teach but are unable to attend every week. Personal or professional responsibilities require many to be out of town on more than an occasional basis. If the choice were to take a class and teach it every week or not to teach, many potential teachers would choose not to teach. If the choice were to share teaching responsibilities with another teacher, personally assume all responsibilities, or not to teach, they would often choose to share the teaching responsibilities for a class.

The *shared class* is most common in churches with a significant segment of younger, white-collar professionals who are more likely to travel and to be cautious in their time commitments. Young professionals may not be less interested in serving, but they are very interested in flexibility. The church that intends to harness the gifts and abilities of its members in Sunday School will need to be creative and flexible in its programs and procedures.

Much of what Southern Baptists have done in Sunday School work is still relevant and effective. Adjustment to current realities and opportunities will always be needed, but the basic principles are still sound. As long as the rules can be bent, many of them will not have to be broken. Perhaps the greatest challenge for the Convention is to keep the Sunday School focused on evangelism rather than nurture as its primary focus, especially as churches move away from the name Sunday School. The use of terms such as *small groups, care groups,* or *life groups,* does put more emphasis on nurturing members than evangelizing the lost.

While the international Sunday School movement shifted away from the priority of evangelism and conversion through Sunday School work, Southern Baptists made a conscious decision to use Sunday School as "the outreach arm of the church." The result was an evangelistic harvest from

Sunday School that was unequaled by other denominations. The aggressive and intentional emphasis on evangelism through Sunday School has declined over the past 30 years in Southern Baptist life and is reflected in the Convention's lack of evangelistic growth and declining numbers of baptisms.

New efforts should be made to refocus Sunday School on evangelism. Teachers need training to teach the lessons evangelistically. While the plan of salvation is printed in all Sunday School literature, lessons that focus on how to become a Christian should be regularly emphasized, not just printed. History has demonstrated that the success of those efforts will have a major impact on whether or not Southern Baptists achieve their evangelistic potential. Without connecting lost people to a process of Bible teaching and relationship building, Southern Baptists are less likely to reach them. If that evangelistic process does not happen in Sunday School, what will replace it? To this point, nothing on the same scale has been developed by Convention entities.

CHAPTER 9

Revivalism

R*evivalism* refers to the use of special meetings inside or outside the church for the purpose of evangelism. For many evangelicals, a revival meeting or evangelistic crusade was an occasional special event. For many SBC churches for generations, the revival meeting was an annual event, an important part of the rhythm of the church year. Individual churches or groups of churches would use a revival meeting as a culmination of all the evangelism efforts of the year, a natural conversion point for those who had been hearing the gospel and thinking about their relationship with God.

In the middle of the twentieth century, William Warren Sweet wrote a classic study on revivalism titled *Revivalism: Its Origin, Growth, and Decline.*[1] He concluded that mass evangelism in the form of revivalism had seen its greatest day and was in decline. In his opinion, the lone exception to that assessment was the Southern Baptist Convention. No denomination has used revivalism with greater effectiveness over a longer period of time than Southern Baptists. In this chapter, an examination will be conducted to see what Southern Baptists have done and why revivalism has been so effective. Attention will also be given to the present and future prospects of revivalism as a method of evangelism.

---

[1] William Warren Sweet, *Revivalism: Its Origin, Growth and Decline* (New York: Charles Scribner's Sons, 1944).

Revive Us Again

During the eighteenth century, a mighty movement of God began in England and North America. Historians call it the Great Awakening. The church had lost its passion and its power, and some critics were ready to pronounce it beyond recovery. Under the preaching of George Whitefield, John Wesley, and others, revival broke out. Thousands were born again; new churches were started; and many believers renewed their zeal for God.

As is often the case, the time of revival was also a time of great controversy. George Whitefield was the early lightning rod of the revival. His dramatic, sensational preaching of the gospel and call for repentance attracted some of the largest crowds ever to hear a sermon in England. He was an itinerant minister and insisted on going to the places where the gospel was not being preached. This boldness earned him the wrath of the official clergy, and he was forbidden to preach in many pulpits. Rejection by the churches led Whitefield to start preaching in the fields.

Whitefield's innovative approach was a scandal in that day, for many believed that preaching in the open air demeaned the gospel and mocked the church. However, the response of the people to his new tactic was enormous. He went to the coal district of England, a very rough area inhabited by uneducated and unchurched people who had little love for the church. Whitefield would stand by the paths used to enter and leave the mines, preaching to them in the morning and evening. One observer noted streaks of white began to appear on their faces as tears of conviction and longing for a new life washed the coal dust away. Revival broke out, and the evangelistic potential of preaching in the fields became evident.

When Whitefield sensed God leading him to preach and minister in the American colonies, he trained John and Charles Wesley to take up his work in the fields of England. John Wesley, in particular, was reluctant to preach in the open air. He had a very strong sense of dignity and etiquette, and field preaching did not seem to him appropriate for a minister of the gospel. The enormity of the response and the closing of the churches to evangelistic preaching eventually persuaded him; so John Wesley took his place among the masses in the fields. At one point he preached a message while standing on his father's tomb in a cemetery next to a church because the pastor of the church had refused to let him preach in the building.

Whitefield made several trips to America, preaching up and down the Atlantic coast. He died on this side of the Atlantic in 1770 at Newburyport, Massachusetts. The results of his ministry in America were much the same as in England. Followed by controversy and resistance from the religious establishment, Whitefield made a great impact as the people flocked to hear him. Much of his preaching was done in the open air. Added to his efforts was the preaching of Jonathan Edwards, Theodore Frelinghuysen, and others. Thousands were born again, and the spiritual life of many congregations was awakened and revived.

During this time called the Great Awakening, the seeds of revivalism were planted. The process that emerged was the gathering of a group of people to hear the proclamation of the gospel. As the Bible was preached, the Holy Spirit brought about conviction of sin and recognition of the need for salvation or spiritual renewal. Many people were born again, and many churches were revived. Like contemporary revivalism, gathering of people to hear the gospel preached, often at a time other than Sunday, was the method. Frequently these meetings took place away from the church building. Unlike contemporary revivalism, the meetings were not planned, nor were the dramatic results always expected. At times what looked like "just another worship service" suddenly became a great moving of the Holy Spirit in the hearts and souls of the hearers. Even at this early stage, Baptists appeared to have an affinity for revivals. Whitefield, an Anglican, is reported to have complained, "All of my chicks have become ducks," meaning that many of his converts, especially in the South, were becoming Baptists after being born again.

For the pastor or a member of a church deeply stirred by an awakening, experience gave knowledge of what can happen when true revival breaks out. As the fire dies down and the church settles once more into a routine, a longing for the passion and intensity of a mighty movement of God's Spirit can emerge. Having tasted the cup of revival, a comparison can occur between the way the church *is* and the way the church *was* when God was doing a mighty work. "Revive Us Again"[2] did indeed become the cry of the church in the aftermath of the Great Awakening. That longing

---

[2] Lyrics of the hymn "Revive Us Again" (1867; originally "We Praise Thee, O God," composed in 1863) were written by William P. Mackay (public domain).

became the first influence in the development of revivalism as a method of evangelism. Planned revivalism was in part a response to a longing for the return of the spontaneous awakening that swept the country during the eighteenth century.

Life on the frontier at the dawn of the nineteenth century was hard, lonely, and dangerous. Christians had few opportunities to interact with others. Churches were in short supply and even fewer ministers were available. Opportunities to observe the Lord's Supper were rare for most Christians in that environment. The Lord used this combination of circumstances as an avenue for sending a revival and awakening to the South and for further development of the methodology of revivalism.

In 1800, pastor James McGready, among others, organized a special communion service at Gasper River, Kentucky. As word spread throughout the rural area, people began to gather from miles away. They came in wagons and on horseback, prepared to camp out for several days. The crowd was far too large for the church, and services were held outside as well. As the preaching services began, revival broke out. Great conviction of sin and repentance occurred. Many were born again, and many more renewed their relationship with the Lord. What happened at Gasper River inspired another Presbyterian minister, Barton Stone, to organize a similar meeting at Cane Ridge, Kentucky. Again the crowds were huge, and the response was dramatic. The crowds who attended those meetings and others like them were probably unaware that they were giving birth to the frontier camp meeting.

The *frontier camp meeting* began as a special form of an open communion service lasting several days. Thousands of people would come to the meetings. Many ministers, usually of different denominations, participated. Preaching continued almost around the clock, with multiple people preaching at the same time in different areas. Often a place would be set aside for those who were "anxious" about their souls. Interestingly enough, the meetings apparently lasted about four days, the most popular length of revival meetings among Southern Baptists today.

The frontier camp meeting began among Presbyterians, Methodists, and Baptists. Although very popular among the common people, the camp meeting created a great deal of controversy among Presbyterians as a whole. Criticism for emotional excess and doctrinal impurity abounded. Eventually, Presbyterians in the South split over the issue. One result was the formation of the Disciples of Christ movement under Stone's leadership. Methodists embraced the camp meeting with open arms and had great success with the movement in the nineteenth and early twentieth centuries. They institutionalized the camp meeting as a revivalistic Bible conference held outside the church, often at campgrounds created for that specific purpose. By the middle part of the twentieth century, the impact and influence of camp meetings among Methodists had waned considerably.

The camp meeting was popular with Baptists as well. Rather than focusing on the gathering of believers or congregations outside the church, Baptists, especially those in the South, institutionalized the camp meeting as a local church meeting, held annually or semi-annually. The *camp meeting* became the protracted meeting—a revival meeting with a scheduled starting date but no planned conclusion. The meeting lasted as long as God's movement was evident through the services. Another variation was the *brush arbor meeting*. To escape the heat of an enclosed building, a brush arbor was constructed for the meeting, often next to the church. To visualize a brush arbor, imagine a roof and supporting columns built from branches and other natural materials. Add benches of some sort inside, and a brush arbor has been created. These variations of the frontier camp meeting eventually developed into the revival meeting known today.

The third influence on modern revivalism unfolded during the nineteenth century in the northern regions of the United States. In 1821, Charles Finney was an agnostic studying for the legal profession and directing the choir of his community's church in rural New York. He was handsome, athletic, and bright. However, he fell under conviction about the state of his soul, and one day he turned from his path to go off into the woods to pray until the issue of his salvation was settled. Shortly thereafter, Finney was dramatically and gloriously converted.

The young man walked away from a promising legal career and entered the ministry. Although he began as a small church pastor, Finney's preaching was accompanied by such powerful signs of awakening and revival, wherever he preached, that he soon became the leading evangelist of his era and one of the most influential evangelists in American history. By the time of his death, Finney had served as an itinerant evangelist, an urban church planter and pastor, and a university president and lecturer. His influence on revivalism was so great that some have called him "the father of modern evangelism."

Prior to Finney, revivalism reflected the theological heritage of Calvinism, emphasizing the sovereignty of God and the penitent waiting of man for conversion and revival. Finney was accused of introducing "new measures," which included the planning and promotion of revival campaigns, praying for persons by name in public meetings, encouraging women to pray publicly, and inviting persons under conviction to come forward to "anxious seats" to seek salvation. Whereas Calvinists of his day emphasized revival as the act of a sovereign God working at the discretion of His will, Finney referred to revival as the result of the right use of the means God described in the Bible. When God's people do what He requires, God sends revival.

This perspective opened up the potential for revivalism as a tool for evangelism. A pastor did not have to wait to catch a wave of revival to see sinners saved and churches awakened. He could set the wave in motion and prepare for a revival to happen, knowing the right use of the right means will result in a movement of the Spirit. If a revival was a great movement of the Holy Spirit, revivalism was the intentional use of revival for evangelism and church renewal. It was positioning the church to be ready for a movement of God.

Modern revivalism is the result of a desire to see God do again what He has done before in a time such as the Great Awakening. The frontier camp meeting and its successors provided a format that allowed churches to focus on the need for and possibility of revival in their communities. Finney and others after him developed methods to prepare a community and church for a revival from God to break out at a designated time and place. These major influences in the background of Southern Baptist practices of revivalism are profound.

Upon This Rock

The development of revivalism in Southern Baptist life is fairly easy to trace. The real question is, Why has revivalism been so effective? What have Southern Baptists done to make revival meetings an effective evangelistic tool? Three words sum up the key ingredients: roots, preparation, and culmination.

The *roots* of revivalism within Southern Baptist congregational life have greatly added to the impact of revival meetings on Southern Baptists personally. The term *revival meeting* is immediately understood in most Southern Baptist churches. Members have a shared anticipation of what to expect. Many people in the congregation will recall a revival meeting as the setting for their own professions of faith. The Southern Baptist emphasis on decisional preaching in weekly worship makes revivalism appear to be a logical way to do evangelism.

S. M. Lockridge, an African-American pastor in California, was one of the great preachers in America for years. He had a classic sermon titled "The Lordship of Christ." I once visited a church and heard an Anglo pastor preach Lockridge's sermon word-for-word. I was not surprised when it had little power. The sermon did not fit that pastor, nor was it connected to his preparation, his background, or his culture. As a result, the sermon was flat. Just as the power of Lockridge's sermon was rooted in his own context, so revivalism has been an effective evangelistic tool for SBC churches because it is rooted in the self-identity of Southern Baptists.

Without the heritage of revivalism, a pastor would have to begin preparing his church members for a revival meeting by educating them. The congregation would have to be taught what a revival meeting is and what having one involves. Negative images of revivals would have to be overcome and replaced with positive images. However, the challenge for the typical Southern Baptist pastor is not education but involvement. In most cases, the pastor will begin his work with a congregation that understands the dynamic of revivalism and has a positive regard for it. The atmosphere for a revival to have a significant impact already exists in many Southern Baptist churches.

Pastors who are in churches without a heritage in revivalism or decisional preaching must proceed carefully in using revival meetings as a tool for evangelism. If the congregation does not have realistic expectations and positive regard for the revival format, the atmosphere for success will not exist. A healthy connection between the congregation and any tool for evangelism must be established. Given unfamiliar tools, few workers would use them properly or enthusiastically.

Preparation is a second important ingredient of effective revivalism in the Southern Baptist experience. A resurgence in the use of revivalism at the denominational level and the evangelistic effectiveness of revival meetings at the local church level occurred in the latter half of the 1980s. Two nationwide simultaneous revival campaigns resulted in increased numbers of baptisms. Most SBC churches participated in both campaigns and found them to be productive. There was little that was new in the technique of "putting on" revival meetings. The most influential factor in the effectiveness of the meetings appears to have been a renewed emphasis on preparation.

As noted earlier, the typical Southern Baptist pastor does not have to deal with the problem of educating his people about the nature and form of a revival, but he does have to secure their involvement. In the middle of the twentieth century, when Southern Baptists were using simultaneous revival meetings for explosive growth, the meetings were usually two weeks in length. Later, the most common length was four days, with many churches opting for a weekend or one-day format. The change primarily reflected the time constraints of the congregation. Life became more complex for families in these times than it was for families in the forties and fifties. Time is a precious commodity, always stretched to the limit by constant demands from a variety of sources. Familiarity with and acceptance of revival meetings does not necessarily ensure participation in them. Southern Baptist churches have discovered the importance of thorough preparation in securing the involvement of their people.

The practice of revival preparation can be traced at least as far back as Charles Finney, the great nineteenth-century evangelist. Evangelists who followed after him continued to refine ways to prepare communities and churches for revival meetings. In fact, Billy Sunday, the flamboyant evangelist of the early twentieth century, got his start in itinerant evangelism as the "front man" preparing the way for Wilbur Chapman's crusades. The principles and techniques pioneered by these evangelists proved to be effective for local churches as well.

The fundamental law for revival preparation on any scale is: *The more people involved in preparation for a revival meeting, the more people are impacted by the meeting.* The people involved in the preparation for a meeting will tend to be present at that meeting and to have positive expectations for it. They are also more likely to involve friends and family members in the event. The moviemakers of Hollywood have discovered that word-of-mouth to friends and relatives is the most critical factor for the success of a movie. In survey after survey, church growth experts have discovered that the invitation of a friend or relative is the most common reason outsiders come to a church. Preparation is the key to involvement, and involvement is the key to impact.

Southern Baptists found that forming a committee is an excellent way to involve the maximum number of people in revival preparation. The size of the church should determine the size and number of committees for revival preparation. The smaller church can have a single revival preparation committee. The larger church will want to have a revival preparation steering committee composed of the chairmen of several subcommittees. The size of the committees is determined by the number of people required to get the particular job done effectively. The committees have a dual purpose: to do what needs to be done to prepare the church for the revival and to involve the maximum number of people in the preparation process.

The basic areas that need specific attention are prayer, visitation, attendance, and follow-up. The prayer committee is charged with the responsibility to mobilize the congregation for prayer, seeking a mighty movement of the Holy Spirit. The visitation committee attempts to organize a campaign to visit lost and unchurched prospects before and during the campaign. The attendance committee is responsible for promoting the revival within the church and the community. The common practice of SBC churches has been to target a specific group for attendance each night of the revival (youth, singles, family, etc.). The follow-up committee plans the process for encouraging and nurturing those who make decisions after the revival meeting is over. Each of these responsibilities can be broken down into other subcommittees or combined into the work of one committee, but these tasks must be addressed to prepare a church adequately for a revival. Other committees (e.g., a music committee to recruit revival choir participants, a hospitality committee to meet the needs of visiting evangelists, etc.) are optional, based on the size and need of the church. Again, the goal is to involve the maximum number of people in preparation in order to achieve the maximum involvement and impact.

The third factor in effective revivalism is *culmination*. In terms of evangelism, the revival meeting appears to make its greatest contribution as a harvest tool. The people who make decisions are generally those who have been hearing the gospel as opposed to those who are hearing about salvation for the first time. Southern Baptist churches have found revival meetings to be effective harvest tools to the extent that their churches are involved in other forms of evangelism.

The classic Southern Baptist approach treats Sunday School as the outreach arm of the church. Experience has proven that those who become involved in a Bible study at the church are likely to make professions of faith at some point. Many Southern Baptist churches have some form of regular visitation program, ensuring that people in the community are being exposed to the gospel. Vacation Bible School (VBS) is often held every summer for children. In the midst of all the activities of VBS are evangelistic Bible stories and presentations of the gospel. Add to VBS decisional preaching every week and an atmosphere of response is created with frequent exposure to the gospel and the need for a commitment to Christ.

In such an atmosphere, the revival meeting "closes the net." When a person recognizes the need for salvation and an event with an especially strong emphasis on accepting Christ is held, the likelihood of a response is significant. When numerous persons respond, the climate of expectation and the visible peer support for making a commitment enhance further the motivation to respond to the invitation to salvation. In other words, given a favorable attitude toward the revival meeting context, the churches with prospects at the point of decision are likely to find that a revival secures those commitments. When the revival culminates the process of cultivation, it can be a very productive harvest tool and has been for many Southern Baptist churches.

"O, Why Not Tonight?"[3]

The strength of revivalism as a method of evangelism among Southern Baptist churches is undeniable. An excellent study conducted in 1988 by Southern Baptist evangelism professor Ron Johnson demonstrated the continuing popularity and effectiveness of revival meetings among churches of all sizes in the Southern Baptist Convention.[4] No other method of evangelism had greater popularity, and the majority of churches continued to hold at least one revival a year. Yet, questions remain about the relevance and effectiveness of revivalism in the contemporary world. Has the twilight of revivalism occurred even in Southern Baptist life? Should a revival meeting be included in the plans of an evangelistic church?

In terms of domination, the day of revivalism in Southern Baptist life has passed. In an earlier day, revival meetings were more than a method of evangelism. They were *the* method of reaching people for Christ. Southern Baptists rarely ignore any method of reaching lost people, but the revival meeting received almost exclusive attention in the heyday of the denomination's growth during the forties and fifties, occupying center stage. That day is gone! It is difficult to imagine any one method of evangelism having that much dominance among the churches again. The diversity and pluralism evident in the United States is found as well in the SBC, which embraces every region of the country, many ethnic groups, and a vast diversity of cultural and socioeconomic backgrounds. Churches, and the pastors who lead them, are not looking for the *one* way to do evangelism. They are looking for some options from which to choose; and when they choose, they do not select just one method. Revivalism is unlikely to dominate the Southern Baptist evangelistic agenda again.

In another sense, the day of revivalism has not passed. For the foreseeable future, this viable tool for evangelism will continue in Southern Baptist churches. Many churches still find revivals to be the most productive

---

[3] The lyrics of this hymn were written by Elizabeth (Eliza) Holmes Reed and were first published in 1842 in *The Hymn Book* and later in the *Wycliffe Chapel Supplement*, 1872.

[4] Ronald Wayne Johnson, "An Evaluation of the Home Mission Board Programs of Evangelism in Local Churches" (D.Min. project, The Southern Baptist Theological Seminary, 1988). This project is a thorough and excellent analysis of the then-current evangelistic practices of SBC churches.

tool they use in evangelism. The reintroduction of a periodic, national, simultaneous revival campaign was very effective. Lost and unchurched people did attend the meetings. Many did make decisions during a revival campaign. In the churches and communities that find the tool a comfortable fit, revival meetings are still a very productive means of evangelism and will remain so. This finding is especially true in smaller churches, and they constitute an often unrecognized majority of SBC churches. The fact that revival meetings are not a good tool for many churches does not mean that they are no longer useful to churches at all.

To assess the evangelistic potential of revival meetings for your church, consider whether or not a revival would be a natural culmination of other evangelistic processes already in place. Are lost and unchurched people being regularly exposed to the gospel and the difference Jesus can make in their lives? Is the atmosphere of a typical worship service decisional? Do people who attend the service expect to be confronted with the need to examine their spiritual lives and consider the need for a commitment to Christ? If the answer to these questions is yes, a revival would provide a more focused and intense experience than what normally happens in the weekly church service. A logical coherence between a regular service and a revival service will encourage a revival harvest or complete the process going on as a typical part of church life.

If the answer is no, the potential for evangelistic harvest is probably not great. By the time prospects adjust to the change in worship style or the decisional atmosphere, the meeting is over. The critical factor is not the revival itself but the relationship between the revival and the normal life and emphases of the church. The evangelistic potential of revival meetings appears to be greatest in churches with a worship atmosphere similar to that of a revival meeting. Though not equally effective in all settings, the dynamic of a mass meeting held for the purpose of evangelism is still powerful.

The culture indicates that the dynamic of a mass meeting such as a revival can appeal to contemporary persons. Consider the attendance of secular events such as concerts, sporting contests, seminars, and such. People will pay a significant sum of money and squeeze the time out of a busy schedule to attend mass events perceived as meeting a need or an interest.

The challenge facing the use of revivalism as a tool for evangelism will be to demonstrate the relevance and value of a mass meeting that focuses on the relationship of individuals to God. Most pastors have learned that even church members will not attend an event just because it is sponsored by the church. People must see the event's relevance and value.

Preparation will become increasingly important for churches using revivalism to reach people. By involving a maximum number of people in preparation, a congregation can be given a degree of ownership in the meeting. The experts say that ownership is essential for reaching and involving many of today's adults, both young and old. Time constraints mean fewer people will attend every session, but focusing on different target groups will give family units and individuals a variety of reasons to attend more than one night. Offering a meal each evening might be an important way to encourage people facing urban traffic and distance to attend.

With an increased emphasis on preparation, a conscious emphasis on the role and significance of prayer must be made as a part of the process. The roots of revivalism lie in mighty, often spontaneous, movements of the Holy Spirit. Techniques of planning and promotion can obscure the necessity of the Holy Spirit's ministry for a truly impactful revival. Establishing an ongoing intercessory prayer ministry is one way to cultivate the anticipation of a deep work of the Holy Spirit. In that kind of atmosphere, God can bless natural preparation with supernatural results.

Often overlooked is the usefulness of revivalism for purposes other than evangelism. Historically, revivalism has referred to an awakening or renewal among the people of God. Conversions were the result of the revival within the church. Practically, Southern Baptists have used revival meetings for the primary purpose of evangelism. In a climate in which Christians, but few lost people, will attend a church meeting, the significance of awakening should be remembered. In days to come, revival meetings might be planned with the church as the primary target audience. Church members are the easiest persons to involve in the meetings. If the awakening of believers becomes the primary goal of the meeting, a greater evangelistic harvest might follow if true revival breaks out among believers. The day of revivalism is not over, but it is different. It will be most useful as one component of a comprehensive plan embracing several evangelistic methods.

The most significant argument for the survival of revivalism is found in Christian history. The roots of revivalism include times of spiritual awakening. Whenever a mighty movement of the Holy Spirit occurs, a mass meeting for the purposes of renewal and evangelism will result. In the aftermath of such movements, meetings will be organized in an effort to recapture the fire. As long as spiritual awakening is a possibility, revivalism as a method of evangelism will have a future. When a mighty movement of God happens in a place, pastors and other leaders will always want it to happen again.

CHAPTER 10

The Southern Baptist Paradigm
for Evangelism

E ach of these four methods—decisional preaching, systematic outreach, weekly small group Bible study, and revivalism—is a proven
evangelistic tool used by churches of all sorts. However, the genius of
Southern Baptist churches has been the integration of all four methods
into the ongoing life of the church, not as a special emphasis or periodic
event but as the rhythm of how to do church every week. It gave a specific
expression of the New Testament teaching of sowing and reaping. Create
an evangelistic atmosphere within the church, share the gospel through the
community, engage the interested in more and more study of the Bible,
connect their lives to the members of the church, and conversions will
come in due time. Old McBaptist did indeed have a gospel farm resulting
in a harvest of new believers.

The Sum Is Greater Than the Parts

A *paradigm* may be defined as an example or model. Because the SBC
is composed of autonomous local churches, to speak of anything as char-
acterizing all of them is dangerous. Yet over the years, Southern Baptist
churches have developed a paradigm for evangelism, a model for reaching
people that is found in most SBC churches. When Southern Baptist evangelism is considered, one or more of the methods discussed in this part of
the book may come to mind. In reality, the Southern Baptist paradigm for
evangelism is the integration of all four methods. To understand the impact

of Southern Baptists, an understanding of the whole and not just the parts must be clear. In this case, the whole is greater than the sum of the parts.

The picture that best illustrates the Southern Baptist paradigm is the farm, especially given the rural roots of most Southern Baptists. A farmer's produce is the result of an appropriate climate, as well as the process of planting, cultivating, and harvest. Each phase is related to the others, and all are essential if a field is going to be productive.

In Southern Baptist churches, decisional preaching creates the evangelistic atmosphere. Each time people come to a Southern Baptist church, they are given an opportunity to be born again. The offering of an invitation is the reminder that a person is not right with God until his or her life belongs to Jesus Christ. A person's family, church, or religious knowledge does not make that person a Christian. A personal commitment to Jesus Christ is necessary for salvation. The more often a person attends church, the more often he is reminded to get his life right with God. And the more often the prospect returns, the more likely he is to see others making a response. Making a decision for Christ can become more acceptable as the process becomes more familiar.

To that atmosphere of decisional preaching is added the process of planting. Personal evangelism, through systematic visitation and relational contacts, exposes people not in church to the gospel and encourages them to come under the influence of decisional preaching. If a person cannot be led to Christ, they can be invited to church. At church, they will hear the gospel and be challenged to consider their relationship with God. Prospects who come to church are visited in their homes, receiving a personal explanation of the gospel and an explanation of any questions raised by the decisional preaching. Visitation and personal evangelism locate prospects and channel them into the witness of the decisional preaching and the ministry of the Sunday School.

People who are identified as prospects and involved in worship are cultivated through the Sunday School (small group Bible study). Two factors make Sunday School a powerful force in cultivation. The first is Bible study. As prospects are involved in studying the Bible, they receive more and more exposure to the gospel. Their study of the Bible is followed by further exposure to decisional preaching in the worship service. The second factor is the strengthening of relationships with Christians. Contemporary surveys have revealed the enormous influence of relationships on those who come to Christ. By emphasizing evangelism through the Sunday School, Southern Baptists have been practicing a form of relational evangelism for years. Unbelievers who come to Sunday School get to know Christians personally. As the class and department have opportunities to minister to a family during times of crisis, sickness, or celebration, bonding takes place. Social interaction can break down barriers and clarify distorted images of Christianity.

All that remains is the harvest vehicle. Decisional preaching creates the appropriate climate. Visitation and personal evangelism programs find the prospects and plant gospel seeds. Sunday School does the cultivation by teaching the Bible and building relationships. The process culminates with the revival meetings as a harvest vehicle. The special emphasis in Southern Baptist revival meetings is the "drawing of the net"—bringing people to the point of commitment. Regular exposure to decisional preaching, personal explanation and application of the gospel through home visitation, and the biblical understanding and relational bonds created by Sunday School all come together when the attention of the church focuses on conversion. For those who are moving to the point of making a commitment to Christ, the revival meeting seems like a natural time to take that last step of a public commitment.

The Genius of SBC Evangelism

The genius of Southern Baptist evangelism is not a particular methodology. Instead, the development of an integrated process finds unchurched people, exposes them to the gospel, bonds them with people in the church, and offers them a logical opportunity to commit their lives to Jesus Christ. Born in the rural South, Southern Baptists were able to glean from the farm a paradigm for evangelism. The paradigm was not the work of a task force on evangelism. It did not begin at a certain point in time, and it has never been officially adopted and promoted as the way Southern Baptists do evangelism. This paradigm for evangelism gradually emerged as an expression of Southern Baptist life and theology. The process is expressed, often unconsciously, in most Southern Baptist churches. The whole, not the individual parts, helped Southern Baptists become the largest Protestant denomination in America.

When viewed as an integrated process, this way of doing church is clearly an embodiment of the New Testament process of sowing and reaping (1 Cor 3:6). The lesson from Southern Baptist history is the importance of making the church a farm. Methods can come and go; but if a church is to be fruitful, it must have an evangelistic climate. The gospel must be planted in the lives of those who do not have a relationship with Christ. For most, the gospel needs to be explained more than once and illustrated through relationships with Christians. Finally, the church must be there when the time for conversion comes, encouraging repentance and faith in Christ. To be an evangelistic church, sow the gospel and reap conversions.

**

Lesson 2

Old McBaptist needs a farm designed to sow the gospel and reap conversions.

To become an evangelistic church that is winning people to Christ and baptizing them into the membership of the church, the New Testament model of sowing and reaping must be implemented. The crucial question is not how engaged is the church in the four classic evangelistic methods that propelled the SBC to greatness. The crucial question is: What is the church's present process for creating an evangelistic climate in the church, for sharing the gospel with people outside the church, and for cultivating and nurturing people who express openness to the gospel? Also, how are the members being given opportunities to yield their lives to Christ and be baptized? Whatever methods are being used, fuel the fire of evangelism by implementing a process of sowing the gospel and reaping conversions. You have seen how Southern Baptists experienced explosive evangelistic growth. How will you and your church sow the gospel and reap more conversions?

***

Questions for Conversation

1. How is the biblical process of sowing and reaping expressed in the evangelism strategy of your church?
2. How do people in your church learn to share their faith with others?
3. How many new Christians did your church baptize last year? Does that seem to be a reasonable number?

LESSON 3

Theological focus enhances evangelistic engagement.

Theology matters! That the philosophical school of pragmatism began in the United States is no accident. By nature, the American people appear to be oriented more toward the question, "What works?" rather than the question, "Why does it work?" However, in the long run, "why" is more important than "what." Time will bring changes to all methods, and there is often more than one way to accomplish the same task. The question is not what Southern Baptists have done to reach so many people over the years, but rather why Southern Baptists have maintained a strong orientation to evangelism and missions for nearly 150 years.

At least part of the answer to that question lies in the theology behind Southern Baptist efforts in evangelism. In this section of the book, the theological distinctives of Southern Baptist evangelism will be explored. While the theological convictions discussed may not be the convictions of all Southern Baptists, these convictions have characterized the Convention as a whole and played a vital role in keeping evangelism in a prominent position on the Southern Baptist agenda.

CHAPTER 11

A Great Commission Hermeneutic

H*ermeneutics* is the science of interpreting the Bible, a standard discipline in the field of biblical studies. The believer should understand
both what the Bible reveals and what it means. Hermeneutics needs attention from those who wish to understand Southern Baptist evangelism as
well. Many who interpret the Bible define their theology and approach to
Scripture in relationship to Calvinism, neoorthodoxy, reconstructionism,
liberation theology, or some other school of thought. Southern Baptists
typically have approached Scripture from a perspective I call a "Great
Commission hermeneutic." What follows will explain the meaning of that
phrase.

A People of the Book

Throughout their history, Southern Baptists have been known as a "people of the Book." Baptists have had a strong and deep commitment to the
inspiration, reliability, and authority of Scripture. Although Baptists are
not a "creedal people," summarizing their convictions in a statement to
which all must adhere, periodically they have produced confessions of
faith that outline the theological convictions generally held by Baptists.
These confessions of faith form a theological snapshot, illustrating more
than precisely defining exactly what it means to be a Baptist. In virtually
all of these statements, reference is made to what Baptists believe about
the Bible. They believe that the Bible is unique among all other books and
that it is the Word of God.

Southern Baptists have produced three confessions of faith. The confessions are actually one statement called *The Baptist Faith and Message*—the original and its two revisions. All three statements reflect an earlier document titled *The New Hampshire Confession of Faith* (1833). That document, composed by a committee of the Baptist Convention of New Hampshire, became one of the most popular theological statements ever produced by Baptists in America. The original *Baptist Faith and Message* statement was formulated in 1925. The first revision was produced in 1963 and the second in 2000. An amendment—Article XVIII on "The Family"—was adopted in 1998 and remained in the 2000 revision. The efforts made to formulate and then revise the statement of faith were due to theological controversies, focused primarily on the nature of the Bible.

In 1925, the nation was in the midst of the controversy between fundamentalists and liberals, highlighted by debate over evolution and the introduction of higher criticism to the analysis of the biblical text. Lest there be any doubt about where they stood, Southern Baptists wanted a statement that would reflect their theological convictions and offer a clear guideline for denominational schools and agencies.

In 1963, controversy was again raging within the SBC. This time the tension was provoked by a book published by Broadman Press. *The Message of Genesis* by Ralph Elliott,[1] a professor at Midwestern Baptist Theological Seminary, reflected very clearly conclusions of liberal higher criticism in biblical studies, awakening many Southern Baptists to concerns about the introduction of liberal and neoorthodox ideas regarding the inspiration, reliability, and authority of Scripture. The Convention decided to adopt a clear statement indicating a consensus among Southern Baptists about the Bible and other theological issues.

The section on the Bible is very similar in both the 1925 statement and the 1963 statement. The 1963 *Baptist Faith and Message* (BF&M) statement regarding Scripture is as follows:

The Holy Bible was written by men divinely inspired and is the record of God's revelation of Himself to man. It is a perfect treasure of divine instruction. It has God for its author, salvation for its end,

---

[1] Ralph H. Elliott, *The Message of Genesis* (Nashville: Broadman Press, 1961).

and truth, without any mixture of error, for its matter. It reveals the principles by which God judges us; and therefore is, and will remain to the end of the world, the true center of Christian union, and the supreme standard by which all human conduct, creeds, and religious opinions should be tried. The criterion by which the Bible is to be interpreted is Jesus Christ.[2]

Among the key elements of this statement for Southern Baptist evangelism is the emphasis on divine inspiration as the source of the Bible. The biblical word for *inspiration* means "God-breathed" (2 Tim 3:16). Scripture does not go into much detail about how inspiration happened, but it does state that God is responsible for the final product called the Bible. He used human beings to record the words, and each writer reflects his own style and approach. But the Bible available today was given by God to His children. There is nothing the Lord would add and nothing He would omit. God used the writers to express what He wanted to reveal to us about Himself and His purposes. The result is a Bible that is "truth without any mixture of error" (BF&M phrasing). Because the source of the Bible is God and the content of the Bible is true, the directives of Scripture are reliable. When readers find commandments and tasks given to believers in the Bible, they may assume that they embody what God expects of those who acknowledge His lordship. The Bible does not tell us everything about God. All our theological questions are not answered. But Scripture does define what we need to know about the character and ways of God, clarifying how the Lord wants His children to live. It also addresses God's purposes for His children. God's Word is an inerrant guide to knowing God's expectations.

In order to further clarify the Convention's conviction that the entire Bible is inspired, true, and inerrant, the 2000 revision removed the language describing the Bible as only a record of revelation and identifying Jesus Christ as the sole criterion for interpreting Scripture. Those two statements had come to be used by some as an indication that Southern Baptists did

---

[2] See "Comparison of 1925, 1963 and 2000 Baptist Faith and Message," Southern Baptist Convention, accessed December 15, 2017, http://www.sbc.net/bfm2000/bfmcomparison.asp. Cp. Herschel Hobbs, *The Baptist Faith and Message* (Nashville: Convention Press, 1984), 18.

not believe all of the Bible is inspired by God. The SBC wanted to clarify its conviction that the whole of the Bible is inspired by God and therefore infallible and true.

Deuteronomy is the book Jesus quoted more than any other book of the Bible. One of its major themes is obedience to the commands and directions given by the Lord to His people. Deut 29:29 teaches that obedience is a greater priority than understanding: "The secret things belong to the LORD our God, but those things which are revealed belong to us and to our children forever, that we may do all the words of this law." One engaged in a relationship with an infinite God will always encounter mystery, but the inability to understand all that God is does not negate the responsibility to obey what God reveals clearly.

As an inspired, true, and reliable revelation of God's character, work, and purpose, the Bible has an authority that is absolute. What the Bible teaches believers to do must be done. What the Bible reveals as doctrine— the truth about God and the Christian life—must be accepted. A court order is an authoritative document that requires response regardless of the recipient's social class, educational attainments, or professional position. As the revelation of God, the Bible is the ultimate authoritative document. Response to its message is required.

Perhaps more than any other adjective describing the Bible, "authoritative" describes the nearly universal Southern Baptist attitude toward Scripture. By declaring themselves to be a "people of the Book," Southern Baptists are expressing their commitment to seek to understand and to do what God has revealed in the Bible. Where there is a clear understanding of what God desires, there must be a response of obedience. As the inspired, true, reliable, and authoritative Word of God, the Bible is the most appropriate guide for the lives of believers and the work of the church.

A Priority in the Book

As Southern Baptists have read and studied the Bible, they have found its focal point to be the relationship between God and His creation, the human race. The Bible begins with the story of creation. Man and woman were created exactly as God wanted them to be, and He placed them in a garden designed for their needs. Tempted by the desire to be like God (Gen 3:1–7), Adam and Eve sinned, corrupting themselves and the human race that would proceed from them. Sin disrupted their relationship with God and with each other, resulting in judgment, expulsion from the garden, suffering, and death. Humanity's sin, however, was followed by a promise of divine salvation to come and the eventual crushing of the evil one who encouraged the Fall (Gen 3:15).

The story of man's creation and fall forms a preamble of sorts, for the remainder of Scripture is a revelation of God's actions to redeem His fallen creation. After Adam and Eve sinned, they attempted to hide themselves from God. But God came seeking them (Gen 3:8–9), providing the first illustration of Jesus's description of His mission—"the Son of Man has come to seek and to save that which was lost" (Luke 19:10).

The purpose and limitations of Scripture are best understood in the context of man's creation and fall. The Bible was not intended to be an apology (defense) proving the existence of God. Nor was it to be a thorough explanation of all the mysteries of God and life. Rather, the Bible is the revelation of who God is and what God has done to redeem those whom sin has corrupted. God's nature cannot be understood apart from His revelation because sin destroyed the ability of persons to know and understand a holy God. The revelation of what God has done to redeem sinners was necessary so that there might be a response to the salvation God has graciously provided and so that there might be hope in an otherwise hopeless world.

Many questions and issues are not addressed in the Bible. Others are addressed, but not to the extent the reader might desire. But the Bible is not incomplete in any matter related to its basic purpose. That purpose is to reveal who God is and what God has done to redeem His fallen creation.

Given this understanding of the purpose of Scripture, one would anticipate that evangelism, the bringing of the lost to salvation and a right relationship with God, is a prominent theme in the Bible. In their study of God's Word, Southern Baptists have found and championed this biblical emphasis on the priority of evangelism. From Genesis, with the Lord's search for Adam and Eve after their sin in the garden of Eden, to Revelation, with the invitation from the Spirit and the church for the thirsty to come and drink freely of the water of life, the Bible emphasizes the priority of evangelism.

In the Old Testament, the priority of evangelism is seen in God's dealings with Israel and in the prophecies of the Messiah who would come to deliver His people. God called Abraham out of Ur, not just to make him a blessed man, but to make him, the nation, and the Messiah who would proceed from him a blessing to all the peoples of the earth (Gen 12:1–3). Moses was sent by the Lord to deliver the Hebrew people from their bondage and lead them into the promised land of blessing. The story of their deliverance from Egyptian bondage by the power of God became the central motif for the self-identity of Israel. The image of God exemplified in the exodus of the Hebrews is that of God as Redeemer.

When a study is made of the important characters of the Old Testament, one discovers that a common denominator among them is the role each plays in the redemption of others. Most often they are fulfilling their redemptive roles at the direction of and in the power of the Lord. Joseph suffered great hardship at the hands of his brothers, but as a result God put him in a position to deliver his family and the people of Egypt during a time of great famine. Judges is filled with the stories of people like Gideon, Samson, Deborah, and others whom God called and used to deliver the Hebrew people during times of oppression. The shepherd boy David delivered the children of Israel during a war with the Philistines by overcoming the apparently unbeatable Goliath. Boaz acted as the "kinsman redeemer" for Ruth, delivering her from a life of poverty and alienation. Even Esther, the only book in the Bible that does not mention the name of God, is the story of a Hebrew woman, who, when raised to a position of influence, acted at great personal risk to save the lives of her people. Through the stories of the great men and women of the Bible, God emphasizes the priority He places on redemption.

The Assyrian people were one of the most cruel and barbaric peoples in history. When the time for their judgment came, the Lord sent the reluctant Hebrew prophet Jonah to warn them of their jeopardy and urge them to repent. The story of God's eagerness to forgive and Jonah's reluctance to bear His message to an obviously sinful people vividly illustrates the priority of evangelism that God insists His people accept. Whatever the attitude of His people, the Lord is committed to the task of redeeming His fallen and sinful creation.

Along with the constant images of redeemers and redemption, the Bible includes prophecies about the ultimate redemption from sin that God will provide through His Messiah. Most biblical scholars, liberal and conservative, agree that a major theme of the preaching of the early church was the presentation of Jesus as the fulfillment of biblical prophecy. In his Gospel, Matthew frequently refers to the Old Testament prophecies that found their fulfillment in the miraculous birth, ministry, death, and resurrection of Jesus. In the encounter of Philip with the Ethiopian eunuch (Acts 8:25–39), Isaiah 53 is used to explain the death of Jesus on the cross as the fulfillment of prophecy about the redemptive work of the Messiah.

A specific example of the prophetic emphasis of the Old Testament on the work of God as Redeemer is found in the use of the imagery of the "Lamb of God," one of the titles for Jesus in the New Testament (e.g., John 1:36; 1 Pet 1:19; Rev 5:12). The meaning of this metaphor is found in the Old Testament. On the night before the children of Israel left Egypt, God sent the angel of death to slay the firstborn of all living creatures in Egypt—human and animal, Egyptian and Hebrew.[3] The only ones spared would be those who marked the doorposts of their homes with the blood of an unblemished lamb. The lamb was sacrificed to avert the judgment of God. Under Mosaic law, the sacrifice of a lamb was one of the sacrifices for sin and part of the prophetic preparation in the Old Testament to help the people of God understand that one day the Messiah would come to die as the sacrifice for man's sin.

In many ways, the Old Testament emphasizes the priority of redemption and evangelism on God's agenda. However, that priority is especially clear in the New Testament. Jesus constantly defined His ministry in terms of evangelism. When He called His disciples, Jesus called them to the work of evangelism. To follow Him and become His disciple meant becoming a fisher of men (Matt 4:19). As His disciples followed Him, they began telling others about Jesus (John 1:40–45). When criticized for associating with the sinful and the impure, Jesus suggested that the redemption

---

[3] See Exod 11:1–5; 12:12–30.

of the sinful has always been the Father's priority (Luke 15). For Jesus, the work of redemption was His great priority.

From the New Testament, one learns of both the unique role of Jesus in making redemption possible and the ongoing role of believers in making known the possibility of redemption. One illustration is John's differentiation between the roles of Jesus and John the Baptist as found in the first chapter of John's Gospel. Jesus is the true light of the world, and He makes salvation possible (John 1:12). John the Baptist was not the light of the world, but he was sent from God to make the light (i.e., Jesus) known, so that others could find salvation by believing in Jesus (John 1:6–8). God is the author of salvation, and He alone can transform a soul. But for His own purposes, the Lord established a role for believers in the work of redemption. That role is making the gospel known and calling those who hear it to respond in repentance and faith.

Perhaps the most compelling passage of Scripture for Southern Baptists in their understanding of the priority of evangelism in the Bible is the Great Commission, found in the closing words of Matthew:

> And Jesus came and spoke to them, saying, "All authority has been given to Me in heaven and on earth. Go therefore and make disciples of all the nations, baptizing them in the name of the Father and of the Son and of the Holy Spirit, teaching them to observe all things that I have commanded you; and lo, I am with you always, even to the end of the age" (Matt 28:18–20).

Following His death and resurrection, Jesus gave His followers a clear agenda to follow upon His departure. Simply put, that agenda is the evangelizing and discipling of the nations of the world.

Each of the Gospels includes a similar statement, calling believers to the task of evangelism, given shortly before or after the death of Jesus (Matt 28:18–20; Mark 16:15; Luke 24:44–49; John 20:21). The last words of Jesus to His disciples before His ascension to heaven extended a similar command for them to take His gospel to the ends of the earth (Acts 1:6–8). The consistent emphasis of Jesus on evangelism during His ministry and in His final instructions to His followers is a powerful indication of the priority evangelism should have in the lives of believers and in the work of churches.

The early church evidently understood clearly the desire of Jesus for evangelism to be the priority of the church. The book of Acts portrays an evangelistic church bearing witness to the gospel at great cost. The gospel spread from Jews to Samaritans and Gentiles, from Jerusalem to Rome. Every effort was made to call all peoples, regardless of race, to repentance and saving faith in Jesus. Acts and the Epistles teach that the early church faced relational problems and doctrinal disputes. There was social ministry and community involvement. But the great priority of the church in the New Testament was the task of telling the world about Jesus.

A Purpose from the Book

Southern Baptists have maintained strong convictions about the inspiration, truthfulness, reliability, and authority of the Bible. They have also found evangelism to be the central theme of Scripture—that is, the action of God to provide salvation for His fallen creation and to commission His people to take the news of that salvation to the world. Given the supreme authority of the Bible and its focus on evangelism, Southern Baptists have made evangelism the logical foundation of their denominational identity and have read Scripture with a *Great Commission hermeneutic* as the logical guide for its interpretation.

The SBC was formed in 1845 by local churches that wanted to work together to evangelize the nation and the world. Through the years, evangelism has continued to be the greatest unifying factor among Southern Baptists. As the Convention expanded beyond its traditional territory in the South, regional, functional, and ethnic diversity began replacing the cultural homogeneity that had characterized Southern Baptist churches.

The rural heritage of the Convention is still reflected in the values, style, and pace of many traditional churches, but there are also sophisticated megachurches in the cities; other churches with a more formal, liturgical worship style; and "new paradigm" churches developing innovative ways to "do church" in order to reach Baby Boomers, Gen X-ers, Millennials, and other unchurched people groups. The controversy that dominated

SBC meetings during the eighties reflected the reality of a theological pluralism that developed in Southern Baptist life. However, evangelism and missions have remained a rallying cry to which Southern Baptists from every spectrum confess allegiance. The purpose of the church, as Southern Baptists understand it, is to evangelize and disciple the world. A resolution passed at the SBC in 1918 illustrates the interpretive significance of the Great Commission for Southern Baptists:

> We must not forget that the main and primary task of all our agencies, preachers, churches, Sunday schools, denominational schools, Seminaries, Boards and all is [to] press a saving gospel to the hearts of men in heaven's power. We must remember that primarily we are fighting this war for freedom to win men to Christ. The winning of the war is a means to the greater end of winning the whole world to Jesus Christ.[4]

Not even the somber reality of World War I took the Convention away from a sense of responsibility to fulfill the imperative to evangelize.

Various suggestions have been made about the distinctive contributions of Southern Baptists to theology. Many suggest their emphasis is on the priesthood of believers or on the separation of church and state. The priesthood of believers is a doctrinal emphasis that emerged during the Reformation. Southern Baptists have emphasized it, but so have other denominations. The separation of church and state was perhaps the first major issue Baptists addressed in the United States. From their earliest days in this country, Baptists have passionately advocated a clear line of demarcation between the authority of the government and the authority of the church. This Baptist issue existed before the Southern Baptist Convention.

The author believes that the most distinctive Southern Baptist contribution to theology and church life is a Great Commission hermeneutic—the use of the biblical imperative to evangelize the world as the lens through which Scripture is interpreted and applied. A lens set in front of the eye affects everything that eye sees. If the lens is colored, the color of

---

[4] *Annual of the Southern Baptist Convention, 1918*, Hot Springs, Arkansas (May 15–20, 1918), 52.

the lens adds a tint to all that is seen. For Southern Baptists, the appropriate lens for understanding and interpreting Scripture is the Great Commission. At the heart of all that God reveals about Himself is His determination to redeem sinful humanity. While there are other important aspects of theology and of congregational life, the biblical mandate to "make disciples of all the nations" provides the most important key to understand and interpret the nature and character of God and His purpose for the church.

Whatever else God may be, He is certainly the Redeemer who has acted to make salvation possible for sinful, fallen humanity. Whatever else the Lord expects of His people, He surely has given them a mandate to take the news of salvation available through Jesus to every corner of the earth. Therefore, the Great Commission must be the hermeneutical principle used to understand God's character and His expectations for His people.

With a Great Commission hermeneutic, Southern Baptists are expected to hold all believers accountable for bearing witness to the gospel. According to the *Baptist Faith and Message 2000*, "It is the duty and privilege of every follower of Christ and of every church of the Lord Jesus Christ to endeavor to make disciples of all nations."[5] A massive emphasis upon evangelism and missions is also expected. Southern Baptists have assembled a huge force of home and foreign missionaries. The largest offering received is the annual Lottie Moon Christmas Offering® for foreign missions. The second largest offering received by the SBC is the annual Annie Armstrong Easter Offering® for home missions. In addition, well over 50 percent of the Cooperative Program budget, which funds all denominational work, goes to the work of the two mission boards (IMB and NAMB) of the SBC.

In the realm of theological discourse, the impact of a Great Commission hermeneutic is evident in the Southern Baptist perspective on the debate between Calvinism and Arminianism. Historically, Calvinism has emphasized the sovereignty of God in saving those whom He chooses to save. Arminianism has emphasized the responsibility and free will of

---

[5] See "Article XI Evangelism and Missions," of "The Baptist Faith and Message: The 2000 Baptist Faith & Message," Southern Baptist Convention, accessed December 16, 2017, http://www.sbc.net/bfm2000/bfm2000.asp. Cf. Hobbs, *Baptist Faith and Message*, 106.

humanity in responding to God's offer of salvation in Christ. There are proponents of each side within the Convention. However, on the whole, Southern Baptists have not deeply engaged that debate. A great many Southern Baptists identify themselves as "traditional Baptists"—neither Reformed (Calvinist) or Arminian. Only a small number would claim to be Arminians. Only in recent years has much attention been given to this theological discussion because most Southern Baptists focus on the Great Commission task. Southern Baptists have emphasized the believer's responsibility to give every person an opportunity to hear and respond to God's salvation in Christ Jesus.

Assuming that Southern Baptists operate with a Great Commission hermeneutic, one would expect evangelism to have been a factor in the controversy reflected in SBC meetings and agencies in recent years. Sociologist Nancy Ammerman analyzed the Conservative Resurgence controversy by means of historical research, collecting data from surveys and observations from a team composed of both Baptists and non-Baptists. Among her conclusions about the purpose and motivation of the conservative group, whom she called fundamentalists, was the following:

> What fundamentalists sought to alter in the Southern Baptist Convention was not so much the structure, but the policies and personnel located within that structure. Although they came in on an antiestablishment platform, it was the establishment's programs and policies they sought to change, not the establishment itself. They wanted programs that would more clearly reflect a single-minded attention to evangelism. . . .[6]

Issues other than evangelism were certainly involved in the controversy. Many decried the controversy because they felt it was detrimental to Southern Baptist efforts in missions and evangelism. In reality, a Great Commission concern was at least one factor in this determinative conflict in Southern Baptist life.

---

[6] Nancy Ammerman, *Baptist Battles: Social Change and Religious Conflict in the Southern Baptist Convention* (New Brunswick, NJ: Rutgers University Press, 1990), 215–16.

In 1990, I wrote an article for a NOBTS publication that suggested the SBC was in the early stages of a rise in Calvinism.[7] I further suggested that this trend could become a conflict as big as or bigger than the Conservative Resurgence. The depth of passions about this Great Commission hermeneutic will ultimately determine how big an issue this discussion becomes in SBC life. Is the simultaneous rise in Calvinism and decline in baptisms a coincidence or a connection? Time will tell if the SBC is shifting its theological focus away from the Great Comission and its implications.

The Great Commission hermeneutic is a distinctive in Southern Baptist life and has affected profoundly the approach of Southern Baptists to theology, the mission of the church, and daily Christian living. One cannot understand the way Southern Baptists "do church"—and the way they approach issues like social ministry, theological pluralism—without understanding their orientation toward fulfilling the mandate of Jesus to "make disciples of all the nations." Southern Baptists believe that the evangelistic imperative is the preeminent concern of God and the priority task He assigned to His people in Scripture. Therefore, they believe that evangelism should be the fundamental purpose of the church today. As one writer has noted, "Southern" is not the most distinctive characteristic of Southern Baptists today.

> So, if the title "Southern Baptist" has outgrown its geographical usefulness, perhaps it has taken on new meaning in describing the people known by the name. "Southern Baptist" has come to be known as a particular kind of Baptist. *The New International Dictionary of the Christian Church* notes: "Individual Southern Baptists have the reputation of being devout, aggressively evangelistic, relatively strict Christians whose lives are oriented about the Bible and the local church. The main features of Southern Baptist life include a heavy emphasis on evangelism and missions, a tradition of ministry to the common people, and a deep independent streak."[8]

A Great Commission focus is, and I hope ever will be, the true distinctive of Southern Baptists.

---

[7] Charles S. Kelley Jr., "Issues in Evangelism," *Theological Educator* 41 (1990): 169.

[8] C. Lacy Thompson, "Who Are These People Called Southern Baptists?" *The Baptist Message*, July 18, 1991, 5.

CHAPTER 12

A Moral Responsibility

A n understanding of the nature and message of Scripture has led Southern Baptists to develop a Great Commission hermeneutic. However,
the passion in Southern Baptist evangelism is not rooted in obedience to
the Great Commission alone. Evangelism is a task assigned by God, but it
is also a moral responsibility. In the midst of many needs and competing
demands, the church must give attention to evangelism because of the implications and consequences of ignoring it. In this chapter, attention will
be given to why Southern Baptists regard evangelism as a moral responsibility, compelling the involvement of all believers and churches.

The Insecurity of the Lost

From Genesis to Revelation, the Bible speaks consistently and somberly
about the reality and consequences of sin. According to Scripture, sin is
neither trivial nor inconsequential but rather a reality that affects every
human life at its core. Sin is more than doing something wrong. It is being
wrong. A bird with clipped wings is made for the sky but is unable to fly.
So man in his sin is unable to fulfill the purpose for which he was created—made by God but unable to know Him; designed for life and blessing, but living in a world of heartache and pain. Sin alienates the creature
from the Creator.

The Bible uses a variety of images to describe sin. One of the clearest pictures is that of rebellion and self-determination. As Isa 53:6 notes,
"All of us like sheep have gone astray; we have turned, every one, to his
own way." The picture is of sheep who will not respond to the shepherd's

leadership. Instead of grazing in the fields or drinking from the streams chosen by the shepherd, the sheep go off looking for their own sustenance. Many people think of sin in terms of doing bad things. A more accurate concept is to think of sin in terms of doing our own thing. As our Creator and Lord, God has the right and the capacity to direct our lives. His desire is for His children to have satisfying and abundant lives. The refusal of the created to accept life on the Creator's terms and the insistence upon living according to man's own terms is the essence of sin.

The self-orientation of sin renders man incapable of being right with God. One of the most common words for sin in the New Testament means "missing the mark." According to Rom 3:23, "All have sinned and fall short of the glory of God." Because of sin, men and women are unable to meet God's perfect standard of righteousness. Self-orientation leaves no room for total submission to God's will and purposes. Sin is not the inability to do anything right. It is the inability to do all the right that God requires.

The results of sin may be described in terms of three types of consequences: relational consequences, experiential consequences, and eternal consequences. *Relational consequences* are those results of sin that affect relationships with God, with others, and even with self. *Experiential consequences* are those results of sin impacting the quality of life. The *eternal consequences* are the effect of sin on one's eternal destiny.

The story of Adam and Eve in the aftermath of their sin is a chilling illustration of how sin impacts relationships. Prior to the Fall, Adam and Eve enjoyed a close and satisfying communion with God. Their attempt to "become like God" not only disrupted their relationship with God but also made being with Him no longer compellingly desirable. Instead of meeting Him in the cool of the day, the guilty wanted to hide themselves from God (Gen 3:8). A result of man's self-orientation is an inability to believe that God has humanity's best interest at heart. God is not trusted because He may not want people to have their own desires. Since humans cannot relate to God on personal terms, they are uncomfortable relating to Him on His terms.

Added to the pain of being out of fellowship with the Creator is the disillusionment of being unable to relate properly with one another. One of the cruelest phrases in the Bible comes from the lips of Adam. When God confronted him about his sin, Adam immediately responded, "The woman whom You gave to be with me, she gave me of the tree, and I ate" (Gen 3:12). As Adam attempted to shift the responsibility for sin to Eve, he was modeling behavior that has become all too familiar. In *Habits of the Heart*, a masterful study of the American people, Robert Bellah notes that people have become so wrapped up in their own goals and values that they find it increasingly difficult to relate to other people.[1] The same self-interest that alienates one from God creates a wall of separation from others as well.

The alienation caused by sin is complete, for man cannot relate well even to himself. People should not have a problem believing that they do not measure up to God's expectations, for most do not even measure up to their own. All the attention on self that is encouraged by our culture does not produce a healthy self-image. It only reveals one's failures and inadequacies more clearly. Sin affects every level of one's relationships.

A very large segment of the United States population is a group called Baby Boomers. These 76 million people born between 1946 and 1964 are well known for their interest in experience. Boomers want to have everything in life, and they want to have it now. However, the reality of sin has made the life of total satisfaction the impossible dream. When Adam and Eve were expelled from the garden of Eden, a life of difficulty and hardship was a part of their judgment (Gen 3:17–19). This consequence does not mean there is no happiness and contentment. It means that life will always be less than ideal. Boomers came of age during the greatest era of prosperity in American history, but even that prosperity was never enough. As *Saturday Night Live* comedienne Gilda Radner would have said: "It's always something." For those without Christ, complete satisfaction will remain an unreachable goal.

The writer of Ecclesiastes devoted himself in turn to the total pursuit of pleasure, work, and learning. He experienced much pleasure and achieved a great deal of meaningful success. He learned and recorded much wisdom. But he never found peace and contentment apart from his Creator. There was an end to every pleasure, a limitation with every success, and fresh questions arising from each new bit of wisdom.

---

[1] Robert N. Bellah et al., *Habits of the Heart: Individualism and Commitment in American Life* (New York: Harper & Row, 1985), 15.

All people will know the sorrow of losing loved ones and the discomfort of illness and other health problems. Natural disasters, unexpected and unavoidable, tragically affect thousands of lives each year. According to the Bible, even nature itself experiences consequences of human sin (Rom 8:22). Life can be filled with many moments of happiness and pleasure, but it will also reflect the reality of pain and suffering along the way. The totally satisfying life is a casualty of sin.

Eternal destiny is a third consequence of sin for unbelievers. According to Rom 6:23, "For the wages of sin is death." Physical death is the immediate consequence. When sin entered the human race, so did physical death. All people have a terminal disease. Each day brings every person closer to the day of his or her death. But physical death is not the end of the story for believers. For unbelievers, eternal death is the final consequence for sin.

Eternal death is not understood completely, but Scripture teaches its reality. "Hell" is the translation most often used for the word describing the place where unbelievers experience the judgment of eternal death. The painful experience of eternal death in hell is as real and lasts as long as the blessed experience of eternal life in heaven, for they are often discussed in parallel fashion in the same verse or passage (e.g., Matt 25:46; John 3:36). Hell is a place of eternal regret (Luke 16:19–31) and eternal suffering (Matt 25:41; Jude 7; Rev 20:10, 15). Jesus spoke about hell more than any other person in the Bible. Often, He warned His hearers urgently to do whatever was necessary to avoid an eternity in hell (Matt 5:29–30; Mark 9:42–43).

The Bible affirms the reality and experience of hell, but this is not at all the major theme of Scripture. There is no excitement or celebration over hell's existence. Instead, there is sober warning. Eternal death and separation from God await the unbeliever on the other side of physical death.

The life and destiny of the unbeliever are not desirable alternatives according to the Bible. All relationships are affected by the basic self-orientation of a sinful life. One's life may have its moments of pleasure and happiness, but there can never be unbroken satisfaction and fulfillment. Physical death is not the end of consequences for sin and unbelief. Eternal death is the destiny of those apart from God.

The Security of the Saved

Scripture notes a marked contrast between the life and death experiences of the believer and of the unbeliever. As sin affects the relational, experiential, and eternal aspects of a person's life, so does salvation. For some, the word *salvation* conjures up images of church or religious philosophies. However, for Southern Baptists, images of life in all its dimensions would be more appropriate.

The most important effect of salvation for the believer is the establishment of a right relationship with God. As a dysfunctional relationship between a husband and wife makes healthy family relationships impossible, so a dysfunctional relationship with God is at the root of all of man's relational failures. When the creation is in right relationship with the Creator, the Creator can help the creation function properly. The believer knows God as Father rather than as Judge. God is no longer feared and mistrusted. Through Jesus Christ, God can now be worshiped, adored, and praised. In Him, the believer has a dependable source of help and hope. From Him, one can learn how to make life's other relationships work.

The Bible teaches that God created man and woman and that He instituted their union in marriage. The family is a divine institution. With salvation, the believer gains more than a right relationship with God. He gains "expert help" on how to have healthy family relationships as well. The Bible deals specifically with how to be a husband or wife, a parent or a child. Guidance is also given for relationships with friends, neighbors, work associates, and even strangers. Salvation can be the path to healthy relationships with others.

Few benefits of salvation are sweeter than the change in one's self-relationship. If one is accepted and loved by God, then one can accept and love oneself. The means of salvation, the sacrificial death of God's Son on the cross, is an undeniable illustration of God's love for us (Rom 5:8). Merchants would say that one indication of value is the price a person is willing to pay for a product or service. God gave persons immeasurable worth and value through the price He paid for their salvation. For believers, the cross becomes the true source of self-esteem and self-acceptance.

The language Southern Baptists use to talk about salvation is also significant. Perhaps the most common phrase is being "born again," which comes from the conversation of Jesus with Nicodemus and highlights the change salvation produces (John 3:3). The believer is in many ways a different person. A sense of self-esteem and self-worth is based upon what God has done *to* the believer as well as what He has done *for* the believer. According to 2 Cor 5:17, "Therefore, if anyone is in Christ, he is a new creation; old things have passed away; behold, all things have become new." Relationships—with God, others, and self—change because the person is changed.

There is also a difference in the quality of life that believers experience. As mentioned earlier, Continuing Witness Training was a Southern Baptist program to train participants to present the gospel to unbelievers. Witnesses were encouraged to explain eternal life as the *quality* of God's life as well as its endless *quantity*. In other words, when a person comes to Christ, he begins to experience God's kind of life. In human terms, that means a life of satisfaction, joy, love, and peace. Jesus described the life of the believer in terms of abundance: "I have come that they may have life, and that they may have it more abundantly" (John 10:10). The believer's life is a life of fulfillment as opposed to a search, one of supply as opposed to need, and a life of possibility as opposed to limitation.

Note that the important difference in life experience between believers and unbelievers is not in *life events*, but in *life quality*. Faith in Christ is not the ticket to a trouble-free life. Pain and pleasure visit every human life. However, the believer's life is characterized more by provision than need, more by help than hurt. The Christian lives with the confidence that when life brings problems, the Lord will provide whatever is necessary to deal with them. While in prison, Paul noted in Phil 4:19, "And my God shall supply all your need according to His riches in glory by Christ Jesus."

As the believer and the unbeliever approach the experience of life, the fundamental difference between them appears to be hope. The unbeliever faces life, and whatever each day brings, with the resources he has at hand and his confidence or lack thereof in his adequacy for what unfolds. The believer faces life, and whatever each day brings, on the basis of his hope and confidence that God will provide whatever is needed for meaningful life. Hope in the abundant resources of God creates the sense of well-being enjoyed by the believer. Whatever limitations one may see in a situation or recognize in oneself are offset by the lack of limitations on what God can do to help and care for His children.

A critical issue for believers arises when the story of a life does not have a happy ending. A woman prays for her marriage to be held together during a difficult time, but the relationship ends in divorce. Were God's resources inadequate for that need? A parent prays for a child to be healed of cancer, but the child dies. Did a lack of faith prevent the healing? The truth of the matter is that not all the stories of believers have happy endings in real life. Where is God's provision for believers when the need is not met?

In one sense, there is no answer to questions such as these. If God is God—spiritual and eternal, and if people are human—physical and finite, there must be aspects of God's nature and work that human beings cannot comprehend. As a child cannot understand why adults say vegetables are healthier than ice cream, so finite people will not be able to comprehend the meaning in all that God does or does not do. Mystery that defies explanation and questions that appear to be unanswerable are to be expected when the finite attempts to understand the infinite.

In another sense, an answer can be found in the cross. If it is impossible for one to understand all that God is or does, the question becomes: "Can I trust the one I cannot understand?" If the death of Jesus is indeed an illustration of how much God loves us (Rom 5:8), then God has demonstrated a depth of love and compassion that indicates He can be trusted even when He cannot be understood. When God does not meet a need by changing a difficult situation, He will meet the need by providing enough strength, comfort, and courage for the wounded to go on. If believers cannot be sure that every story will be happy, they can be confident that every story will be hopeful. God will be there to see His children through whatever life brings.

The third area of experience impacted by salvation is the eternal destiny of the believer. For the unbeliever, death brings eternal separation from God. For the believer, death brings eternal fellowship with God. Although the Bible says more about heaven than hell, neither the eternal destiny of the saved nor that of the lost is discussed extensively in Scripture. Enough is revealed to give an indication of what to expect, but not enough is given to answer all questions. One thing is made perfectly clear. Heaven is a place of surpassing beauty and blessing, exceeding the ability of the human mind to conceive.

Believers who have endured stories with endings more hopeful than happy will not be disappointed. Heaven will be without death, pain, and suffering; God Himself will wipe away every tear from the sorrowful eye (Rev 21:4). Paul notes that any sufferings experienced in life will appear insignificant when compared with the glorious blessings that will belong to the believer in eternity (Rom 8:18).

The rich imagery of gold, silver, and precious stones that informs the popular imagination regarding heaven point to eternity's abundance. What is rare and precious on earth is so pervasive in glory that it becomes common and ordinary enough to use for building materials. In other words, the believer will not have a need that cannot be abundantly and extravagantly met by God in heaven.

Perhaps the most beautiful image of all is the description of praise, adoration, and worship as the ongoing activity of heaven (Rev 5:11–14). Gratitude is an emotional state that fills body and soul with a sense of well-being. When a great service is rendered or a very precious gift is given, one's soul and body can be overcome with a marvelous combination of emotions and physical sensations—a sense of well-being, warmth, and security floods the consciousness. Such thankfulness produces a profound bonding with the one to whom you are grateful. Remember your most profound experience of gratitude, and you will have a sense of how you will feel in heaven. For those who dwell in heaven, the reality of God's love, grace, and blessing will be so complete that the normal mood and disposition will be one of deep gratitude. The passing sense of gratitude experienced on earth will become a permanent state of being in heaven.

In Christ, the believer is absolutely secure. One's salvation cannot be lost or removed (John 10:27–28; Phil 1:6). Salvation puts the believer in right relationship with God and makes it possible to have healthy relationships with others and a healthy acceptance of oneself. Salvation also makes an immediate impact on the quality of life for believers, bringing hope into their lives. That hope is the confidence that God will supply every need and help with every hurt. Even death is not to be dreaded, for beyond death are eternity and the believer's destiny of heaven. In life or in death, those who are in Christ are secure.

The Moral Imperative to Witness

For Southern Baptists, there is a stark contrast between the state of those who are lost and the state of those who are saved. To sum up the condition of each with a phrase: the lost are absolutely insecure, and the saved are absolutely secure. That being true, the responsibility of every Christian becomes clear. Each believer must be a witness. It is a moral imperative. Those who know Christ must speak to others about the salvation and new life available through Him.

This responsibility supersedes one's vocational calling. Some denominations and groups have emphasized the responsibility of the professional minister or priest to handle matters of the soul's relationships with God. This practice cannot suffice when salvation is at issue. When a driver loses control and the car filled with his family runs off the road and into a lake, it is not just the passing firemen or policemen who should stop. They may have superior training and ability in rescue techniques, but the rancher with a rope and the teacher who can swim must help when they are the first ones on the scene. A saving relationship with Jesus is qualification enough for any person to be able to tell another how to be born again. More than that, it is a qualification that requires a person to be a witness.

Bearing witness to others is more than a matter of one's spiritual gifts. The Bible teaches that the Holy Spirit gives one or more gifts to all believers so that every believer can have a place of service in the church and an opportunity to minister in the world. Some would say that sharing Christ is the responsibility of those with the gift of evangelism. Although those who have the gift of evangelism should be active in telling others about Christ, bearing witness is a responsibility that cuts across the lines of all gifts. Witnessing is the universal responsibility of all who are already secure in Christ.

The story of the Good Samaritan is a biting indictment of those who would ignore someone in need because they were on their way to do some other ministry (Luke 10:29–37). Some believers have the spiritual gift of giving (Rom 12:8). Even when giving is not one's spiritual gift, believers must tithe. All believers are responsible for a basic level of giving. Extraordinary giving is a spiritual gift. Likewise, all believers are responsible to bear witness to what Jesus has done for them and can do for others.

Evangelists will do the extraordinary evangelism. In fact, Eph 4:11–12 indicates that the responsibilities of the evangelist include equipping the people of the church to tell others about Jesus. Southern Baptists have given greater emphasis to the role of those called to evangelism than many other denominations or groups. Still, they have insisted that all believers share the responsibility to bear witness to Jesus.

Bearing witness to Christ even supersedes opportunity. Any person who lives as Christ lived will have an opportunity to tell others about Jesus. The Christian way of life contrasts sharply with the worldly way of life. From time to time, lost people will want to know why a believer's behavior is different. Such opportunities are to be used to bear witness to the difference Jesus makes in a life, but those opportunities are not enough. They happen too rarely. The believer must attempt to initiate situations in which a witness can be shared.

Two o'clock in the morning is not a good time to go visit a neighbor. The family will likely be asleep, and the house may be a mess. The neighbor will not be expecting a visit. However, if you look across the street and see the house on fire, you would not wait until the next morning to sound a warning. The question is not, When should I go? The question is, How can I wake them and tell them? Those who are secure have a responsibility to help those who are insecure. The believer must not only wait for opportunities; he must actively seek to create them.

The passion that prompted Southern Baptists to emphasize evangelism and missions is due in part to a sense of moral obligation and responsibility. Believers and the churches they form are obligated to make evangelism a priority. The understanding that all people without Christ are lost and that lostness means dysfunctional relationships, unfulfilled lives, and eternal separation from God in hell leaves no other moral choice. D. T. Niles defined evangelism as "one beggar telling another beggar where to get food."[2] Those believers who are secure in Christ must go to the insecure with the news of what Jesus can do. It is a moral and ethical responsibility.

---

[2] D. T. Niles, *That They May Have Life* (New York: Harper & Brothers, 1951), 96.

CHAPTER 13

A Possible Task

For a variety of reasons, people who are Christians generally want other people to be Christians as well. When a believer's life is full and satisfying, he has a natural desire for others to experience the same satisfaction. The values and lifestyles associated with active Christians become more appreciated as the world grows increasingly violent, bitter, and disillusioned. Many Christians long for a world in which people would live and act in accordance with the teachings of the New Testament. The reality of hell and eternal separation from God adds a sense of urgency to the desires for others to be born again. The longing for a "Christian world" is common among believers, especially in one's feelings for family and friends. Those people who are best known and loved are the ones believers would most like to see give their lives to Christ.

The presence of these desires in many, if not most, believers indicates that churches should attempt to mobilize their memberships for training and involvement in personal evangelism. Not all agree. Some feel that faith-sharing is the task of the vocational Christian worker. As a plumber would not attempt to do the work of the surgeon, some church members believe that the work of evangelism is best done by the Christian professionals (i.e., the clergy).

However, for many Southern Baptists, the provision God has made for all believers to be effective in personal evangelism confirms the importance of mobilizing the whole church for bearing witness to Christ. Evangelism is not just a task assigned to the few with special gifts for leading others to Christ. God made personal evangelism a possibility for every believer, a discipline for every disciple.

The Work of Christ

The work of Christ makes involvement in sharing the gospel possible for all believers. The work of Christ began with creation. Both the first chapter of the Gospel of John and that of Colossians strongly affirm the role of Jesus in creating the world. He is the one responsible for all that exists. When sin corrupted His creation, Jesus started the process of redemption and evangelism. In terms of evangelism, the work of Christ began with His incarnation. In taking on flesh and blood, He who is all of God that God can be and all of man that man can be (John 1:1, 14). Absolutely unique, Jesus is the God/Man, combining divinity and humanity in one person.

The New Testament is filled with references to His humanity. Jesus was born as a child and experienced normal human development (Luke 2:52). He grew weary and slept. He was the life of the party at banquets, and He cried at funerals. Scripture records some of His battles with temptation (Luke 4:1–13) and notes that He "was in all points tempted as we are, yet without sin" (Heb 4:15). His life included much of our contemporary experience, for in many ways Jesus lived the kind of life people live today.

The parallels between the life of Jesus and the lives of believers indicate that the example of Jesus can serve as a model or guide. Of particular significance for evangelism is the fact that the life of Jesus can serve as a model for sharing the gospel. Several Southern Baptist authors have written books on evangelism based upon the evangelism of Jesus. Among them are L. R. Scarborough's *With Christ After the Lost*;[1] Gaines S. Dobbins's *Evangelism according to Christ*;[2] and Delos Miles's *How Jesus Won Persons*.[3] That these men were serving as seminary professors when the books were written and that the publications were intended to be used as

---

[1] See chapter 7, n. 1.
[2] See chapter 7, n. 2.
[3] Delos Miles, *How Jesus Won Persons* (Nashville: Broadman Press, 1982).

textbooks is an indication of the significance of Jesus for the Southern Baptist philosophy of evangelism.

Those authors who have written about the evangelism of Jesus emphasize that He considered any setting to be appropriate for evangelism. Some of His evangelism took place in the context of the miraculous. However, much of it took place in the more ordinary setting of a conversation (Nicodemus), a meal (Zacchaeus), a spontaneous encounter (woman at the well), or a life crisis (woman caught in the act of adultery). For Jesus, evangelism often took place outside of worship services and in the midst of any given day's events. Talking to people about God did not require a particular place or setting.

Jesus also used a variety of ways to explain the Gospel to those who would listen. With Nicodemus, Jesus talked about being born again (John 3:1–21). With the woman caught in adultery, He talked about forgiveness as an opportunity to start over (John 8:1–11). With the rich young ruler, He spoke of turning away from the material in order to find the spiritual (Mark 10:17–27). In each encounter, Jesus explained the essence of the gospel in different ways. The variety of His approaches indicates the validity of multiple approaches to evangelism today. The greater the variety of ways to tell others about Christ, the more likely all believers can expect to find some way to witness.

Another critical factor in the example of Jesus was the priority He gave to evangelism. Although His ministry was brief, it was busy. Jesus received much advice about how to spend His time: from His family, His disciples, and from the religious leaders of His day. His family wanted Jesus to leave the crowds and be with them (Matt 12:46–50). His disciples wanted Him to stay close to home, teaching and healing the many who wanted to be near Him. The religious leaders wanted Jesus to avoid the people who were social outcasts and moral failures (Luke 15:1–2). Jesus insisted that their problems were the very reason that He came.

In every case, Jesus clearly affirmed His commitment to the priority of evangelism. As Paul affirmed in 1 Tim 1:15, "Christ Jesus came into the world to save sinners." As a boy, when He was questioned by Mary and Joseph about remaining in the temple after they left Jerusalem, Jesus reminded them that He had to be "about My Father's business" (Luke

2:49). When the disciples bickered about their place in the kingdom, Jesus told them He "did not come to be served, but to serve, and to give His life a ransom for many" (Mark 10:45). Jesus was criticized for having a meal with the corrupt tax collector Zacchaeus, but He answered His critics by saying that "the Son of Man has come to seek and to save that which was lost" (Luke 19:10). The determination of Jesus to herald the coming of salvation and to go to the cross for the redemption of humanity illustrates the priority evangelism should have, even in busy lives.

A fourth component of the model of Jesus in evangelism is found in His embodiment of evangelism with integrity. In His earthly life, Jesus engaged in evangelism through being, doing, and telling. In His lifestyle, Jesus was sinless and pure, perfectly obeying the law of God. He illustrated God's righteousness by being righteous. To His righteous character, Jesus added loving actions, serving and helping those in need. Jesus demonstrated God's righteousness by doing righteous deeds. He did not stop with the witness of His character and His deeds. Jesus told those who would hear how to be right with God. Evangelism with integrity includes being, doing, and telling. One's moral *character*, daily *deeds*, and spoken *words* should communicate the same message about who God is and what God can do with and for a human life.

Although the example of Jesus in evangelism is important, it is not the most important aspect of His evangelistic work. The atonement is the supreme work of Christ in evangelism. *Atonement* is a theological term meaning that Jesus acted to make a right relationship with God possible. What did He do? According to the Bible, Jesus died for our sins and was buried. On the third day, He rose from the dead and gave evidence of His resurrection by appearing to several people who saw Him die and who then recognized Him as being alive again (1 Cor 15:3–8). The sinful life and moral imperfection of humanity required the judgment of eternal death and separation from God (Rom 6:23). The sinless life and moral perfection of Jesus qualified Him to act as a substitute for the human race, experiencing the wrath of God's judgment against sin in man's place (1 Pet 3:15). When a person turns away from sin in repentance and places his faith in the atoning work of Jesus, that person is saved and transformed. As the new believer's Savior, Jesus is also his Lord, the supreme authority in his life.

The act of atonement by Jesus was His most important work related to evangelism because salvation thereby was made possible for those who put their faith in what Jesus did (John 3:16). The possibility of salvation enhances the possibility of believers becoming involved in sharing their faith. Knowing that faith in Christ can make a difference in the life of a friend, neighbor, or person in need encourages a believer to give others the opportunity to place their faith in Jesus and be changed. In His life, Jesus illustrated how to do the work of evangelism. Through His death and resurrection, Jesus made involvement in evangelism meaningful and important.

The Work of the Holy Spirit

The work of the Holy Spirit also plays an important role in the possibility of evangelism. Historically, Southern Baptists have not placed a major emphasis on the doctrine of the Holy Spirit, although the doctrine is included in the *Baptist Faith & Message 2000*. The growth of the charismatic movement in the 1970s brought renewed attention to understanding the work and ministry of the Holy Spirit, especially in regard to spiritual gifts. However, the aspect of the Holy Spirit's work that has received the most attention from Southern Baptists is inspiration. Because of their very strong convictions regarding the Bible, Southern Baptists have devoted careful thought and extensive discussion to the role of the Holy Spirit in the production and interpretation of Scripture.

Yet, along with the concern about inspiration and the confusion and controversy surrounding spiritual gifts, the Spirit's role in evangelism has received some attention from Southern Baptists. The regular use of the invitation as a part of the worship service keeps before congregations the Spirit's role in drawing the lost to Christ through the pastor's exhortations, the words of invitation hymns, and the prayers of believers for the unsaved to respond to appeals. Personal evangelism training programs, often highly promoted in denominational evangelism emphases, generally include some instruction about the work of the Holy Spirit in evangelism.

The popularity of such programs in the churches has provided another avenue for keeping before the people of the denomination the Spirit's role in evangelism. As a result, active Southern Baptists have a general awareness of the work of the Holy Spirit in evangelism. His work will often be discussed or understood in terms of three main categories—the role of the Holy Spirit in the life of the believer, in the life of the unbeliever, and in the process of conversion.

In terms of evangelism, the work of the Holy Spirit in the lives of *believers* is *enablement.* When the disciples expressed concern over the coming departure of Jesus, He reassured them with a promise about the Holy Spirit: "And I will pray the Father, and He will give you another Helper, that He may abide with you forever" (John 14:16). The word translated "another" means another of the same kind. Jesus promised that the Holy Spirit would do the same things for His disciples that He had been doing—that is, equipping them for ministry and sending them out to preach, heal, and help. The Holy Spirit would continue that work of equipping and sending in the lives of the disciples and all believers.

The Holy Spirit equips believers for evangelism by giving them *power.* In Acts 1:8, Jesus promised the disciples, "But you shall receive power when the Holy Spirit has come upon you." The fulfillment of His promise was evident at Pentecost when Peter preached and thousands responded to his message. The power of the Holy Spirit in evangelism is rarely manifested outwardly or physically. In 1 Cor 1:26–29, Paul noted that God is much more likely to use the weak than the mighty. The power given by the Holy Spirit is effectual power. When shared by a believer, the gospel has the power to change the life of the hearer. The Holy Spirit empowers the witness of a believer, giving it the impact and power necessary to change lives.

The Holy Spirit also brings *boldness* into the lives of believers, giving them the courage to share their faith. A sense of inadequacy or fear is a common barrier to be overcome by those who become involved in evangelism. That was as true in the early church as it is among believers today. In Acts 4, Peter and John were arrested for their witness about Jesus. Before being released, they were warned that continuing to bear witness to Jesus would result in severe punishment. When they told the other believers about the new penalty for engaging in evangelism, the church responded by praying for boldness to continue. In response to that prayer, the disciples were filled with the Spirit and proceeded with great boldness to tell others about Jesus (Acts 4:31). The Holy Spirit enabled them to witness by providing the boldness they needed to continue sharing in the face of opposition.

A third way the Holy Spirit equips believers for evangelism is by providing *guidance* during witnessing conversations. Before His death, Jesus warned His disciples that they would face persecution and opposition. Jesus promised that when they had spontaneous witnessing encounters for which they could not prepare, the Spirit would guide them in knowing what to say (Matt 10:16–20). This promise was not meant to comfort preachers who fail to prepare sermons but to encourage believers who fear not knowing what to say about Jesus during a witnessing encounter, especially during a hostile encounter. Many times, in witnessing conversations, I find myself saying something I have not said or thought about before. That is the guidance of the Holy Spirit at work.

The enabling ministry of the Holy Spirit makes bearing witness to Jesus Christ a possibility for all believers. The background and experience one has to offer as a witness to Christ is not as important as what the Holy Spirit does through the person who chooses to be available as a witness. The Holy Spirit enables all believers to have confidence in being equipped adequately to share the gospel with others.

In addition to enabling believers, the Holy Spirit performs an *evidential ministry* in the lives of *unbelievers.* The Spirit both equips the believer to witness and prepares the lost person to receive this witness. The most specific teaching regarding this aspect of His ministry comes from Jesus and is found in John 16:7–11. The setting for this instruction is the anxiety of the disciples over the coming departure of Jesus. He has told them that His departure is for their benefit because of the coming ministry of the Spirit. Jesus explains that the disciples will profit from the Holy Spirit's ministry both to them and to unbelievers.

The Holy Spirit gives evidence and confirmation to unbelievers that the message they are hearing is true. According to Jesus, the Spirit "will convict the world of sin, and of righteousness, and of judgment" (John

16:8). He helps unbelievers recognize that their failure to believe in Jesus is evidence of the reality of their sin. Since the life of Jesus is no longer visible as an illustration of the righteousness God requires, the Spirit will convince them that Jesus is the only source for the righteousness God demands. Then the Spirit will confirm for them that sin does have serious consequences in the form of God's judgment (John 16:9–11).

Although the Bible does not make clear the exact ways in which the Spirit will work, the implication is that He will use the witness of the believer. As the Christian shares the gospel with a lost person, the Spirit speaks to that person and affirms that what he is hearing is true. The Holy Spirit gives the statements of the witness the ring of truth. He adds an internal witness to the external witness of the believer. Without the inner witness of the Spirit, the verbal witness of the believer would never be accepted. The unbeliever can resist the witness of the Spirit but does so at his own peril. Some believers would suggest that the unpardonable sin of which Jesus spoke is a rejection of the witness of the Holy Spirit to the truth about Jesus (Matt 12:30–32). The work of the Holy Spirit in affirming the witness of the believer emphasizes the possibility of the involvement of all believers in the work of evangelism.

The third aspect of the Holy Spirit's work in evangelism is His role in the process of *conversion*. The anticipated result of evangelism is the conversion of the lost. For the believer and the unbeliever, a total change in one's life, resulting from a witness about the saving power of Jesus Christ, can be difficult to imagine. But conversion is not the result of a witness. It is the result of the transforming work of the Holy Spirit. Through His death and resurrection, Jesus made salvation possible. By His work of regeneration, the Holy Spirit makes salvation actual in the life of the person who responds to the gospel. The Holy Spirit applies the redemptive work of Christ to the individual who places his faith in Jesus.

In His conversation with Nicodemus, Jesus spoke of the need for persons to be "born again" (John 3:3). When Nicodemus struggled to understand how this could happen, Jesus explained that transformation was possible only through the power of the Holy Spirit to make a sinful person into a new being reconciled with God (John 3:6, 16; 1 Cor 5:17).

The work of the Spirit in salvation underscores the supernatural nature of salvation. Salvation is by grace—what God does—and not by works—what someone does for God. The Christian witness does not call the unbeliever to change but to be changed. The impact of evangelistic efforts on the life of an unbeliever does not depend upon the witness or the lost person but rather upon the work of the Holy Spirit. The Spirit enables the Christian to share. The Spirit prepares the unbeliever to receive the message. The Spirit transforms the life of the one who turns to Jesus. Evangelism is made possible through the work of the Holy Spirit.

The Work of the Witness

The final factor Southern Baptists have emphasized in considering the possibility of evangelism for all believers is the work of the witness. The responsibilities of the witness can be fulfilled by all believers; they are not duties requiring a trained professional's competent handling. The roots of the Southern Baptist Convention are in the rural South. For many years, their churches were led by farmers/preachers. While Southern Baptists have become more urban and more educated, even today about half of the pastors in the Convention do not have a seminary degree. However, formal training is not a prerequisite for effective involvement in evangelism.

Nor does personal evangelism require a certain spiritual gift or gifts for effectiveness. The existence of the gift of evangelism has been the subject of debate inside and outside of the SBC. The New Testament is largely silent on the matter. The term *evangelist* is used only three times in the New Testament. Philip, a layman, is described as "the evangelist" (Acts 21:8). Paul tells Timothy, a pastor and church planter, to "do the work of an evangelist" (2 Tim 4:5). In the third reference, "evangelists"—along with apostles, prophets, and pastors/teachers—are themselves described as gifts to the church (Eph 4:11–13). None of the references includes a clear definition, description, or identification of the gift of evangelism.

Through the years, Southern Baptists have recognized the function or role of evangelists in relationship to the local church. Traditionally, the evangelist is an itinerant who travels from church to church or community to community, focusing his ministry on inviting lost people to come to Christ. Billy Graham, the most famous Southern Baptist evangelist, has described his gift as the ability to extend an evangelistic invitation to which unbelievers respond. The revivalistic heritage of Southern Baptists has helped evangelists to be more accepted in their denominational life than are evangelists in some other denominations.

Despite the acceptance of and appreciation for the role of the evangelist in Southern Baptist life, the SBC has not let evangelism become the work of the professionals. Southern Baptists have emphasized the personal responsibility of all believers to be witnesses. In earlier years, revivalism was the basic method of evangelism for Southern Baptist churches. In recent years, a slow but steady shift has developed toward personal evangelism and worship evangelism (evangelism through the weekly worship services of the church), supplemented by revivals and other evangelism methodologies. In Southern Baptist life, evangelism is a task that is possible for every believer. The work of the witness involves a personal walk with Jesus Christ, prayer, and sharing one's personal experience of the work of Christ.

In Matt 4:19, Jesus told His disciples, "Follow Me, and I will make you fishers of men." The responsibility of turning believers into witnesses is assumed by Jesus Himself. He told His disciples that if they would follow Him, He would make them become witnesses. Our involvement in evangelism is not a result of a certain personality type or spiritual gifts. The work of Jesus in our lives results in evangelistic outreach. The focus of the believer is to *follow Christ*—spending time with Him through Bible study, prayer, and doing as He commands. The result will be a witnessing life.

One of the most effective witnesses I have known did not begin as an effective witness. She came to New Orleans Baptist Theological Seminary from a very difficult background and was painfully shy for physical and psychological reasons. But she loved Jesus and was planning to be a missionary. She became burdened about her work as a witness and asked for prayer as she attempted to follow Christ into a witnessing lifestyle. Her long journey involved many small steps, but by the time she left New Orleans, she was taking pastors and students to evangelize with her so that they could learn more about sharing their faith. Nothing about her personality or appearance made her a "natural" witness, but her walk with Jesus led her into a witnessing lifestyle.

The work of the witness also includes *prayer*. The Bible gives little explanation about how prayer works, but it is filled with exhortations to pray. A definite relationship between the practice of prayer and the practice of evangelism is apparent in believers. In Matt 9:35–38, Jesus commented on the number of people who were in need of help by comparing them to an overripe harvest. In a striking turn away from the expected, Jesus did not exhort His disciples to get busy working to bring in the harvest. Instead He urged them to pray and ask God to raise up sufficient laborers for the harvest.

Perhaps God uses the process of prayer to give believers a sense of responsibility to become involved in telling others about Jesus. In any case, Jesus intends the work of the witness to include prayer. Mention has already been made about the work of Jesus as a model for witnessing. The disciples noticed that prayer was deeply woven into the private life of Jesus. According to the biblical record, the only thing His disciples asked Him to teach them was to pray. Those who pray will witness. Those who witness must pray.

Continuing Witness Training, discussed earlier as one of the popular evangelism training programs in Southern Baptist life, required all participants to have prayer partners who would pray with them and for them as they learned about the witnessing process and went out to witness each week. One of the fastest-growing ministries among Southern Baptist churches is an organized intercessory prayer ministry. At one point, the evangelism section of the Home Mission Board created a staff position to promote prayer and spiritual awakening. Denominational evangelism workers are encouraging churches to strengthen the relationship between a prayer program and an evangelism program. For Southern Baptists, the work of the witness must include the task of prayer.

The third component of the work of the witness is *sharing one's personal experience* with Jesus Christ. Many different methods of evangelism are available to share a testimony. Pulpit evangelism, media evangelism, literature evangelism, social media evangelism, and event evangelism are just a few of the many ways to tell others about Christ. A common denominator exists among the many methods being used today. That common denominator is telling others what Jesus Christ has done for you personally.

When Peter and John were arrested and forbidden to speak of Jesus again, they responded by saying, "We cannot but speak the things which we have seen and heard" (Acts 4:20). In the first chapter of his first epistle, John rooted his testimony about Jesus in the experiences he and the other disciples had when they lived with Jesus (1 John 1:1–4). Several times in the missionary journeys recorded in the book of Acts and in his epistles, Paul used his personal testimony to explain the gospel to others. The Greek word translated as "witness" was adopted by the early church as a word for evangelism because much of what they did was to tell others what Jesus had done for them. Today virtually all Southern Baptist witness training programs include teaching participants how to share the gospel by sharing their personal testimonies.

Christians can discuss many aspects of the gospel with unbelievers. The better one's knowledge of Scripture and understanding of the faith, the easier it is to engage in evangelism. However, Bible knowledge and theological maturity are not essential equipment for involvement in evangelism. When a believer understands what Jesus has done for him well enough to share the experience with others, he is capable of doing effective evangelism. In a court of law, a witness is someone who has seen or experienced something about the event under discussion. A witness for Christ is someone who has evidence to offer concerning what Jesus Christ can do to change human lives. That work is possible for anyone who has had a personal encounter with Jesus.

Southern Baptists have emphasized the mobilization of the church for evangelism because evangelism is believed to be a task for all Christians. It is possible due to the work of Christ, the work of the Holy Spirit, and the work of the witness. Evangelism is not the responsibility of trained professionals alone. God has made it possible for all believers to participate in the fulfillment of the Great Commission.

CHAPTER 14

A Transferable Gospel

One of the most interesting aspects of Southern Baptist theology related to evangelism involves its packaging. To the passion for a biblical theology, Southern Baptists have added a determination to make that theology transferable. If believers are going to witness, they must be able to explain the process of salvation to others. Rarely does the conversation require the technical expertise of a theologian. Believers simply need to explain how to become a Christian, using plain language that can be understood by people outside the church. Southern Baptists have excelled in developing an understanding of the gospel for popular use but not without some cost along the way.

The Focus on Faith

Evangelism cannot be reduced to a single theological concern. Attempts to fulfill the Great Commission raise a wide variety of theological issues. Some of the most intense theological debates, in fact, are a result of grappling with the task of evangelism. God's sovereignty versus human freedom is a debate that has raged for centuries. The relationship between the death of Christ on the cross and the forgiveness of sin is a crucial issue in understanding the doctrine of salvation. The reality of hell versus the universality of salvation is a discussion growing in intensity among evangelicals. The theology of evangelism touches many areas of great concern in the development of a sound and biblical theology.

Southern Baptists and their theologians have addressed the issues listed above and a host of others. However, amid their theological musings, the issue that keeps surfacing is the response issue. To echo the question of the Philippian jailer in Acts 17, What must one do to be saved? Without downplaying the priority of God's initiative in redemption and recognizing man's utter reliance upon God's grace in salvation, Southern Baptists tend to focus on faith. In light of what God has done, how should man respond?

As Baptist work began in America, two major Baptist groups developed: General Baptists and Particular Baptists. The General Baptists were associated with an Arminian tendency, emphasizing man's responsibility and free will. The Particular Baptists tended toward a more Calvinistic emphasis on God's sovereignty. During the Great Awakening of the eighteenth century, churches and communities along the eastern seaboard, especially in the Northeast, were deeply stirred. The revival fires spread southward, in part through the ministry of Baptists like Shubal Stearns and Daniel Marshall. Southern soil proved fertile for the Baptists, who experienced explosive growth. One congregation, the Sandy Creek Baptist Church in Liberty, North Carolina, gave birth by itself to more than 20 churches.

As the Baptists grew in the South, they developed a unique identity. Combining the evangelistic zeal of the more Arminian General Baptists with the theological framework of the more Calvinistic Particular Baptists, these "new" Baptists were reflecting Baptist distinctives from a Reformed theological perspective, which emphasized an activist approach to evangelism and missions. As the identity of Southern Baptists coalesced around evangelism and missions, it was only natural for an interest in a transferable gospel to develop.

If church and denominational leadership were to emphasize the involvement of all Christians in evangelism, the doctrine of salvation needed to be in a form that believers could share with their neighbors. A missionary facing the challenges of cross-cultural evangelism needed an explanation of the gospel emphasizing essentials more than details. The focus on faith encouraged expressions and discussions of the faith that could be easily passed on to others, both by the rank and file believers and by the trained leadership.

While the theologians—like James Boyce, E. Y. Mullins, W. T. Conner, and others—were writing their systematic statements, pastors and evangelists were reducing the issues to the transferable essentials. The focus of the theologians was on understanding the faith. The focus of the people in the field was on sharing the faith with others. Among Southern Baptists at grassroots level, the transferable gospel, emphasizing how to become a Christian, made the deepest impression. Many Southern Baptists, if asked how to become a Christian, would respond, "Believe on Jesus." Those who could not cite a biblical reference for the doctrine of election or the doctrine of the Trinity probably would be able to cite John 3:16 as a reference on how to become a Christian. The theology that reached the people in the pew was a theology that focused on faith.

The Presentation of a Plan

As Southern Baptists found their identity in the task of evangelism and missions, they focused their theology on faith. That focus on seeking a response to the gospel of Christ stimulated the search for ways to present the gospel, making it transferable from believers to unbelievers. There was an inevitable need to develop various ways to present the gospel or plan of salvation. Over the years, Southern Baptists developed multiple gospel presentations. Some were formulated and promoted as integral parts of denominational evangelism programs. Others were developed outside of the SBC but were assimilated into the life of many SBC churches. *The Four Spiritual Laws* tract of Campus Crusade for Christ and the model presentation from Evangelism Explosion are two examples of gospel presentations from outside the denomination that were embraced by many SBC churches. Still others were developed by various individuals for use in the churches they were serving.

For many believers within the SBC, these explanations of the gospel became their systematic theology. Their heavy promotion in evangelism efforts gave them visibility. Their simplicity made them memorable. The doctrine of salvation became the theological framework for most Southern

Baptists because it was the doctrine most discussed. The result was a conversion-driven theology.

In an effort to understand the emphasis Southern Baptists have given to the doctrine of the lordship of Christ, Robin Jumper conducted a thorough and excellent study of the gospel presentations promoted by the Convention.[1] He noted that the evangelism department of the SBC began to develop and promote presentations of the plan of salvation for personal evangelism in the late 1930s.

Study course books, taught in conjunction with the education programs of churches, were the primary means of propagating the gospel presentations and training people to use them. In the 1960s, a movement toward a more organized and sophisticated training process began. The growing sophistication of the training methodology produced a more sharply defined explanation of the gospel.

Due to the large number and great diversity of their churches, at no time have Southern Baptists used only one expression of the plan of salvation. However, Jumper's research did indicate that when the Evangelism Department of the Home Mission Board began to emphasize personal evangelism training, one presentation in each era did appear to be more popular and receive more promotion. Jumper documented four of the most significant and influential gospel presentations promoted by the denomination.

One of these was "God's Way of Salvation," promoted by Roland Q. Leavell before and during World War II, and published in his book *Winning Others to Christ*. The plan of salvation was presented using a simple outline with three points: salvation needed, salvation provided, and salvation accepted. The sequence of scriptural references included Rom 3:23; 6:23; 1 John 1:7; John 3:16; Eph 2:8; Acts 20:21; Luke 13:3; and John 3:18, 36.

The years following World War II were dominated by an emphasis on mass evangelism. In the 1960s, the denominational evangelism program was more balanced and included the first formal program of relational

---

[1] George Robin Jumper, "An Investigation of the Concept of Committing to Christ as Lord in Conversion in Selected Southern Baptist Convention Gospel Presentations" (Ph.D. dissertation, New Orleans Baptist Theological Seminary, 1990).

evangelism for Southern Baptists called *Cultivative Witnessing*, by C. E. Autrey. A clearly defined plan of salvation was not included in the training, but general references on how to become a Christian were placed in the brightly colored, 16-page brochure used for home visitation. The gospel was presented most obviously under the headings of the Bible's vital message of Christ as God's answer to man's need. The themes used were unbelief, satisfaction, and security. The sequence of Scripture references included Rom 3:23; John 3:18; Rom 6:23; John 5:24; 3:16–17; 10:10; and Rev 3:20. This technique was a "soft" approach to personal evangelism, especially for Southern Baptists, but it reflected the context of the United States during that turbulent period.

The Lay Evangelism School was introduced in the early 1970s as a training process for teaching the laity to share their testimonies and the plan of salvation. A tract titled *How to Have a Full and Meaningful Life*[2] was used to present the gospel. Its major points included God's love, Christ's death and resurrection, the spiritual birth, man's sin, and how to receive Christ. The sequence of Scripture references included 1 John 4:9, 13; 5:11; John 1:12; 3:3, 16, 18; 5:24; 10:10; Acts 3:19; Rom 4:25; 5:8, 12; 6:23; 8:16–17; 10:9–10, 13; 2 Cor 6:2; Eph 1:7; 2:8–9; Phil 4:19; Heb 10:23; and Jas 2:19.

The most prominent plan of salvation in the evangelism program was developed originally for the Continuing Witness Training program. Other denominational evangelism programs incorporated it as well. Regarded as the model presentation, its outline is: God's purpose, our need, God's provision, and our response. The design includes elements of explanation, illustration, and application. Among the Scripture references used are Matt 7:21; John 1:1, 12, 14; 3:16; 10:10; 14:3, 6; Acts 3:19; 26:20; Rom 3:23; 4:25; 6:23; 10:9–10, 13; Eph 2:8–9; 1 Pet 3:18; Jas 2:19; and 1 John 5:13.

The plan of salvation being promoted by NAMB at this writing is called the *3 Circles: Life Conversation Guide*. Released after Robin Jumper's study,[3] it is the most significant plan of salvation produced since 1990. The three circles represent "God's Design," our "Brokenness," and the

---

[2] This tract is published by LifeWay Christian Resources in Nashville.
[3] See n. 1 in this chapter.

"Gospel."[4] The sequence of Scriptures used is Gen 1:31; Psalm 19:1; Rom 3:23; 6:23a; and 1:25; Prov 14:12; John 3:16a; Col 2:14; 1 Cor 15:3–4; Mark 1:15b; Eph 2:8–9; Rom 10:9; Phil 2:13; Eph 2:10; Rom 10:13; John 20:3; Matt 6:33; and Col 2:6. The presentation is available in printed form and in a video accessed through a smartphone app.

There are three distinctives about this plan of salvation. First, it is easy to learn and can be drawn on a piece of paper or napkin for use without referring to all Scriptures. Second, it does use more Scripture than most gospel presentations. Third, I can recall no other diagram of the plan of salvation that places repentance and belief before the gospel news of Christ dying for our sins on the cross. The booklet and video explain the gospel and go backward to add repentance and belief. Its overall simplicity is its greatest strength.

The common elements of the gospel presentations are God and His purposes, sin and its consequences, Christ and His work, and faith and its effect. Many Bible doctrines are included in these understandings of salvation. The doctrine of God, the doctrine of man, the doctrine of sin, the doctrine of Christ, and other doctrines are all aspects of the doctrine of salvation. However, the primary focus is on what one must do to be saved. The unique feature of developing theology in light of the evangelistic task is that the goal is not so much the understanding of God but the conversion of men and women. The theological agenda is framed by the questions: What do people need to know in order to be converted? and What do believers need to understand in order to engage in evangelism? The result is a theology that is practical, relevant, and transferable to others. This conversion-driven theology is a logical complement to the Great Commission hermeneutic discussed earlier. Through the years, however, Southern Baptists have discovered that there is a cost involved in focusing on a functional theology.

---

[4] See "3 Circles: Life Conversation Guide," *Life on Mission*, accessed December 16, 2017, http://lifeonmissionbook.com/conversation-guide.

The Completion of the Commission

For many Southern Baptists, theological discourse takes place most often in the sermon and the Sunday School lesson. SBC churches offer no formal catechism for the young to learn as they grow up, and no creed is taught to adults as a part of the membership process. Doctrinal training programs exist, but Southern Baptist churches are not uniform in their usage of any one formal process of instructing believers in doctrine. For the most part, Southern Baptists learn their doctrine through sermons from their pastors, lessons taught in Sunday School and absorbed in personal Bible study, and through the songs and hymns sung in church.

Over the years, Southern Baptists organized both Sunday School and worship around the evangelistic task. More is said about this fact in another section of the book, but in both theory and practice, the Convention attempted to make evangelism the main business of worship and Bible study. An evangelistic invitation is given in most worship services of the typical SBC church, and Sunday School is described as the outreach arm of the church. Pastors preach about a variety of topics and, over a period of time, will address a host of doctrinal concerns. The Sunday School literature is designed to deal systematically with the entire Bible and the whole range of theological issues and doctrines. Even *The Baptist Hymnal*, an official hymnal of the SBC, intentionally reflects a variety of theological issues. The doctrinal issues that the typical Southern Baptist is most likely to absorb are the reliability and authority of the Bible and the necessity for all persons to experience conversion.

One consequence of a conversion-driven theology is that the experience of conversion is celebrated as such a great event that magnifying conversion can retard further theological development. People who follow football have seen one team race to a large lead, only to lose the lead while the other team suddenly begins to dominate the action. Coaches and commentators often explain the change as the result of one team's getting an easy and early lead. Because the game seems to be under control, the players have difficulty maintaining the intensity necessary to continue to dominate play. When the mission of winning seems well in hand, distraction sets in. When conversion is presented with such emphasis, other aspects of spirituality may appear less important. The presence of this attitude can result unintentionally in a deemphasis on the process of sanctification (i.e., maturing in Christian life and thought).

To at least some degree, Southern Baptists have experienced this problem. C. E. Matthews led the Southern Baptist program of evangelism during the period of greatest growth, but even he noted Southern Baptists' historical weakness in following up on professions of faith and discipling the converts. Leading people to a commitment to Christ is easier than involving them in growth and nurture through a local church.

The problem has not been overlooked. When Southern Baptists chose to make Sunday School the outreach arm of the church, another program was created to focus on the discipleship of believers. The Sunday night program in most Southern Baptist churches known as Discipleship Training was designed from the beginning to provide doctrinal and leadership training for believers. As the aggressive process of discipleship waned, spiritual maturity became an even greater problem for Southern Baptists.

Robin Jumper concluded that the gospel presentations used in denominational evangelism training programs have emphasized the lordship of Christ and the necessity for a truly changed life following conversion. More contemporary programs and resources such as *MasterLife*[5] and *The Survival Kit for New Christians*[6] were written to provide systematic training for spiritual growth and development. When the CWT program was revised, a section on the doctrine of baptism was added to prepare witnesses to talk to converts about the meaning and significance of baptism. Experience had revealed that a person's attitude toward public baptism is one indicator of the person's willingness to become active in a church as well as to grow and mature in personal faith.

As an orientation toward conversion in one's doctrine can tend to slow down the growth and development of the converted, Southern Baptists

---

[5] Avery T. Willis Jr., *MasterLife: A Biblical Process for Growing Disciples* (Nashville: LifeWay Press, 1997) is the title of the Leader Guide for the four-volume set of workbooks (see http://www.lifeway.com/n/Product-Family/MasterLife); originally published in another format as *MasterLife: Discipleship Training for Leaders* (Nashville: The Sunday School Board of the Southern Baptist Convention, 1980).

[6] Ralph W. Neighbor Jr. and Bill Latham, *Survival Kit: Five Keys to Effective Spiritual Growth* (Nashville: LifeWay Press, 1979, rev. 1996); originally published as *Survival Kit for New Christians* (Nashville: Convention Press, 1979).

made conscious efforts to emphasize the importance of follow-up and nurture. Their experience has been that the focus on faith and conversion do not stop growth. As they wrestled with the issues of discipling the converted, the SBC continued to grow in baptisms, membership, and number of churches. The cost of a conversion-centered theology is not the inability to develop theological maturity in believers. The cost is that the task of spiritual and theological development requires intentional, creative work. The evangelistic members will not necessarily be the spiritually mature. To fail to engage fully in discipleship following conversion is to sow seeds of spiritual immaturity that can later undo evangelistic effectiveness. In fact, this failure is happening to Southern Baptists today.

When the driving force of a denomination is the fulfillment of the Great Commission, the critical question becomes, When is the Great Commission fulfilled? Three possible responses are:

(a) when the gospel is proclaimed to the nations,
(b) when the nations are converted, or
(c) when the converted of the nations are baptized and taught.

The proper answer is (c).

The problem faced by Southern Baptists is not an overemphasis on the Great Commission and evangelism. The problem is inadequate communication of what the Great Commission entails. True evangelism includes making the gospel known, bringing hearers to a point of decision, and nurturing the faith of those who respond. To have a transferable gospel is not inappropriate for the contemporary church. However, to have a transferable yet incomplete gospel is to build spiritual immaturity and its resultant problems into the life of congregations.

The path chosen by Southern Baptists produced some great churches and tremendous denominational growth. As seen in this book, that path is not without some risks. Church members who think the risks outweigh the gains should consider the experience of Paul the apostle. Most Christians would agree that he was one of the most important theologians in the early church. The majority should recognize also that Paul focused his life and ministry upon the fulfillment of the Great Commission. The churches he produced included the spiritually immature church at Corinth, but the spread of the gospel ultimately turned Rome away from paganism. Linking their denominational life to the fulfillment of the Great Commission did not produce a trouble-free denomination for Southern Baptists, but the emphasis on evangelism did produce a growing one.

***

Lesson 3

Theological focus enhances evangelistic engagement.

Southern Baptists maintained a passionate focus on evangelism for an extended period of time because their basic theological convictions drove them to do so. The Great Commission and theological perspectives about the role of the church in evangelism must be connected if evangelistic engagement is to be maintained. Without proper theological foundations and processes guiding believers to grow in spiritual maturity, even the most effective approaches to evangelism will eventually be undone. To fuel the fire, connect the dots between theological convictions and evangelistic engagement.

***

Questions for Conversation

1. Should every Christian be involved in sharing the gospel with others?
2. Could you explain how to become a Christian to someone who is lost?
3. Does the Great Commission appear to be the most important of all the activities of your church?

LESSON 4

*When the winds of change are blowing,
the adjustments you make will
determine the direction you sail.*

The twentieth-century storyline for the Southern Baptist Convention was explosive growth for its churches and ministries. However, with the coming of the twenty-first century, a far different storyline began to emerge. Growth slowed and became a statistical plateau that eventually turned into a decline reflected in nearly every statistical category the Convention measures. As both the culture and its churches changed over time, the SBC made adjustments. What were those adjustments, and how have they affected the evangelistic focus and growth of the Convention? A task force report at the 2010 meeting of the SBC called for a Great Commission Resurgence among SBC churches. However, in the years following that report, the statistics reported by the Southern Baptist churches indicate results looking more like a Great Commission Regression. The changes have led the Southern Baptist Convention and its churches to sail in a different direction in terms of evangelistic effectiveness.

CHAPTER 15

A Great Commission Update

O ne could make a case for saying that if there were no Great Commission in the New Testament, there might not be a Southern Baptist Convention. The missionary imperative was clearly a factor in bringing Baptist churches in the South together, and throughout their history they have drawn inspiration and direction from the text famously known as the Great Commission. Given its prominence in SBC life, a fair question to ask is what progress the Convention is making in the task Jesus assigned to His disciples, and the biblical text itself could be used as the standard of measure.

The Great Commission Standard

As noted earlier, the last words of Jesus to His disciples in the closing chapter of Matthew's Gospel have always been extremely important to Southern Baptists. From the founding of the Convention to the present day, this passage of Scripture is cited at SBC gatherings more than any other. Here is the full text of the Great Commission passage:

> And Jesus came and spoke to them, saying, "All authority has been given to Me in heaven and on earth. Go therefore and make disciples of all the nations, baptizing them in the name of the Father and of the Son and of the Holy Spirit, teaching them to observe all things that I have commanded you; and lo, I am with you always, even to the end of the age" (Matt 28:18–20).

From the beginning Jesus sets a tone of command for these words, spoken as the risen Christ—victor over sin, death, and the grave. He commands with the authority of the exalted Lord, giving an order to be obeyed, not a suggestion to be considered.

The task the Lord assigns is simple and clear: "make disciples of all the nations." His emphasis is on the role of the church in the conversion and spiritual growth of new believers. Those who follow Him are to go to the nations of the world with His life-transforming gospel, calling all peoples to repentance from sin and faith in Christ. The discussion of what makes one a disciple of Jesus can be lengthy and complicated, but Jesus offers a very simple measure for progress: Baptize—in the name of the Father, the Son, and the Holy Spirit—all who respond. In addition, they are to teach those who respond to the point of obedience to His commands. If new disciples are obeying His commands, those who are baptized and taught will themselves become witnesses, further extending the gospel to more and more people.

Progress in fulfilling the gospel is not merely making the gospel heard. People will need to hear it in order to repent and believe, but increasing the number of people who have heard the gospel is not equivalent to increasing the number of disciples among the nations. Making the gospel known to a larger and larger number of people is not Great Commission progress. People will need to understand what they hear, realize who Jesus is, and accept what Jesus has done for them; but that knowledge alone does not make them disciples. Great Commission progress is measured by making disciples, which means, at a minimum, new believers are baptized, taught the commands of Jesus to the point of obedience, and therefore become witnesses themselves.

This Great Commission standard of measure is why Baptists are sensitive to the number of people they baptize. Baptism is not the only measure of discipleship, but it is at least one basic indicator identified by Jesus as important. The aggressive, comprehensive attention to discipleship and membership in a local church through much of SBC history flows from the Great Commission as well. To be driven by the Great Commission is to be subject to the Great Commission standards of progress.

The SBC and Great Commission Progress

Having studied evangelism in the SBC most of my adult life, I cannot estimate the number of charts and graphs I have prepared and utilized through the years. When I asked Dr. Bill Day of the Leavell Center for Evangelism and Church Growth at New Orleans Baptist Theological Seminary to prepare a simple chart showing the total number of SBC churches and the total number of SBC baptisms over an extended period of time, I did not realize that this chart would be the most stunning snapshot of the Convention I had ever seen. The timeline begins in 1881 and goes through 2016:

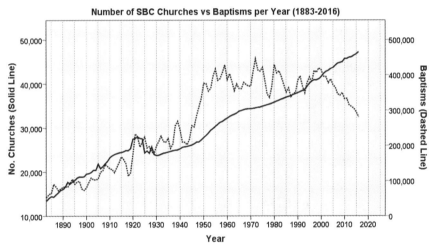

Graph by Dr. Bill Day, New Orleans Baptist Theological Seminary (June, 2017). Data: ACP of the SBC (June, 2017)

The graph has only two lines. One line shows the total number of SBC churches. With the exception of the Great Depression, a continual growth in the number of SBC churches for a long period of time is indicated. More churches—indeed, many more churches—are still needed, but the clear pattern of growth in churches is visible. The line indicating the number of baptisms stays close to the number of churches in the early part of the chart. The line dips during the Depression. And then, as World War II opened a new chapter in the story of our nation, the number of baptisms exploded, and SBC churches began reaching people and growing faster than the population of the United States. The chart makes it easy to see when the SBC became so large. After years of up-and-down numbers, an unprecedented trend began.

In the year 2000, the two lines on the graph crossed and continued moving in different directions. Total baptisms dropped, but the number of churches was still growing. As the years rolled by, the number of churches continued to increase, but the number of baptisms continued to fall. The gap between the two grew steadily larger. At this writing, the SBC is experiencing the longest decline in baptisms in the Convention's history. And the trouble runs deeper than the decline in baptisms of new converts. For much of the last decade, SBC membership has declined; the number of SBC members attending worship has declined; and the number of SBC members attending any form of small group has declined. At the annual meeting of the SBC in 2010, Southern Baptists overwhelmingly adopted a resolution calling for a Great Commission Resurgence. Thus far, statistics indicate that the Convention is having the greatest, deepest Great Commission Regression in its history. The Southern Baptist Convention is adding more and more churches each year, but SBC churches are baptizing fewer and fewer people and keeping fewer and fewer of the people they have engaged.

What Does This Trend Mean?

Conclusion #1

The lost world is making a bigger impact on Southern Baptists than Southern Baptists are making on the lost world. Not only are SBC churches baptizing fewer and fewer people, they are losing the people who are already members. Fewer members, fewer members attending worship, and fewer members attending small groups are key indicators that decline is real. The SBC has long been accustomed to open-ended growth. The challenge facing the churches today is twofold—both how to reach new people and how to keep the world from drawing members, and their children and grandchildren, away from church.

Conclusion #2

Southern Baptists are becoming a shrinking presence with a diminishing voice in our nation. The Convention has long been a focus of attention in the evangelical world and a denomination watched and studied by those outside the world of churches. People have wondered what Southern Baptists thought about issues, both religious and secular. If you wanted to understand where Americans stood on things, you needed to give at least some attention to the nation's largest Protestant denomination. Southern Baptists are still a major player in the American religious scene, but the conversation is likely to include attention to their decline as well as to their opinions on various issues.

Conclusion #3

The SBC is closer to losing the South than to reaching North America. Pluralism and secularism are rising even in the Baptist stronghold of the South. Not many southern cities or towns are more Southern Baptist than they were 20 years ago. Much attention has been focused on planting churches outside of the South, whereas little attention has been given to the struggles of existing churches in reaching lost and unchurched people in their communities. The generation known as millennials is the most unreached generation in the history of the SBC. When millennials were children and youth, SBC baptisms of children and youth dropped dramatically. Now they are young adults and young families, often without a connection to any church.

Nevertheless, there are some very bright and exciting things happening in Southern Baptist life. Growth in membership and baptisms among ethnic minority churches is a very encouraging trend, and there are others. Yet the challenge of reaching people in their local communities is growing steadily for the typical SBC church.

Conclusion #4

The deep passion of Southern Baptists to take the gospel to people who have not heard the name of Jesus cannot be sustained if churches fail to reach locals who are unsaved and unchurched. If Southern Baptists do not replace the members that time takes away, there will not be enough dollars to fund missions and other evangelistic work that Southern Baptists love to do. To remain fresh, a church needs to make new disciples in its community. When that process stops, growing smaller in members, ministries, and budgets is inevitable.

Conclusion #5

The Great Commission health of local churches is a crucial question for the SBC today. So much of what the SBC does is based upon the assumption that its churches are steadily reaching people and making new disciples. This assumption is wildly inaccurate. Great Commission struggles at the local church level constitute perhaps the greatest crisis ever facing the SBC as a denomination. Can SBC churches learn to grow again? What kind of resources will they need to become more fruitful? What kind of support do they need to reach people in their communities with the gospel, to baptize the people they reach, and to engage them in a disciple's life of obedience to the commands of Jesus? The path to taking the gospel to the nations goes through the fields of lost people surrounding churches in their local settings.

CHAPTER 16

The New Methodists

For much of American history, Baptists and Methodists shared many commonalities, including a passionate commitment to evangelism and discipleship that drove the extensive growth in both denominations. When Methodist growth peaked and began to decline and that decline began to accelerate, Southern Baptists noticed. Many a Southern Baptist conversation discussed how, unlike Southern Baptists, Methodists had "lost their way." Today, the SBC is following very similar trend lines. A look at the factors stimulating the decline in each denomination shows how important a healthy discipleship process is for fruitful evangelism.

Fresh Eyes, Fresh Insight

Following the ravages of Hurricane Katrina, I was immersed heart and soul in the recovery and restoration of New Orleans Baptist Theological Seminary. After a couple of years, an invitation to address the SBC evangelism directors at a meeting in New Orleans came as a breath of fresh air, allowing me to lay the burden of recovery down for at least a while and return to the passion of my adult life—the study of Southern Baptist evangelism. That time away from research I began as a doctoral student and continued through my years as a professor of evangelism and even as a seminary president proved to be extremely valuable. When I picked up my research again to prepare for the assigned presentation, I quickly noticed two things: the SBC had moved from a statistical plateau to an accelerating decline, and a factor I had largely ignored was, in fact, having a major influence on evangelism in Southern Baptist life.

Perhaps the best place to begin is with a brief review from Lesson 2[1] of the prolific evangelism paradigm of SBC churches. In 1945, Southern Baptists baptized approximately 257,000 people into their churches. In 1955, only 10 years later, approximately 417,000 people were baptized, almost *doubling* the recorded conversions in just 10 years. Southern Baptists developed a way of doing church very similar to the way a farmer raises crops.

Farmers know which crops will grow best in their *climate*. You can grow cotton in Mississippi, but it does not do well in northern Canada. To have evangelistic results, churches needed a climate *continually* affirming for the congregation the importance of sharing Christ with the lost. Southern Baptists used *decisional preaching*, preaching that calls for an immediate and public response, to help create and maintain a climate emphasizing evangelism in the worship services of our churches. In many ways, the format of evangelistic crusades and revival meetings was absorbed into the normal style of worship for Southern Baptist churches. The invitation following every sermon was a weekly reminder that no one is right with God until he has made a personal response to Christ. This public appeal was a constant reminder of *why* evangelism must be a priority in the programs and ministries of the church.

Farmers know that a harvest will not result without *planting seed* in the soil. Southern Baptists realized that most unconverted people did not come to church. They knew that the gospel must get outside the walls of the church, that *personal evangelism* throughout the community was needed. For example, the typical Baptist church would devote at least one night a week to *evangelistic* visitation, going out to the families in the community for the specific purpose of sharing the gospel with them. Evangelism was not limited to pastors in the pulpit. It also involved the people of the church in face-to-face conversations with people they knew and people they did not know in the community.

---

[1] See pages 115–18.

Farmers know that planting seed will not, in and of itself, produce a crop. Once planted in the soil, that seed must be *cultivated*. Enough water is needed for growth, but not too much. Pests and diseases must be kept at bay. Southern Baptists knew that sharing the gospel one time with a lost person usually would not result in conversion. A process of cultivation was necessary for people who had heard the gospel but did not respond immediately. *Sunday School*—the only program in an SBC church one could join without being a church member—became the cultivation strategy for SBC churches. Churches expected most Sunday School classes to have lost and unchurched people present on a regular basis.

Why Sunday School? This program was an efficient way to harness the power of *Bible-lationships*, my word to describe the combination of Bible teaching and relationship building at the heart of the Southern Baptist approach to Sunday School. All ages were involved in Sunday School. Those who came heard the Bible, promoting a better understanding of the gospel, *and* formed meaningful relationships with Christians in the class. Sunday School classes taught the Bible and had ice cream fellowships. There were devotionals and hymns, but they also sent members to visit classmates in the hospital and prepare food for those who lost loved ones. The *Bible-lationship* combination of teaching Scripture *and* nurturing relationships was a powerful tool for cultivation, often used by the Holy Spirit to draw closer people from all age groups who had heard the gospel but not yet responded.

With the right climate, proper planting, and cultivation, the farmer knows his crop will ripen and be ready for *harvest* in due time. Southern Baptists used *revival meetings* as their primary harvest tool. For at least one or two weeks each year, the whole attention of the church was focused on the simple question, What is the status of your relationship with God? Many revival messages included simple explanations of how to become a Christian and powerful appeals to repent and believe. The revival became a very normal time for *those who had heard the gospel clearly explained over time, and who had formed meaningful relationships with Christians in the church,* to come to the point of faith themselves.

What is important to understand? The true nature of the genius of Southern Baptist evangelism was not the individual methods used that produced such an incredible harvest. Rather, the interaction of those methods with each other created an *integrated process* described in the New Testament as sowing and reaping. Wheels alone can generate power. But if cogs are added to those wheels so that a gear is formed, the power those wheels produce is multiplied. Old McBaptist, integrating decisional preaching, personal evangelism, Sunday School, and revival meetings, had a great farm that produced much fruit, creating growth throughout the SBC. For an expression of the biblical process of sowing and reaping, see 1 Cor 3:6: "I planted, Apollos watered, but God gave the increase."

What Happened to the Farm?

Let's go back to those baptism statistics. In 1945, the SBC baptized about 257,000 people. In 1955, the SBC baptized about 417,000 people. But since 1955, the SBC has not reached the mark of 450,000 baptisms. After doubling in baptisms in 10 years, SBC churches could not increase baptisms by 35,000 in more than 50 years. What happened to the harvest? What happened to the farm?

For many years, the primary problem appeared clear to me. There was a growing lack of attention to and engagement with the components of the SBC paradigm. I often said, "Southern Baptists are a *harvest-oriented* denomination living in the midst of an *unseeded* generation." Churches ignored the continual renewal of an evangelistic climate, reduced the planting of gospel seeds in the lives of those outside the church, and neglected the cultivation of those who had heard the gospel but had not responded. Not surprisingly, the harvest results were smaller. After all, the size of the harvest can never be greater than the amount of seed planted by a farmer. Southern Baptists have become more like gardeners working in window boxes for a bouquet than farmers working the fields for a harvest. They are more like the grandchildren of farmers keeping harvest stories alive over coffee and dessert at family reunions. The elements of the farm are still in place in many SBC churches, but not on the same scale; and they are not being implemented with the same vigor. However, as I continued seeking to understand the dwindling evangelistic harvest in SBC churches, a factor began to emerge with steadily growing clarity. The problem was deeper than the aging of a paradigm.

The particular methods being used by SBC churches are not the crucial issue. The Bible speaks little of methods. An open fire, an oven, or a microwave can all accomplish the same purpose of cooking food. Tasks will always outlive methods. There will always be more than one way to approach any mission God gives His church.

The amount of money available to spend on evangelism is not the crucial issue. In 1906, W. W. Hamilton created the first Department of Evangelism for the SBC. With no budget allocation at all, he found a way for the Department to grow to include more than 20 evangelists and to make a great impact. After a tragic embezzlement by the treasurer of the Home Mission Board, the Board was nearly bankrupt and shut down the Evangelism Department for a decade. In 1936, Roland Q. Leavell was asked to relaunch the Department with only one staff member—himself! With little money and no assistance, he laid the groundwork for the greatest period of fruitfulness in the history of the SBC. During that legendary period of 1945 to 1955, when the annual number of baptisms doubled, the staff of the Evangelism Department never grew larger than three people, including a secretary. Money is very important, but it is not the crucial issue reducing our fruitfulness. Having more money will not turn things around.

The gospel's power is not the crucial issue. God's message has the same power to transform any human life today that it had in the first century of the church. Here is just one example. Louisiana has a single maximum-security prison for men, located in a place called Angola. Long known as the bloodiest prison in America, Angola houses more than 5,000 prisoners, making it the largest collection of violent people in the United States. One would think that a prison must be the worst possible setting for ministerial training and that these men must be the worst possible candidates for salvation, much less for a call to the ministry.

In 1995, New Orleans Baptist Theological Seminary began a program of training for ministry in the Angola prison, teaching a small group of Christian prisoners the same curriculum being taught at the seminary's Leavell College in New Orleans. The results have been stunning! More than 200 inmates have graduated to date. Upon completion of their studies, each graduate becomes engaged in church planting or ministry in some area of the prison. Violence has dropped dramatically. The prison has become a different place, amazing people in the justice system all over the United States. The impact of these prison preachers has been so great that they are now being sent out two-by-two into other prisons to teach there what they learned in Angola. The gospel of Jesus Christ is still a message of incredible power today!

A lack of attention on evangelism had a noticeable effect in Southern Baptist life, but it does not appear to be the fundamental issue shrinking the harvest. I cannot remember, and have not found in research, a time when there was so little conversation about evangelism in the face of such glaring evangelistic problems among SBC churches. The growing number of baptism-less churches, the lack of baptisms among those under the age of 19, and the worst-ever ratio of Southern Baptists per baptism should be matters generating a much higher level of concern in a denomination that places such a high value on the Great Commission. Even churches that are giving evangelism-focused attention in the rhythms of congregational life are not seeing the size of harvest they expect to see. Yet, there is no great hue and cry among the churches.

The Crucial Issue

Discipleship is the crucial issue driving the lack of evangelistic fruitfulness in the SBC today. The spiritual state of the farmer (our churches and leadership), not the abundance of the harvest, is the root of problems in SBC evangelism. Every evangelistic method, every evangelistic program or plan from the days of the New Testament until this present day is based upon one common assumption. That assumption is that the life of a person in Christ is different than the life of a person without Christ. In Acts 11:26, the followers of Christ "were first called Christians in Antioch." The believers did not choose this name for themselves. Apparently, the pagan people of Antioch created and used the term, meaning "belonging to or identified with Christ," because their observations of those early believers clearly revealed that their lives were different. Christians looked like they belonged to Christ. They obviously wanted to be identified with Christ.

Those early Christians lived distinctively in their culture. The Christian is the living illustration of what the gospel is and what it does in a human life. Without that living illustration, the gospel is less likely to be noticed or heeded.

For many years, Baptists and Methodists were known more for their similarities than their differences. As a Presbyterian minister told his son in the book and movie *A River Runs through It*, "Methodists are just Baptists who can read." That began to change as theological differences became wider and wider and as lifestyles also moved in different directions. However, the stories of Baptists and Methodists today are once again converging as a similar path is being charted. A problem and an outcome are shared. The problem is diminished discipleship. The outcome is decline. Southern Baptists are becoming the New Methodists.

The New Methodists

I love Methodists! They played a key role in the First and Second Great Awakenings. Their concept of a circuit-riding preacher was a brilliant strategy for the circumstances of the day. With their strategy, Methodists were able to multiply church starts faster than they multiplied church pastors, enabling them to evangelize the American frontier in the nineteenth and early twentieth centuries. They made holy living a core value and were called Methodists because personal holiness was cultivated in a systematic and methodical way. Much of what Southern Baptists know about evangelism, especially evangelistic harvesting, was learned from Methodists. Through the years, many have observed Methodists and Baptists and noticed their kinship.

However, the Methodists of today have changed dramatically. Although there are numerous Methodist people and churches that would still be recognized by John Wesley, many would say the American denomination has been moving in directions significantly different than he could have imagined. Their efforts in evangelism and missions have greatly diminished. For many Methodists, the passion for holy living has been replaced by behavior mirroring that of the culture. Their greatest theological fight today is over the normalcy of homosexuality. Most surprising, they have set new records for the most rapid loss of membership in the history of the church in America.

Methodists did not choose their name; it was given to them. As noted earlier, what stood out to those who observed Methodism was the methodical way personal holiness was cultivated. From the perspective of those who observed its development, earnest, intentional discipleship gave Methodists a distinctive identity noticed by Christians and non-Christians alike. They would not likely be given the same name today. Having observed these changes in Methodism, I find myself admitting today that although Southern Baptists do have a distinctly different theology, in many ways the SBC is following in Methodist footsteps.

In what ways are these two denominations similar? Universalism is settling into SBC pews as more and more Southern Baptists believe and behave as though a personal relationship with Christ is not necessary for one to be right with God. Tolerance is beginning to overtake conviction as growing numbers, particularly of younger Southern Baptists, are less comfortable with taking a firm stance on moral or doctrinal issues. The way Southern Baptists live their lives is blending more and more with the surrounding culture as behavior is becoming less distinct and recognizable in the crowd. It is as easy to get drunk at a Baptist wedding reception as any other kind of wedding. Baptists go to the same movies, watch the same TV shows, and seem comfortable using the same coarse language as their neighbors. A Baptist family is just as likely to choose to attend a school or community soccer tournament on Sunday as any other child in the neighborhood. It is not a coincidence that Baptists are also moving from growth to plateau to decline in the membership of our churches. Never in the history of the Southern Baptist Convention have there been this many declining churches and this many churches recording zero baptisms in a year. Southern Baptists are the New Methodists, and discipleship is the heart of the problem.

The Untold Story

The history of discipleship in the Southern Baptist Convention is a story that has never been told. This reality is unfortunate because discipleship has played a crucial role in Southern Baptist life. Although Southern Baptists often have been criticized for overemphasizing conversion, the opposite is true. In the era of the denomination's greatest evangelistic growth, typical SBC churches had more discipleship activities than evangelistic activities. Aggressive evangelism was matched by aggressive discipleship. Southern Baptists were "disciple-istic" (my word), combining both evangelism and discipleship, without giving priority to one over the other. Evangelistic discipleship constantly sought to incorporate both evangelism and discipleship at the same time. This dual strategy was the defining characteristic of Southern Baptists for many, many years.

Lesson 2 described in some detail the components of the SBC paradigm for evangelism. Here is a brief snapshot of some of the elements of the discipleship process found in the typical SBC church of any size and location. Sunday School was viewed as the outreach arm of the church as well as the primary place for collecting the weekly offering. The offering envelopes included a checklist for members to report whether or not they read their Bibles daily, prayed, contacted others about coming to church, and so on. Sunday nights were viewed as the specific time for discipleship. The Sunday night program included small group discipleship training for all age groups and an evening worship service for further instruction in the Bible. A three-to-five-day Bible conference was held each January in many SBC churches to teach one book of the Bible to all ages. At least once, and often more frequently, special events called study courses were scheduled to train members in some aspect of Baptist doctrine, church polity, or the Christian life. In addition, a weekly missions training program for young girls and a separate program for young boys were organized, as were Vacation Bible School, youth camp, and children's camp in the summer. A daily devotional guide that was typically made available included a daily Bible reading, devotional thought, and list of missionaries having birthdays on that day. Furthermore, churches engaged in "disciplism," an aggressive approach to discipleship paired with an aggressive approach to evangelism.

For many years, I failed to observe the significance of discipleship in the story of Southern Baptist evangelism. However, Southern Baptist history clearly indicates that there will be no evangelistic resurgence in

Southern Baptist life without fresh attention to the crucial nature of discipleship in SBC churches. When efforts are made to intensify evangelism efforts without an accompanying emphasis on intensifying discipleship efforts, one can expect the results to be less than satisfying.

Many readers will remember churches being challenged to be seeker-friendly. Unfortunately, many churches put so much emphasis on how a congregation's way of doing church affected the lost they failed to notice how it was affecting the saved. Changes and innovations were added to make the church more welcoming to the lost and unchurched, but little was done to improve the way churches inspired evangelistic discipleship in believers. When did the SBC emphasis on aggressive discipleship begin to fade? During the late sixties. When did the Convention's evangelistic fruitfulness begin to fade? During the seventies. When baptism numbers started to weaken, our focus on harvest strategies and evangelism methods intensified. This evangelist has concluded that more attention should have been paid to our discipleship process. Upon reflection, the most significant and influential death in the modern history of the SBC was the death of a strategic plan or template for discipleship in Southern Baptist churches.

Why Disciplism Matters

Disciplism is a passionate evangelistic discipleship that seeks to incorporate both evangelism and discipleship at the same time. A refusal to give one the priority over the other is the key. Disciplism is absolutely essential because those who come to Christ must begin and continue the journey to be like Him. The problem is not a lack of witness to our neighbors. That is a symptom. The problem is that more Christians do not look like and live like Jesus. If we did, more of us would witness to our neighbors. When we do not produce children, youth, and adults who live out a biblical worldview, no strategy for doing church will make us salt and light in the world. Aggressive evangelism without aggressive discipleship will eventually undo itself. The Great Commission commanded those who follow Jesus to make disciples.

Any fan of country music can instantly recognize the voice of country music legend Johnny Cash. His voice is unique and therefore easy to recognize. You know who he is when you hear his voice. Southern Baptists are not losing our voice; we are losing the distinctiveness of our voice amid all the sounds of today's culture. We are blending in more than we are standing out. We do not recognize our own voice. The world does not recognize our voice. Our lost friends and neighbors do not recognize our voice. Baptist believers must be taught how to be the distinctive presence of Christ as both missionary and minister in the culture. We must be the salt our neighbors cannot fail to taste and the light the world around us cannot fail to see. We must be the voice they cannot fail to recognize. To paraphrase Jesus's verdict, "Salt that is not salty is not good for anything but throwing out. . . . Light that is under a bushel is useless" (Matt 5:13–14).

The Christlikeness of church members living distinctive lives in a community is essential for any evangelistic strategy to be fruitful. Without question, the SBC and its churches need to give much more attention and intentional effort to evangelism. However, if the evangelistic efforts are to bear the fruit of multiplying changed lives, the evangelistic efforts must be accompanied by the living illustration of transformed lives.

The Bottom Line

Is there more to SBC problems than this? Yes! But there is at least this observation: We are becoming the New Methodists. We must be aware of where the road the SBC now travels will lead. I am a man of immense hope in what the future can bring to the Southern Baptists of today. God is not necessarily through with us yet! I do have reasons for that hope, but they will have to wait for another day. Yet, I am deeply moved by the serious realities that we are facing today.

One of the most popular sites to visit in Jerusalem is called the Western Wall or Wailing Wall. The large stones forming its base are all that is left of the structure supporting God's temple during the time of Jesus, making it a place of great significance to Jews as well as to Christians. Every day of the year, rain or shine, people gather at the site. Many visitors are Jews who weep and remember what they once had, what they lost, and pray that one day all will be restored. In times past, God has worked through

Southern Baptist churches in a mighty way. In times present, God is not working in that same mighty way through SBC churches. If we continue in the direction we are going now, only one question remains: To what wall will our children return to *weep* and *remember* the glory of what the SBC once was and what the SBC once did?

CHAPTER 17

Mega-Shifts in SBC Life

The rhythms of church life in a great many SBC churches have changed through the years. These changes, intentional or unintentional, had no moral quality—none was inherently good or bad, right or wrong. However, key changes did have a disruptive effect on the processes in place that had been producing the fruit of conversions, baptisms, and growth. The former processes were disrupted, but to date they have not been retooled or replaced with a fresh, widely embraced paradigm for evangelism. The wind changed, but despite the present lengthy decline, the sails were not adjusted in a way that maintained the evangelistic course of the typical SBC church and produced a similar level of conversions, baptisms, and growth. That said, what follows is a description, not an evaluation.

Mega-Shift #1: From the Priority of Discipleship to the Priority of Worship

Although evangelism is widely recognized inside and outside the Convention as the defining characteristic of Southern Baptist life, discipleship was actually the engine that pulled the train in SBC churches. The synonyms for discipleship for much of the twentieth century were Christian education and training. The primary statistic that most pastors monitored in their own ministries and those of others was Sunday School attendance. If a church needed a new worship center and additional education space, the education space would normally be built first. After the pastor, the staff member with the most influence, authority, and compensation was usually the minister of education. Most of the weekly offering was collected in Sunday School, and the offering envelope itself included a weekly checklist of personal discipleship activities, such as daily Bible reading and witnessing.

The discipleship program in Southern Baptist life was multilayered, including plans and activities for every age group. For example, Sunday School was heavily promoted as the outreach arm of the church, the only organization people could join without joining the church. Church members were encouraged to find a role in a ministry of the church, and there was a strong emphasis on continually training people for those roles. As noted earlier, the Southern Baptist approach to discipleship was even more aggressive than the approach to evangelism.

This priority began to change in the late sixties and early seventies. The Jesus Movement introduced new styles of worship to the nation and, along the way, elevated the role of worship in Southern Baptist life. Slowly, pastors began to focus on worship attendance rather than Sunday School attendance. Worship became the new, larger "front door" for visitors and new members. More of the offering was collected in the worship service than in Sunday School classes. In churches with multiple staff members, the worship leader gradually displaced that of the minister of education in terms of influence and compensation, and a graded choir program became the popular new activity for children and youth. Today, if a church needs both education space and worship space, the worship space will be built first.

In many churches in the SBC, this shift revitalized worship services that had grown stale and tired. Worship gives adoration to God and feeds the passion of the soul in the grip of Jesus. However, the experience of that passion became as much a measure of the impact of worship as the number of people who gathered, particularly for the younger generations of a church. Some pressure was exerted on pastors to make similar kinds of connection with people in their preaching styles. Worship became as much a matter of style as of content, and these changes gave rise to the term *worship wars.* Conflict over worship could affect a church more deeply than harmony in worship. The strong feelings that would often surface in churches facing transitions in their approaches to worship led many churches to offer multiple services, in part to offer multiple styles of worship. In many churches, increased attention on attendance in the worship services masked a decrease in the number of people attending Sunday School or small groups. Perhaps more people were attending the worship services, but often those who came had a lower level of engagement with the larger church program.

At the same time, the strategy for discipleship in Southern Baptist churches began to fade and was not reinvented or replaced. It simply moved closer to the margins of church life. Strategies and resources for discipleship and attention to discipleship did not disappear, but they were diminished. A series of short-term studies, each lasting a few weeks at a time, replaced an ongoing discipleship process. Instead of pulling the train, discipleship was along for the ride.

Mega-Shift #2: From "Mayberry" to "Lake Wobegon"

The fictional TV town of Mayberry, featured in *The Andy Griffith Show*, captured the heart of America. Each television episode featured average people in an average town having average problems that somehow, some way, worked out in the end. There were no superheroes or dazzling beauties. There were no wild car chases or explosions or scenarios in which the future of the world hung in the balance. The problems that arose were not unlike the problems of many people. The solutions were believable solutions. Long after the last episode was filmed, America's love affair with Mayberry continued. It was a celebration of the common, the ordinary, the average.

That is a wonderful metaphor for the Southern Baptist Convention through much of its history. The operating assumption was that our churches were of average size, with average leadership, and average people. This assumption was gladly embraced because these average churches were also assumed to be united by a great and extraordinary mission. They were deeply and passionately committed to a vision to reach the whole world for Jesus Christ. Because they knew they were average, Southern Baptists recognized a need for each other in order to make a maximum impact. By acting in concert, SBC churches could achieve profound results. "Average" was enough to change the world.

This assumption that the typical church was average drove the development of Southern Baptist strategies and resources. The strategies for the Convention were ones in which any church could find ways to participate. The resources produced were such that any church could use them without a great deal of preparation or significant expense. Above all, the assumption of average drove a culture of training throughout the SBC.

The growth of the SBC was driven by an internal culture that emphasized training, training, and more training. Many of the books from that era are among the most boring books I have ever read. Why? They were not designed to inspire. They were designed to take you step-by-step through the process necessary to accomplish a particular task. To all those small books were added national training conferences, associational training conferences, and local church training conferences. Southern Baptists knew they were average, but they also knew their great vision could have great success if they accomplished it with excellence and hard work.

To use a more modern term, Southern Baptists thrived through the development and distribution of *templates*. A template is a clearly defined way to accomplish a task so that it requires little creativity to implement. Southern Baptists developed templates for every aspect of church life: Sunday School, Vacation Bible School, stewardship, deacon ministry, and music ministry. The churches received the templates and implemented them, finding they usually worked as advertised. Those templates were usually accompanied by training processes on how to implement the templates.

Denominational leaders and heroes of the SBC were those who developed transferable templates that others could use and who supported and promoted the templates. You do not have to have a large number of big churches producing much fruit if you have a large number of medium-to-small-sized churches producing some fruit. That's who Southern Baptists were: medium-to-small churches, most of which were producing some fruit, not big churches producing a lot of fruit. First Baptist Mayberry and a great many of its sister churches found many of the transferable templates developed in Southern Baptist life to be useful and fruitful. They were able to see progress year-by-year in accomplishing their extraordinary mission. This strategy was the glue holding the Convention together.

Lake Wobegon is a different place than Mayberry. In Lake Wobegon, the fictional town made famous by Garrison Keillor on public radio, "all the women are strong, all the men are good-looking, and all the children are above average."[1] A different assumption drives this approach to church. The assumption is that every small church can be large. Large church is in fact the base assumption of an ideal church. The emphasis is more on personal leadership than on templates. Exceptional churches with excellent leaders craft creative strategies that perfectly fit their context. The distinctive church and its leader or leaders are celebrated rather than the notable church doing with great effect what typical churches are also able to do within the scale of their resources and circumstances. Many assume that every church desires and is able to craft its own distinctive strategic plan. "Average" is more often associated with "inferior" than with "common."

Let me say that in another way. Today's templates are often developed from the model of what worked well in an exceptional church with excellent leaders as opposed to what is transferable among typical churches with average leaders. The effect of this shift can be summed up with a few simple questions: Where have all the templates gone on how to do church in Southern Baptist life? What is the template for discipleship? What is the template for mobilizing our congregation to bear witness to Jesus?

The key feature of a template is that when church leaders see it, they know with confidence that they can follow the model. The need for and interest in creating something different and new in a church is not as great as the need for and interest in finding something that a church is confident will work for the problems and opportunities it faces. The template-driven SBC always had room for and usually affirmed and celebrated the more gifted or the better resourced churches. Excellent leaders will always move beyond templates, but the templates focused on the typical church body and, to be productive, required execution rather than exceptional leadership. If nothing else, the templates provided a place to start.

---

[1] See Sarah Begley, "Garrison Keillor to Say So Long to Lake Wobegon," *Time*, July 20, 2015, accessed December 17, 2017, http://time.com/3965277/garrison-keillor-retiring/.

Mega-Shift #3: From *All in the Family* to *Let's Make a Deal*

To read SBC publications from the first six decades of the twentieth century is to notice immediately a very strong sense of Southern Baptist identity and a great deal of pride in that identity. Over and over again, leaders called SBC churches to do everything in a Southern Baptist way. The attention of the Convention was almost entirely focused on what we as Southern Baptists were doing. And all of the entities kept nearly all of their attention on the Southern Baptist world. What others were doing was not of much interest because what the SBC was doing was working so well. We were absorbed in our own mission and our own strategies. We wanted to keep our money, our energy, and our attention "all in the family."

The idea sounds very odd today, but Southern Baptists did not view themselves as evangelicals. We had no sense of identity with the evangelical world. Why? We were Southern Baptists. We saw ourselves as an entirely different category. We had a distinct theology, a distinct polity in our churches, and a distinct approach to missions. When we went shopping for ideas and strategies and our resources, it was usually in a mall that we owned. Thus, the things we did and the resources we used all reinforced that very distinctive strong identity as Southern Baptists.

That began to change in the latter part of the twentieth century and the change accelerated in the early twenty-first century. Churches began to look outside the Southern Baptist Convention for resources to utilize and for conferences to attend. Some seminaries hired professors with little or no life experience with Southern Baptists. The value of doing things in a Southern-Baptist-kind-of-way was replaced by the value of looking more widely afield to find whatever worked.

Because of our interest in evangelism, much of this motivation was driven by attention to the bottom line—that is, by a hunger to bring increased numbers of people to Christ and to grow our churches bigger and bigger. Perhaps the best illustration of this shift is *Evangelism Explosion*, a witness training strategy developed by an evangelistic Presbyterian pastor. Southern Baptists became one of the largest single groups using EE as a strategy. Another illustration of this shift is the number of non-Southern

Baptist vendors to be found at the annual SBC Pastors' Conference. That phenomenon would have been unthinkable in an earlier era.

To state this as simply as possible, Southern Baptists began behaving more like consumers than like a family. That was a profound shift indeed. The effect of this change has been an erosion of Southern Baptist identity and the introduction of non-Southern Baptist elements in church polity as well as church strategies.

Mega-Shift #4: From a Laser to a Collection of Flashlights

I speak here as a layman and not as a scientist, so please understand the limits of this analogy. Both a laser and a flashlight produce a beam of light. However, one is far more powerful in a way the other is not. The laser gathers, focuses, and amplifies light in a tight, narrow beam. The other uses light in a much more ordinary, common way.

Through most of the twentieth century, Southern Baptists worked diligently on a very simple strategy for funding the Great Commission. Every church, every week, set aside a locally determined portion of their tithes and offerings for the work of the SBC. That portion of the income was used to form a common fund—the Cooperative Program—to be used for Great Commission ministries. The state, national, and international ministries all drew from that fund, which generated dollars for the home mission field and abroad. It has been a phenomenal success!

The Cooperative Program provided affordable theological education for ministers and missionaries on a scale unmatched today, placing thousands of missionaries on the field, both around the world and all over the North American continent. However, the most important point of focus is not the size of the income stream but rather the scale of the buy-in to the strategy. The universality of participation in the Cooperative Program was the key to its success. The number of churches choosing to do missions from a common pot gave the CP its punch rather than the individual efforts of single churches. The deferral of a local church's particular control over missions giving in lieu of missions giving through the Convention allowed entities to reduce overhead and maximize the amplified offerings of thousands upon thousands of churches every week. The cooperative impact became a great point of pride. A Convention composed of typically small churches was able to do great things on a grand scale. The progress and growth of SBC ministries were viewed as the progress and growth of the local church's ministry.

What we were able to do together became as thrilling as, or even more thrilling than, any one congregation was able to do separately as a simple local church. "Me" was overwhelmed in a tide of "we." In our surrounding culture, the baby boom generation became famous for self-centeredness. Called by media outlets the "me" generation, boomers introduced a sense of individualism into Southern Baptist life. It is expressed now in a growing number of SBC churches finding their greatest source of pride not in the massive scale of what we can do together but rather in the more immediate and tangible ways that individuals and congregations are able to do ministry directly. "We" is now being overshadowed by a growing tide of "me." In effect, churches are beginning to break down the tightly focused laser and turn it into a collection of flashlights. Clearly, the light is not lost. Clearly, nothing evil or immoral or ungodly is going on. We are simply beginning to use light in a different way. Time will tell how much the power of the laser will be diminished and how great will be the impact of a collection of flashlights.

Mega-Shift #5: From the Great Commission as a Marathon to the Great Commission as a Sprint

The marathon and the sprint are both legitimate races requiring a great deal of physical energy and effort. Each one leaves the runner tired at the end. However, the strategy for running each type of race varies dramatically. Everything hinges on the question: How long are you going to run? The answer to that question determines everything. In the past, Southern Baptists viewed the Great Commission as a marathon, having no idea how long it would take. We did not know how the end result would look. We simply labored every year to push the gospel further and further. The goal was to give every man and woman, every boy and girl—nation by nation—an opportunity to hear about Jesus. A passion for spreading the gospel was very deep and consuming, but the end point—when the marathon would be finished—was not defined. However, in recent years, the task of fulfilling the Great Commission is being presented as more like a sprint than a marathon. The end is more clearly defined, more nearly at hand. So, "the time is now" to finish the job because we *can* finish the job.

Why do some think of the Great Commission as a sprint? Some note Matt 24:14, "And this gospel of the kingdom shall be preached in all the world as a witness to all nations, and then the end will come." They think that speeding the fulfillment of the Great Commission will speed the return of Christ. Others note Acts 1:7, when Jesus said, "It is not for you to know times or seasons which the Father has put in His own authority." They think the Father's decision, not the activity of the church, will determine when Christ returns. All would agree that the necessity of salvation in Christ alone makes the Great Commission an urgent assignment for the church. The view of the Great Commission as a sprint, however, is a newer development in SBC life.

The evangelical world has had this vision before. The Student Volunteer Movement in the nineteenth century called for the evangelization of the world in their generation. I do not recall this sentiment being as close to the surface in Southern Baptist life as it is now. Why does this viewpoint matter? What does it effect? That missions is urgent is beyond dispute no matter what the viewpoint. Leaders of the International Mission Board invariably testify to the passion of these missionaries for reaching the world. That we do missions with urgency is not debatable. The key questions are: How will you use your resources to fulfill that objective? and How long do resources need to last?

If the gospel race is a sprint, every possible dollar and every ounce of effort is invested in extending the point of the arrow of the gospel as far as possible and as fast as possible into the lost world. However, if this race is a marathon, the point of the arrow is extended as far as possible while the base of churches is continually built up. Some have not understood that the Cooperative Program was designed according to this marathon approach. It was not designed only to raise money to get the gospel to the ends of the earth in the mission field. That was certainly a priority. However, the Cooperative Program was also designed to build up the base of local SBC churches. As the base grows larger and stronger, the arrow of the gospel can be pushed farther into the lost world. If this race is a marathon, the mission must be extended *and* the base must be built stronger so that resources for the mission can be increased. Attention is paid to the health of churches in addition to reaching the world. If the health of the churches declines, time will erode the resources available to push the gospel farther. The question is momentous: Is this race to fulfill the Great Commission a marathon or a sprint? Are we using time to make our mission efforts stronger and stronger, or are we squeezing time and expending resources to get the job done as quickly as possible?

In considering these mega-shifts in SBC life, one should keep in mind that there are no moral issues involved in these changes. We are not talking about good and evil here. We are talking about a whole Convention that is genuinely wrestling with the best ways to fulfill the Great Commission. Always remember that the person with whom you may disagree most deeply and most passionately likely has the same degree of commitment to Jesus Christ as Lord and Savior of the world as you do. We all love God's Word. We all love His church. We all want the whole world to come to Christ. We are not trying to figure out who is right and who is wrong. We are trying to find the best and most effective way to be fruitful in kingdom work and to extend the gospel to the ends of the earth.

***

Lesson 4

When the winds of change are blowing, the adjustments you make will determine the direction you sail.

Change is inevitable. Whatever the ministry setting, change will happen in some ways over time, and those changes will affect the outcomes of the ministry. The key question is: Have the changes enabled the ministry to continue having the desired effect? If not, are there additional adjustments that need to be made? Remember that there are no points scored for making changes unless those changes continue or improve the desired results. The bottom has been falling out of the number of baptisms recorded by SBC churches. This number will continue to decline unless adjustments are made to help SBC churches become more fruitful in reaching the lost and unchurched in their communities.

***

Questions for Conversation

1. What is your church doing to focus attention on reaching lost people in your community?
2. How do members in your church learn to pray, to read and study the Bible, and to share the gospel with others?
3. Does your church approach missions to the world as a marathon or a sprint?

LESSON 5

The knock of opportunity is useless unless you answer the door.

T he churches of the Southern Baptist Convention are facing the greatest evangelistic challenge in their collective history. The challenge is fruitlessness—a lack of baptisms on a massive scale over a prolonged period of time. That is the bad news. The good news is that every challenge carries with it a host of opportunities. The gospel is as relevant and powerful as it has ever been. With the nation and the world becoming both more secular and more pluralistic, the witness of the church to Jesus is less familiar and can be viewed as fresh and distinctive. The message and the benefits of the gospel match up amazingly well with the questions and needs of our culture and the world. While it is important to recognize the very serious problems the SBC is facing, it is perhaps even more important to recognize the great opportunities on the table for today's churches.

CHAPTER 18

Four Places to Start

M ost church leaders can readily accept the fact that countless numbers of people are spiritually lost, separated from God and having no relationship with Christ. It is a day of great opportunity to share the gospel because so many people need to hear it. The challenge is where to begin to get a church connected with its evangelistic task among the people living and working in the community the congregation serves. An entire community need not be reached at one time, but seeds of the gospel must be planted and the process of reaching the community must begin. Here are four places to start.

Focus on Prayer

Personal needs, family concerns, and the physical needs of people we know tend to crowd out evangelistic concerns in our prayer life. Recognition of the need for engagement and fruitfulness in evangelism is crucial for building a specifically evangelistic component into your prayer times. Jesus taught His disciples to have confidence that the world around them was more like a field ready to harvest right now than a field just beginning to be cultivated (John 4:35–38). He also taught them that the present harvest was bigger than the available laborers could handle; therefore, they were to pray that the Lord would send out more laborers into the harvest (Matt 9:37–38). A good way to begin praying evangelistically is to begin praying that the Lord will burden His people to share their faith and invite others to salvation. Make a list of church leaders and begin praying for them to develop a passion for people to come to Christ. Create some prayer partnerships, asking others to join you in praying for a greater number of people with whom to begin sharing your faith. When appropriate, include in your public prayers a request for more witnesses. In meetings of church leaders, include as part of the meeting a prayer for the harvest. The point is to follow the direction of Jesus and incorporate the prayer for laborers into the ongoing fabric of your prayer life and that of your church.

In Rom 10:1, Paul prayed passionately for the salvation of his people. In Rom 9:1–3, Paul shared the anguish in his heart over the lostness of his people. He was so hungry for their salvation that he expressed his willingness to be accursed himself if only they could be saved. If you have not already done so, start a prayer list of people you know who need to be saved. Pray for them by name. Ask the Lord to give you opportunities to share Christ with them. Pray that the Lord will bring others into their paths who will bear witness to Christ. As you pray for others, you will find God giving you a greater burden for their souls. That growing burden will connect you with an expanding number of people who need Christ. I have found the greater my awareness and focus on people who are lost, the more sensitive I am toward opportunities to start gospel conversations, even with people I do not know.

Prayer walking and prayer driving are important ways to pray for the lost you do not know but who live and work around you. Take some time to walk through your neighborhood and pray for the people living in each home to come to know the Lord. Do a prayer walk in other areas of your town or city as well. As you drive about in your normal travel pattern, pray for people in the homes and businesses you pass, that they might come to know Jesus if they do not yet know Him. Let every traffic light become a call to prayer. Pray for the joggers and bicyclists you pass on the street, but don't close your eyes! With eyes wide open, ask God to open their eyes to their need for salvation. When your church or Bible study has a time of prayer, let one part of it be designated specifically for the salvation of people in the community who do not know Christ. As you make praying evangelistically a continual part of your prayer life, you will find God using prayer to increase your passion to share your faith. Your eyes will begin to see what God sees. Your heart will begin to feel what God feels.

A visionary donor group approached New Orleans Baptist Theological Seminary with an unusual idea. Their idea was to create a scholarship fund that would pay all tuition and fees for students to earn any undergraduate or graduate degree offered by the seminary, with two requirements for eligibility. The first was that the applicant had to be on the staff of a smaller SBC church. Such churches are actually typical for the Convention. On any given Sunday some 70 percent of all SBC churches have 100 people or less in attendance. Nearly 90 percent have 250 people or less.

The second requirement was even more unusual. Scholarship recipients would be required to share the gospel with a lost person at least one time each week during any and every semester in which they received the financial aid. Students responded with great enthusiasm to the program. Their biggest question was uncertainty over whether or not they could have an opportunity every week to share the gospel. Many of these students are serving churches in small towns and rural areas. Others are in hectic, busy urban areas. A solution emerged that has provided a steady stream of witnessing opportunities for these students.

Dr. Mark Tolbert is the founding director of the Caskey Center for Church Excellence at NOBTS. An experienced pastor and frequent witness himself, he began to teach our students the "Monday Morning Prayer." Dr. Tolbert encourages the students to begin praying a very simple prayer every Monday morning. Specific wording is not important, but the prayer goes something like this: "Heavenly Father, I ask You to give me at least one opportunity to share the gospel with someone who needs it this week." As students began praying this prayer each week, they found witnessing opportunities coming to them. Those opportunities came in a variety of ways, but they kept coming,

Here is an experience I had after beginning to pray this prayer. I stopped in a Waffle House for a quick meal while traveling. I had my iPad open, and as the waitress refreshed my coffee, she asked a question or two about it. That started a running conversation. As she brought me the check, I told her that I liked to pray for people and asked if she had any prayer requests. She got very still, and then told me she was having a tough day and would appreciate my prayers. When I asked if she could share any specifics, she told me that while she and the cook were on break several days before, a robber had approached and beat her, then shot the cook. It was her first day back at work. Talk about an opportunity to share hope! A little later another server stopped by to talk with me. That was a gospel conversation just waiting to happen. My intentionality and openness were all God needed to connect us.

At last report, our Caskey Scholarship students had engaged in 3,319 gospel conversations with 2,179 opportunities to ask someone to give their lives to Christ. What a joy to know that 456 people have made professions of faith, most living in the communities where these ministry students are serving.

If you are wondering how to get engaged in evangelistic encounters, consider joining the NOBTS family in praying the Monday Morning Prayer. There are a variety of ways you can incorporate evangelistic praying into your life. Perhaps the Monday Morning Prayer will be a key in helping you recognize those moments when the Lord has put someone in your path to hear about Jesus.

Set a Goal

Virtually every church sets a financial goal for the budget. A church must be able to pay its bills and have enough money to do the ministries of the church. Most churches report each week on the progress toward the budget goal. Setting a specific goal and reporting regularly on progress toward the goal indicates that the offering each week is important. Most Christians would agree that it is important for people to be born again, but few churches set a goal of how many people they would like to win to Christ and baptize or how many times they would like to share the gospel in the community. To encourage a church to be more evangelistic, set a church goal for the number of people your congregation will seek to win to Christ or how many witnessing conversations members will have with others.

A baptism goal should not be an arbitrary number. How many people has your church baptized each year for the last several years? Can you reach as many people for Christ this year, or do you think you can reach more? A baptism goal should be the result of prayer and discussion among church leaders. A baptism goal should be formally approved by the congregation, as is a budget goal. A realistic goal is better than a goal so large that it is unattainable, but it is also important to have a goal large enough to engage the whole congregation in reaching people in the community. A goal specifying the number of witnessing conversations the church can have in a week, a month, or a year is a good companion to a goal for the number of baptisms. It also indicates the source of those baptisms and reminds the congregation of how people come to Christ.

After setting a goal for the number of baptisms, two questions need to be answered. First, what will you do to make it likely that you will reach the goal? Pray, of course, but what else will you do to share the gospel with the lost during the church year? How can you connect with unbelievers who need Christ, and how can you explain the gospel to them? The second question involves reporting. How will you report progress to the congregation? Will you report every week or once a month? Will the progress report be included in the weekly bulletin or shared from the pulpit? I have found it interesting to observe that few church members have any idea how many people were baptized in their church during the last year. One of the surest ways to increase baptisms is to increase congregational engagement with evangelistic goals and activities.

Share Your Testimony

People share the gospel more often by sharing the story of how they came to Christ than by using any other evangelism tool. Paul's conversion on the Damascus road has become well known because he shared it often (Acts 9:1–31; 22:1–21; 26:1–23). All Christians should be able to explain, in two or three minutes, how they came to know the Lord. I have shared the gospel by sharing my testimony more times than I can count. I have shared it in churches, in personal conversations, on the street, in airplanes, and many other places. Hardly ever does anyone take offense. Hardly ever do I feel threatened or intimidated. If a pastor wants to have a more evangelistic church, teaching the congregation how to share personal testimonies is a great place to start.

I teach people to use a simple three-point outline: (1) my life before Christ, (2) how I met Christ, and (3) my life after meeting Christ.

Personally, I have a plain, not dramatic, testimony because I was born and raised in a strong Christian home. Nevertheless, my life was changed when I met Jesus. I talk about discovering there is a world of difference between knowing about Jesus and actually having a relationship with Him. Over and over again, I have found that my plain, undramatic testimony connects with all sorts of people, from the Hispanic boy who was the first person I led to the Lord, to the doctor with whom I shared during my annual physical.

When I teach people how to share their testimonies, I ask them to write it out on a single sheet of paper. That keeps it brief. You can always add details when appropriate, but you are far more likely to have a brief time in which to share. I also ask them to practice sharing the testimony with someone right after they put it in writing. Many times, while teaching a group how to share their testimonies, someone in the group realizes that he has never actually given his life to the Lord. Be prepared for this realization when you teach a group how to tell others what Jesus has done for them. After teaching people how to share their testimonies, I challenge them to share it at least one time with someone during the next week and to tell someone what happened when they shared. There is no easier way for Christians to begin conversations about Jesus than by sharing their testimonies with someone else. When they do so, a further conversation about the gospel is often the result.

Share a Gospel Explanation

Another important key to becoming an active, effective witness is learning at least one way to explain how to become a Christian. This skill matters, in part, because it helps believers gain a clear understanding of their own salvation experience. It is also important that the witness be prepared when the Holy Spirit is drawing someone to Christ, and they need an explanation of what to do. While it is a very good thing to be able to talk for hours about all that is included in the doctrine of salvation, when the Philippian jailer asked Paul and Silas what he had to do to be saved, they went right to the heart of the matter: "Believe on the Lord Jesus Christ, and you will be saved" (Acts 16:30–31). Sharing my testimony has been a very effective evangelistic tool because it leads me into sharing how one can come to Christ now. I like to close my testimony by asking, "Has anything like this ever happened to you?" If the answer is "No" or unclear, I ask for permission to explain what the Bible says about becoming a Christian. To be confident as a witness for Christ, a Christian needs to be able to explain clearly how one can be saved.

An explanation of the gospel is often called a plan of salvation. There are many ways to explain how to be born again. Any explanation should address sin, the Savior, and salvation. The underlying assumption of any presentation of the plan of salvation is that there will be further instruction in the faith after one is born again. The moment of salvation is the beginning of a journey, not the end. To be a witness is to have the responsibility for introducing people to Jesus and for helping them to know Him better and to live for Him the rest of their lives. Learning how to explain the plan of salvation and teaching others how to do so are great ways to get started in evangelism.

Another approach is to use a worship service to equip the congregation to share the gospel. Every Christian should know how to use the Bible to explain how to become a Christian. A worship service is a great format for teaching people a simple gospel explanation. Designate a Sunday as "Gospel Sunday," and encourage everyone, including the youth and children, to bring a Bible and a pen. Ask people to mark the verses for a plan of salvation as you explain it to them. They can write the major points in the margins or in the back of their Bibles. Two possible texts to use are John 3:16 or the "Roman Road." Explain each Scripture one phrase at a time.

John 3:16 is one of the most familiar verses in the Bible. If people are told how to use it to explain salvation, they are likely to remember it. The Roman Road is a series of verses in the book of Romans that has long been a widely used way to explain how to be saved. The verses often used are Rom 1:16; 3:23; 5:8, 6:23; and 10:9–10. Also, Rom 12:1–2 is an excellent reference to use as you begin the follow-up process with a new Christian. People can be encouraged to write the first reference and the page number in the front of their Bibles and then underline each verse, putting the page number and reference of the next verse at the bottom of each page. Consider delivering a sermon on "The Gospel Explained" at an annual event when you can teach people to use their Bibles to tell someone how to be saved.

Some churches teach members to share the gospel in conjunction with a project to distribute Bibles in the community. On a designated Sunday, give everyone present a Bible to give away. Ask people to mark the Bible with a plan of salvation as it is explained, and then challenge them to give the Bible away in the next seven days. Challenge them to attempt to share their testimonies with the one who receives the Bible.

Another way to teach people to explain how to become a Christian is with a gospel tract. Use of a printed plan of salvation can be modeled in a worship service or as the focus of a workshop or seminar. There are many helpful gospel tracts. *Four Spiritual Laws* by Bill Bright and *Steps to Peace with God* by Billy Graham have been widely used for years. The *Eternal Life* booklet is one of the most popular tracts ever produced by the North American Mission Board. At this time, the *3 Circles* booklet is being widely used. The advantages of a tract are that very little training is required to use one effectively and that they are usually small and easy to carry. Perhaps most important, they can be given to someone to keep. I have been amazed to learn of the continued witness of tracts long after their initial presentation. They can be passed around to multiple people and go places you never expect. As is the case with teaching people to share their testimonies, providing an opportunity to practice using a tract for the first time is highly recommended.

A third way to explain the gospel is with a memorized presentation of the plan of salvation. This approach usually requires a formal training process and includes pairing an experienced witness with a learner for practice as an evangelistic visitation team. Advantages include the lingering effect of the training. People who have engaged in these processes tend to be consistent witnesses after the training has concluded. The witness is taught always to be ready to share, even without a Bible or tract. The experience of going out with a mentor or experienced witness is very powerful and encouraging. Such programs are less popular now, but they have had an excellent track record.

I taught Continuing Witness Training to seminary students for a decade. Most students were as afraid and reluctant to witness as the people filling church pews, even though they were ministers. Every year I watched changes take place, usually near the halfway point of the semester. Students would lead someone to the Lord for the first time and realize they could do it. They would share stories of starting to witness without even realizing it because the model presentation had become so familiar that the gospel found a way into all sorts of conversations. One student, who had been very angry about the class as the semester began, shared her shock at what happened in the middle of the night. She was awakened by an obscene phone caller. Before she knew what she was doing, the evangelism student engaged the guy in a conversation with the questions she had learned. Before the conversation ended, the caller was in tears wondering how God could love someone like him. The conversation had a horrible beginning, but it ended with prayer. She said, "I would have never done that if I had not memorized the gospel presentation. Without realizing it, sharing the gospel had become second nature to me, and the Lord pulled it out in the most unlikely of times." This type of training should never be the only evangelism tool in one's toolbox, but programs such as CWT do provide a tool that can be useful.

The bottom line is simple. Get started. Do something. Get engaged yourself in sharing the gospel with the lost in your community, and help others learn to share the gospel with them. As Paul told Timothy, "Do the work of an evangelist" (2 Tim 4:5). There will never be a better time than now.

CHAPTER 19

Next Steps

The Southern Baptist Convention is in a difficult place. The reality of statistical decline in its churches is no longer debatable. The culture of evangelism that formerly was so deeply rooted in its entities and churches is fading in some notable ways, but it is not gone. Unless that culture is refreshed and restored, however, the future of the SBC can be summed up in one word—smaller. But this is not necessarily so, for there are opportunities to enlarge the harvest once again. Here are some steps that could take the Convention in that direction.

Emphasize Christlikeness

Southern Baptist churches need a rebirth of *disciplism*,[1] a passionate emphasis on both evangelism and discipleship. The gospel must be both illustrated and explained. Put as simply as possible, more Southern Baptists must look and live like Jesus, being a distinctive, notable presence as they live and work in their communities. Every evangelistic strategy and method from the days of the New Testament to the present day is based upon a simple assumption: The Christian life is observably different from the life of a non-Christian. Teaching church members of all ages to live distinctively as Christians in a secular, non-Christian culture is essential for improving evangelistic impact. We do not become more effective in reaching our neighbors by becoming more and more like them. We win

---

[1] See discussion of this term on page 186.

the attention and hearing of our neighbors by being notable in our resemblance to Christ. If your church is going to take steps to become more evangelistic, steps must be taken to be more intentional in discipleship, encouraging spiritual growth and Christlikeness.

When the Sanhedrin, the group who had condemned Jesus to death and urged Pilate to crucify Him, brought Peter and John to stand before them, they were reminded of Jesus.

> Now when they saw the boldness of Peter and John, and perceived
> that they were uneducated and untrained men, they marveled. And
> they realized that they had been with Jesus (Acts 4:13).

The impact of their testimonies came from the Christlikeness that members of the Sanhedrin saw in them. When the pagans in Antioch heard the witness of the believers to Jesus and observed how those believers were living, they began calling them Christians (Acts 11:26). They noticed the conscious effort of the believers to be like Christ.

Christians should never fear that an intentional effort to pursue a holy life will drive others away. Being snobbish about holiness is not attractive, and such snobbishness and pride about being holy is not Christlikeness. People may assume you do not care about them because they do not share your values. You have to seek ways to express love, warmth, and hospitality to those who are unlike you. That is what Jesus did. My wife and I live in the very non-Baptist city of New Orleans. Our habits are strange and different to many of those whom we seek to reach. We have found that creating social opportunities, especially in our home, is an important way to give lost people a chance to observe our hearts and not just our habits.

Some nonbelievers may find your devotion to Christ annoying, but when we are truly Christlike, we seek to express His love as well as embody His righteousness. Jesus was sinless, but the outsiders and sinners of the day were comfortable in His presence because He clearly cared about them and their problems. Restoring and cultivating the perception of Christlikeness in the eyes of the community is a key to being able to tell the community about the gospel.

Gospel Conversations

If a church is going to be effective in evangelism, the church members must take the gospel outside the church. Since most people who need the gospel are not attending church, the people of the church have to be willing to take the gospel to them in their natural settings. One of the best ways to accomplish this task is to seek gospel conversations. Gospel conversations are opportunities to introduce Jesus into life encounters. These conversations can occur at work, in school, during hobbies, and many other settings. Gospel conversations may give little more than an opportunity to say a good word about Jesus. However, they may give an opportunity to explain how to be saved or may even lead to asking someone to give his or her life to Christ. There is no standard approach and no specific script. The only requirements for a gospel conversation are to start talking to make a connection with a person and then to keep talking until you have an opportunity to say something about Jesus. Once the conversation gets to Jesus, seek to explain how to have a relationship with Him.

The way to begin a gospel conversation is simply to start. Engage someone in a conversation about whatever is appropriate to the moment. Is football the subject in the air? Talk football. If food is the topic, share a favorite place to eat. The important thing is to start talking with the person or people at hand about any topic that could give you a connection. In John 4, Jesus had a gospel conversation with a woman at a well. He started the conversation by asking for a drink of water. Why did he start there? He was thirsty. Ask a question or make an observation. Initiate a conversation and follow where it leads. This is a very common practice in New Orleans. You simply start talking and see if a connection develops.

When our nephew moved to New Orleans to begin a new job, he had to take a national certification test. I offered to buy him a study guide for it, and as we were driving to the book store, I thought I would do a little New Orleans coaching. I suggested he go to the section of the store where the study guides for this certification are kept and see if someone else was looking through the same books. If so, I encouraged him to start talking to the person and ask if they know anything about which one might be the most helpful. I assured him no one would think he was strange or inappropriate because that is what people in New Orleans do. They start conversations. As we drove back to the house after the purchase was made, I asked if he had seen anyone else looking at those books. "Yes," he said, a young lady was there. You know my next question. "Did you talk to her?" I asked. "Actually," he replied, "she started talking to me first." The most important thing about gospel conversations is to start talking. If you don't start talking and looking for a connecting point, you cannot have a gospel conversation. Begin and see where the conversation takes you.

I read widely and keep up with many subjects and issues. I do this because I am curious by nature and because I want to be able to say something about as many different topics as possible. I once got into a conversation with a rancher who was quite interested in cattle breeding. We talked about the strengths and weaknesses of various breeds of cattle, advances in artificial insemination for cows, the differences between raising cattle for breeding and for meat, and other such things. When the man found out I was a Baptist preacher, he was shocked. He could not understand how I stayed engaged in that conversation. The secret? My wife has an uncle who breeds cattle at a high level. When I was around him, I listened. When we visited, I would look through the magazines in his home, which were always different from the ones in my house! Staying curious is a great help for gospel conversations. But you do not have to know much about any topic as long as you are truly interested in people. Ask a person a question about his life or an area of interest, and you will quickly be in a real conversation.

The second step in a gospel conversation is to look for an opportunity to say a word about Jesus. I know a Mexican cafeteria that makes great sopapillas, a wonderful type of fried pastry not unlike the beignets in New Orleans. Every table has a flag that you can raise or lower. For more sopapillas, raise the flag and the server will bring them. For gospel conversations, raise a flag that says you are ready to talk about Jesus. I often tell people that I like to pray for others and ask if I can pray for them about some concern. I may ask if they think much about God. The important thing is to start a conversation, and once started, look for the place where Jesus fits in.

When you introduce Jesus to the conversation, the person usually makes it clear whether or not he wants to discuss spiritual things. If the individual seems open or curious, I look for some opportunity to share my testimony and allow the conversation to flow. If a person does not seem ready to discuss spiritual matters, I change the topic and continue working to build a relationship that may lead to other conversations at a later time. I find it fascinating how often I discover people who have spiritual questions or issues on their minds. I believe in every community there are people with whom God is dealing. Spiritual things are on their minds. Seeking gospel conversations is one way to find those people. Keep talking to enough people, and God will connect you with someone who is waiting for an opportunity to talk about God.

Uncertainty is one of the big fears people have about starting gospel conversations because you do not know where they will lead. Many worry about being asked a question they cannot answer. Actually, getting a question you cannot answer is a great opportunity. I never hesitate to say, "I don't know" when asked a question that stumps me. My full response is typically: "I don't know, but I will find out and get back with you." Questions are invitations from someone to have a second conversation. That second conversation is definitely going to be on spiritual things and will come at the invitation of the other person. Don't be nervous about questions. Questions are your friends in sharing Christ. Do the best you can; and if you don't know a satisfying answer, use the moment to set up another conversation after you have an opportunity to prepare.

Any Christian can engage in gospel conversations. Gospel conversations are essential to bring Jesus to the attention of those who are not attending church to hear the gospel preached and taught. Start talking and see where the conversation takes you. Here is an amazing reality: When you connect the gospel with someone who is living life unconnected to anyone's church, that person will bring you into contact with other people who are unconnected to the gospel. A gospel conversation can be the fast track to more evangelistic prospects than you will find in a worship service through a month of Sundays.

Our seminary created an app (a computer application for a mobile device) to give people a chance to report on gospel conversations. Go to either Apple or Android app stores to look for "Gospel Conversations." Download the app and post what happened when you had a gospel conversation.

Children and Youth

An analysis of SBC baptisms during the years of decline reveals the biggest issue driving the decline. Southern Baptists stopped reaching their own children. Numbers of baptisms have been down in every age category for nearly all of the past 16 years, but they dropped off the charts for people ages 18 and younger. As I travel among Southern Baptist churches, I often ask the crowd to raise their hands if they came to Christ when they were age 18 or younger. Without fail, most people in any section of the country indicate that they came to Christ by the time they reached age 18. Having seen the overwhelming number of Southern Baptists who came to Christ by the time they finished high school, I am convinced that the failure to reach the children of church members, as well as the failure to reach the lost and unchurched children who are the friends of the children of church members, is an extremely serious issue with profound implications.

As a teenager, I was deeply committed to Christ, actively seeking to live for Christ and bear witness to Christ. Had I not come to Christ until I was an adult, all the people who heard about the Lord from me, including the big crowd at my high school graduation who heard my commencement address, would not have heard my witness. When Christians fail to reach children and youth, they are also failing to reach all those who would otherwise hear the witness of these individuals. Paying specific attention to sharing the gospel with children and students should be "Priority #1" for the church. Being prepared to begin the discipleship process immediately after children and youth come to Christ is also a crucial priority. If Southern Baptists are going to improve their evangelistic impact, the resources of the SBC and the focus of local churches must be brought to bear on reaching the children and youth of the church and community.

Sharing the gospel with children and youth must be done carefully and thoughtfully. Anyone who works with or has children knows there can be vast differences in maturity and understanding among children and youth who are the same age. Attention must be given to them both as individuals and as a group. Acknowledging this fact, we should not hesitate to have spiritual conversations with the young simply because they are young. In Mark 10:15, Jesus taught His disciples that there would be no entry into the kingdom of God unless one receives it like a child. Faith, not adulthood, is required for salvation. Care must be taken not to manipulate a decision or assume a level of understanding that is not there. That being said, Christians must seek occasions to share Jesus with the young and give them an opportunity to be born again.

The best place to begin sharing Christ is in the home. Equipping parents to know when and how to explain the gospel is very important. Each year a church should plan something to help parents know how to witness to their own children. Every pastor must connect with parents and ensure that they know he is available to help if needed. One possible approach is to select an age when major attention is given to explaining salvation to the young. For instance, imagine selecting the ages of 10 and 15 as a time to do a special emphasis on the gospel. A church could sponsor a workshop giving special attention to informing parents of appropriate ways for their children to know and understand the nature of salvation. The pastor or church staff could set a goal of going to each home with a child of that age to share the gospel with that child. The strategy is to be sure that in the setting of the home, each child is able to hear an appropriate presentation about the necessity of salvation, and each child is given an appropriate opportunity to respond in faith to Jesus.

Church activities should also be planned to include age-appropriate gospel presentations. Every Sunday School or Bible study group for children and youth should carefully explain the gospel at least once each year. The meaning of the Lord's Supper and its role as an illustration of the gospel should also be explained at least once a year at a level designed for the young to understand. When youth or children are baptized, an explanation should be given from the baptistery on what baptism means and why it is important for the believer. Children are paying more attention when other children are involved on the platform.

Vacation Bible Schools, youth camps, and other activities designed specifically for children and youth should always include an evangelistic component featuring an appropriate presentation of the gospel, and an invitation to respond to the gospel should be extended in an appropriate way. A prayer list with names of children and youth who need salvation can encourage the church family to pray for the salvation of the younger members. Such a list would have to be handled carefully, especially with the names of teenagers who are so very sensitive to what their peers think. Occasionally asking an older child or youth to share a personal testimony in a worship service or at the time of their baptism can be a very powerful testimony to the others in the church. The most important point is taking the time to look at your church calendar each year and ask what will be done this year to present the gospel to the children and youth in the church, to the parents of children and youth who have connected with the church without parental involvement, and to the friends of the children and youth in the church who have no connection with the church or Christ.

When Southern Baptists fail to reach the children and students in their own churches and communities, SBC churches are not likely to be fruitful. That failure will set in motion other consequences with ever more serious challenges for the churches. If we passionately want to get the gospel to the whole world, we must never forget that this quest should begin with getting the gospel to our own children and youth, as well as to their friends. In many instances, the conversion of a child or teenager will open an opportunity to introduce the gospel to parents or other family members. A change in this one trend line for Southern Baptists would have a greater impact than changes in any other. In order to reach the world, Christians must start in our homes.

***

Lesson 5

The knock of opportunity is useless unless you answer the door.

If you want to see a greater evangelistic harvest in your church or ministry, do something evangelistic. Start. Nothing will change unless you identify the best place to begin engaging in evangelism and then do something to engage in sharing the gospel. After you start, keep at it. Reaching people with the gospel is like farming. It is a process. Find your place to start and begin now. According to Jesus, the harvest is ready. The opportunities are there. It is time to go reap!

***

Questions for Conversation

1. How would you explain the gospel to a child, including an invitation to be born again?
2. When did you become a Christian, and how did it happen?
3. What would be an appropriate way to establish an evangelism goal for your church?
4. How can your church get engaged in praying for the lost in your community?

All Is Vain Unless the Spirit of the Holy One Comes Down[1]

T he Southern Baptist Convention formed in 1845 as a collection of churches that were evangelistic and mission-minded with a passion to reach the nation and the world for Christ. These churches wanted to reach the unreached places in the nation and the world, but they also wanted to reach the lost and unchurched in their communities. Southern Baptists have always kept an eye on what's working, and they noticed other American church families getting help from a denominational evangelist. That help seemed to make a difference, especially in cities. Southern Baptists knew they had to reach the cities if they were to reach the nation. To coordinate their cooperation, the churches assigned responsibility for reaching the nations and for reaching the United States, but they had not assigned a responsibility for assisting the churches in evangelism.

These concerns crystallized in a long, controversial battle to create a Department of Evangelism, which finally did put in place a structure for evangelism in the SBC. As the Department matured and developed, so a paradigm for evangelism became deeply rooted in the way Southern Baptists did church. The New Testament model of sowing and reaping was embedded in the normal rhythms of church life. If you attended a Southern Baptist church, decisional preaching, personal evangelism, Sunday School, and revival meetings were familiar features in church life. With

---

[1] This statement appears in the lyrics of the hymn "Brethren, We Have Met to Worship," by George Atkins, first published in 1819.

a leader in place at the Department of Evangelism who had a plan and an evangelism paradigm widely embraced in the churches, Southern Baptists churches exploded with evangelistic growth. The theological convictions of Southern Baptists reinforced the role and priority of evangelism, and the evangelistic culture of the SBC remained in place for decades, even when the statistical growth turned into an extended plateau.

Things change. They always do. The evangelism structure and paradigm present for so many years began to fade. Attention to both discipleship and evangelism weakened, and with their waning influence, an unprecedented decline began. The decline in numbers of baptisms, membership, worship attendance, and small group attendance became normal. A stunning gap between the number of churches and the number of baptisms recorded by those churches began and continued to widen, putting the SBC in the unusual position of having more and more churches but fewer and fewer people being baptized and engaged in ministry. As of this writing, that gap is now 16 years old and continues to grow. Southern Baptists are still a driving force in the evangelical world, but the decline of the SBC is a very serious issue.

What lies ahead for the Southern Baptist Convention? There are some key questions that must be addressed. Will the North American Mission Board return to making attention to evangelism in SBC churches a major priority? Reducing attention on church evangelism has not been very productive to this point. Will there be a sustained intensification of attention to evangelism? If so, will it come in time to reverse the direction of the churches that are struggling? Will there again be a widely embraced paradigm for evangelism shared by most SBC churches? Getting a process of sowing the gospel and reaping conversions as deeply embedded in congregational life as it once was will be a difficult challenge. Methods and approaches can change, but the process of sowing and reaping is essential.

Will the theological convictions shared by most Southern Baptists reinforce the priority of aggressively seeking to reach the lost in a community for Christ, or will the theological focus be on other areas of church life? Theology does matter, and ultimately theology will affect behavior. In the past, Southern Baptists felt responsible for seeking out the lost in their communities and urging them to give their lives to Christ. Will that be the passion of today's SBC caught up in the dynamics of this present decline?

The little amount of attention given to the connection between discipleship and evangelism, in contrast to the large role both historically have played in SBC church life and culture, is remarkable. The discipleship templates that played such a key role are largely gone. Will new ones emerge and capture the interest and confidence of today's churches? One of the most important questions is whether or not Southern Baptists will be able to reach and disciple their own children. That has been the greatest evangelistic struggle of the last two decades.

The answers to all these questions become irrelevant unless one thing happens. The deepest need of the Southern Baptist Convention today is for God to do what only He can do. In the words of a great old hymn: "All is vain unless the Spirit of the Holy One comes down." The writer of "Brethren, We Have Met to Worship"[2] is correct. Southern Baptists tend to be pragmatists. They are always looking for what works. Southern Baptists have always been willing to work hard and to take on difficult, even dangerous, tasks for the sake of souls. This present day is one in which effort is not enough. God must move for a fresh vitality to be released in SBC churches. Prayer on the part of God's people is the necessary prelude to a movement of the Holy Spirit of the magnitude needed today.

I undertook this project to get a conversation started. The SBC has changed and is facing some challenges never before faced. We need to talk about these matters as we all search for a way forward. We need to trust each other as we talk, so that even when we disagree, we do so knowing we share the same commitment to the Great Commission. If we can move the conversation along, I am hopeful that action will follow. Conversation alone will not be enough. Simply maintaining the status quo will have heartbreaking consequences. However, neither talking nor doing is the most important destination. Prayer is the true necessity. God must intervene for these circumstances to change. We need a stirring of the Holy Spirit.

---

[2] See n. 1.

May we meet together before the throne of God seeking His mercy and grace, and one day, may we find ourselves rejoicing in wonder over a mighty work of God that revitalizes Southern Baptist churches and brings a flood of the newly redeemed into the kingdom. Fuel the fire, O Lord, in our lives and our churches. Let the passion for lifting up Christ and calling all peoples to repentance and faith burn as it never has before!

APPENDIX A

Motion to Create a Department of Evangelism, 1904 [1]

36. L. G. Broughton, Georgia, presented the following paper, and the time for its consideration was referred to the Committee on Order of Business to report later, by a vote of ayes, 439; noes, not counted:

> *Resolved*, That the Convention appoint a committee of twelve pastors, not members of any Convention Board, to be known as the Committee on Evangelism for the Needy Sections of our Convention Territory;

> That this committee, in cooperation with the Secretaries of our Boards, shall employ a general evangelist, who shall also be the Secretary of the Committee;

> That said evangelist shall, in addition to his evangelistic work, gather statistics, disseminate information and call to his aid such help and helpers as the Committee may approve;

> That the cooperation of State Boards be secured as far as possible, where work is to be done in needy and destitute fields;

---

[1] *Annual of the Southern Baptist Convention, 1904* (Nashville, Tennessee: May 13–16, 1904), 7; see "Resolution on Evangelism: Nashville, Tennessee - 1904," Southern Baptist Convention, accessed December 17, 2017, http://www.sbc.net/resolutions/501/resolution-on-evangelism.

That the salary of the general evangelist be paid by the three Boards of the Convention, and other expenses, including the salaries of special evangelists, be arranged for by the field or cooperating board;

That collections be taken at every meeting held by the evangelists for the work of the Evangelistic Committee;

That annual reports be made to the State Boards in all the States where work has been done;

That the Committee also report annually to the Convention.

APPENDIX B

Report of the Evangelism Department Study Committee[1]

80. A. J. Thomas, South Carolina, read the following report from a committee appointed at the preceding session (1904, item 36) on

Evangelism.

At the last annual session of this Convention Bro. Len G. Broughton offered the following resolutions:

> *Resolved*, 1. That the Convention appoint a committee of twelve pastors, not members of any Convention Board, to be known as the Committee on Evangelism for the Needy Sections of our Convention Territory;
>
> 2. That this committee, in co-operation with the Secretaries of our Boards, shall employ a general evangelist, who shall also be the Secretary of the Committee;
>
> 3. That said evangelist shall, in addition to his evangelistic work, gather statistics, disseminate information and call to his aid such help and helpers as the Committee may approve;
>
> 4. That the co-operation of State Boards be secured as far as possible, where work is to be done in needy and destitute fields;

---

[1] *Annual of the Southern Baptist Convention, 1905* (Kansas City, Missouri: May 12–15, 1905), 35–41.

5. That the salary of the general evangelist be paid by the three
    Boards of the Convention, and other expenses, including the
    salaries of special evangelists, be arranged for by the field or
    co-operating board;
6. That collections be taken at every meeting held by the evange-
    lists for the work of the Evangelistic Committee;
7. That annual reports be made to the State Boards in all the
    States where work has been done;
8. That the Committee also report annually to the Convention.

By unanimous consent the resolutions were referred to a committee of five to report to this Convention. Soon after the meeting
of the last Convention a communication was addressed to the members of the Committee for the purpose of ascertaining their views.
A communication was also addressed to the several State mission
secretaries with inquiries as to what special evangelistic work was
being undertaken in their respective States; whether a State evangelist, or evangelists were employed; as to results reached, and as
to the general estimate of the work accomplished. We ascertained
that in some States evangelists are employed with most satisfactory results, in other States the missionaries of the State Boards
are considered evangelists and are doing good work. All of the
replies showed an unusual degree of interest in the work of evangelism, and expressed desire for its enlargement, with the belief
that more could be accomplished in immediate and far-reaching
results. We have not found any general conviction in favor of a
separate board and secretary to be appointed to take charge of this
as a special and distinct department of our work. Your Committee
therefore has not deemed it wise to recommend the appointment
of the committee of twelve and a paid secretary called for the resolutions quoted above. In making this report, however, we feel sure
that the subject is worthy of the attention and consideration of this
Convention, and we submit more at length the following:

It is manifest to all that there has come about an awakened
interest in the subject of evangelistic work. There is an atmosphere of evangelism. By evangelism we mean no new thing.

It has been recognized and felt through all these years—special efforts, earnest preaching, and private personal work, which has for its end the salvation of the lost and the edification of the saved—that edification which has as its aim the better, fuller, more complete equipment of the individual member of the church; edification from an intelligent, spiritual, Biblical bottom. The work needs a more earnest purpose on the part of pastors and churches to press home upon the sinner immediate decision, submitting to the Lordship of Christ, trusting to the value of his atonement, believing in the power of his resurrection, accepting his terms of discipleship and then being trained into loving service for his Lord. This is not a new doctrine, but it is something which seems to be getting hold of many of God's people with greater force. There must, of course, be made the distinction between the evangelist which is needed, and that which has gained a reputation. There is a great difference between the real God-sent evangelist, and peripatetic, non-responsible traveler whose sound is heard but whose affiliation and connection are as uncertain as the doctrine he preaches. The pure and true New Testament evangelism greatly needs a larger place in our lives and work today because of the widely prevalent, vague, and superficial views on the subject.

That this special work of evangelism is receiving much more attention than formerly is evident in the frequent and prominent discussion of it in the newspapers, magazines, and reviews. Scarcely a week passed but may be found in some of the public prints soul-stirring articles from thoughtful pastors and others on evangelistic methods and preaching. Not only so, but the new books on this subject show that there is new interest and an increasing demand for published thought; such books as Torrey's "How to Organize and Promote a Great Revival," and "The Soul-Winner—How to Bring Men to Christ," Riley's "Perennial Revival," Broughton's "Soul-Winning Church," and Campbell Morgan's "Evangelism." Men who have tried it, and who have been blessed in their work, are telling others how to reach the individual. Thousands of others might bless the world if they would more frequently tell their brethren how the Spirit has used them and their messages to bring men to immediate decision and sent them forth to tell others "how great things the Lord hath done for them."

That this work of evangelism is receiving awakened attention is seen also in the organized agencies already at work, with marvelous results. For instance, the Northfield work and its evangelists, and the Evangelistic Committee of the Northern Presbyterians, this latter organization, with Rev. Wilbur Chapman as Secretary and general evangelist, is doing a vast work in awakening general interest and in adding members to their churches and in developing the membership. They show an increase of 12,000 members through this agency within the past year. The Baptists of London have organized their Baptist Evangelistic Society and the active campaign has already begun. We have heard of recent evangelization agencies in some of the Southern cities among the business men of the several evangelical denominations. The Baptists of America have no special evangelistic agency, as such, and this fact, and the further fact that they have always been blessed with men of evangelistic gifts in a remarkable degree, may help to explain how it comes about that there are some among us who are seriously considering today whether is it [sic] not time to bring together into some kind of organization those brethren who are adapted by nature and by grace to this special work. There are men so gifted, some of who [sic] already wholly given to this form of service. There are others gifted with the evangelistic spirit and qualification, and they only need to be drawn out and properly directed and sent forth backed up by some agency of the denomination. There are men of means too who are willing to make special contributions for this work in addition to what they are doing for missions and benevolence in other directions. Special evangelistic work will appeal to very many of our business men, and experience has already proven that it receives from them a liberal support. It is altogether probable that we shall soon have to consider the wisdom of a separate, distinct evangelistic agency; not only to emphasize the thought, but also to press the work in connection with the regular organizations that we now have. Some of our brethren who wish aggressive and organized evangelistic work, urge, "if the time will ever come to do definite work in this direction, that hour has struck; that there never has been such a demand for evangelistic work as now; that we ought to read and heed the signs of the times; that the work of evangelism in the Southern Baptist Convention is not in 'destitute' regions, those places our State Boards are caring for, that the need is a wise movement to free the hands of able pastor-evangelists, accredited men, who can meet the demands of our cities, and strong churches in town and villages; that our churches in cities, towns, and villages need the reinforcement of strong evangelists." One of these city pastors says: "As Baptists we are not strong enough in cities and towns, and we seldom gain anything in inter-denominational meetings, but generally lose. Our city churches could be increased twenty-five percent within two years in Baptists [*sic*] union meetings directed by some great Baptist evangelist."

Your committee would not have the impression created that we are ignorant of what is being done in special evangelistic work in the several States connected with the Convention. Much is being done by the missionaries of the Home Board and the several State Mission Boards, especially in destitute regions and in mission fields. We have every reason to believe that this will continue and even be enlarged. Our correspondence with the State Mission Secretaries was in every way encouraging and gratifying. We find that they are giving much attention to evangelism. They are seeking men who have special gifts in this kind of work. One of these Secretaries writes: "Our State Board has employed men who give their entire time to holding meetings in that season of the year in which such meetings are usually held, and their work has been very satisfactory to the Board. We pay them a stipulated salary. They are expected to aid in the dissemination of knowledge concerning our work of State, Home, and Foreign Missions, and in every practicable way assist in moving the churches to will to do greater things. If there is a more excellent way, I shall be glad to adopt it." Another Secretary writes, that in his State "has been inaugurated an evangelistic corps of missionaries. These men are directed to labor in destitute sections. They are required to report monthly, to give a detailed statement of each meeting, the attendance, general statement of the religious condition of the section, what religious influences are at work, the number of days of meetings, with the results. We have found that this evangelistic work appeals very strongly to business men, and so we have been enabled to get special pledges from different business men to support these evangelists." Another Secretary writes: "We are beyond the experimental stage with evangelists. We have called them general missionaries for years. These men have been selected with reference to their abilities to give the churches a strong uplift for work, also with reference to their evangelistic gifts. Their work has been for years most gratifying in results. They have gone to many churches run down, held good meetings, and while the welding heat was on have brought them into the front ranks for progress, and collected more than their salaries. The Board has determined to greatly enlarge this work, and we are just now entering upon an evangelistic campaign which we hope will enlist the pastors and create a great forward movement. There is no question as to the value of the movement or its Scriptural-ness either, the only question is the proper direction of it." Another Secretary urges the necessity of reviving pastoral evangelism, and the importance of developing more of evangelistic preaching among the pastors, and adds: "I have often employed a brother to go to a destitute point or pastor-less church and hold a meeting which resulted in saving a weak church or the organization of a new one. Let the question of evangelism be discussed in all our papers; it will do great good. Baptists must continue to be aggressive, or perish." Another Secretary says: "Our State has three evangelists besides missionaries who do evangelistic work in the bounds of the associations in which they work. We have a man whose special work is among mill people. He is admirably adapted to it and has accomplished great good. He collects from his meetings about two-thirds of his salary and expenses. The two remaining general evangelists frequently hold meetings with self-sustaining churches. I think we could employ several additional men with profit." Still another Secretary says: "In our State from four to ten evangelists are employed; some of them by individual churches and some by the State Board. Some of the latter are colporters, but they all do the same work; hold protracted meetings with churches." Every Secretary of State Mission Work heard from laid stress upon the idea of evangelism, expressed the wish that more evangelistic work might be done by the missionaries and pastors, or special evangelists, and, whether they endorsed the Broughton resolution or not, they fully agreed in, and realize the importance of the work.

The Southern Baptist Convention territory is an inviting field for distinct, specific, Scriptural evangelism. Perhaps there is not a more inviting field in the world at this time than the territory of this Convention for organized evangelistic agencies and effort. It is largely a Baptist territory to begin with, and the edification part of evangelism has already called into service special talents, and hence we have the Sunday school evangelists now at work, and others are needed, and are eagerly sought. The need of trained workers is felt, and we hear of training schools where workers are taught to be better equipped for soul winning and the training of those who are won. An inviting territory because of the large influx of new people, unsaved, un-evangelized, people coming into the States from every nation under heaven. An inviting territory because of the rapidly changing conditions even in the communities formerly staid, fixed and conservative, the changes wrought by the partial depletion of rural districts in some sections, and the marvelous growth of the mining and mill districts; districts rapidly filling with people who may be evangelized in the truest sense. Inviting because of the growing cities, some of them for many years considered as hard fields for the Baptists, and hard because the true work of Bible evangelism was there neglected, and is there needed, viz: the triumph of the New Testament principles over the hearts and lives of the people. An inviting territory because our people have long been trained to believe in evangelistic services, and they have reaped richly from these special efforts. The statement has been made time and again, and it has not been seriously questioned, or successfully contradicted, that the majority of the members of our churches were converted under evangelistic preaching. Say what we will, our protracted meetings, special efforts, revival services, or whatever we may be pleased to call them, and wise are we if we study the sanest and safest methods of conducting these services. We believe in these special methods to such an extent that we experience a spiritual refreshing when we read or hear of one of these blessed, old-time revivals of religion.

Surely it is not improper to give this subject of evangelistic work some special thought, and some emphasis in our meetings. It has been forcibly remarked by one of our most consecrated pastors: "There is no doubt of the fact that the evangelistic sentiment among the Baptists of the United States and Canada is widespread and strong enough to be crystallized into a great organization, but, in our judgment, there is no need of it, provided the existing societies and conventions will give to evangelism the place in their policy its importance demands." These are wise words. It is not an unfriendly imputation, it is not an un-fraternal reflection upon pastors, churches, existing agencies, and boards that some of our seers and consecrated workers have come before us asking that this great subject shall receive that annual consideration of these messengers of the churches. Believing, therefore, that it is a subject that may properly come before this Convention for special consideration, and with the wish that our hearts might become more burdened for the salvation of the lost and the edification of the saved, and that there might be a great revival wave sweeping over our land and through our churches, we respectfully recommend:

1. That this Convention appoint a special committee of five brethren whose duty it shall be to take this whole matter under advisement and into consideration, and to report at the next Convention on the "Work of Evangelism in the several States of the Convention."

2. That the committee be instructed to seek information as to the wisest methods in the work of evangelism consistent with our church polity and our denominational policy; to ascertain as far as practicable the special needs, and what is being done in the several States, as to the number of evangelists employed, where, and how employed, and as to the general results obtained; to agitate the whole subject of evangelism, and to gather any statistics in connection with the work, and any other information or intelligence touching the spiritual condition of our people, and the work of the denomination in reaching the unsaved massed at the very doors of our churches.

3. That in the prosecution of this work the committee shall solicit the co-operation of our religious newspapers, the State mission secretaries, and the secretaries of our general boards, and that these brethren be requested to render any aid they can to this committee in seeking the desired information.

4. That this committee, after a careful study of men and methods, shall feel it their privilege to discreetly recommend to inquiring pastors and churches such brethren as in their view possess the true evangelistic gifts, and who can acceptably do the work of an evangelist.

5. That it is understood that the committee in their work shall not entail any expense upon the Convention, or its boards, but that the committee is at liberty to receive any contributions that may be furnished by the friends of this cause for any necessary expenses that may be incurred in the successful prosecution of its work.

Respectfully submitted,
A. J. S. THOMAS,
MILFORD RIGGS,
JOHN E. WHITE,
T. B. RAY,
W. S. RYLAND

The Convention was addressed by L. G. Broughton, Georgia, the report was adopted.

81.The Chair announced the following as the committee called for in the foregoing report: L. G. Broughton, Georgia; G. W. Truett, Texas; W. W. Hamilton, Kentucky; W. M. Vines, Virginia; A. J. S. Thomas, South Carolina.

APPENDIX C

Report of the Second Evangelism Department Study Committee[1]

36. The report of the committee appointed by the previous Convention, on the subject of "Evangelization," was read by L. G. Broughton, Georgia.

37. After discussion by L. G. Broughton, Georgia, the report on motion of R. G. Bowers, Arkansas, was made the special order for Sunday at 3 P.M.

53. On a motion to reconsider the action of the Convention fixing 3 P.M. Sunday as a special Order for the consideration of the report of Evangelism, the house divided: Ayes, 188; noes, 252. Whereupon, a number of motions being made, which were decided to be not in order, it was finally determined, by general consent, that this report should be made the subject of discussion at 3:30 P.M. Sunday, without passing upon the business details involved, which, on motion of J. J. Taylor, Kentucky, were made the order for 4 P.M. Monday. It was further ordered that a memorial service for the distinguished dead should be held at 2:30 P.M. Sunday.

66. In the interest of the general subject of "Evangelism," addresses were made by G. W. Truett, Texas; F. C. McConnell, Missouri; M. P. Hunt, Kentucky; J. B. Gambrell, Texas; and L. G. Broughton, Ga.

92. The special order for the hour being the consideration of the report of the Committee on Evangelism, the Convention was addressed by B. H. Carroll, Texas, and the report was adopted.

---

[1] *Annual of the Southern Baptist Convention, 1906* (Chattanooga, Tennessee: May 11–14, 1906), 7, 19, 25, 40–43.

Evangelism

The spirit of evangelism is abroad in the land. From every part of the country there come the tokens of increased revival fervor among the churches of all denominations of Christians. The man who has failed to see this has failed to keep abreast with the religious movements in our country.

In many of our great cities there has been very distinct and extraordinary evangelistic enthusiasm. More people have been reached by the gospel in our great cities through evangelistic agencies within the last year than ever before. This seems especially to be true of the centers of population, where it has hitherto been so hard to reach the masses.

Generally speaking, the notable revivals of this year have been of a co-operative character, either different denominations coming together or groups of churches of the same denomination. The large central meeting, or a number of simultaneous meetings in the same general movement, has usually been the order of the evangelistic work of the past year so far as the cities are concerned. Great halls, theaters, skating rinks, and other large central meeting places have been utilized by evangelists, and thousands of non-churchgoers have been reached in this way. This seems to have been the general order for much of the evangelism in the great cities for the last few years. Upon much of this God seems to have put his seal of approval.

The country sections and small towns have likewise shared in the evangelistic sweep of the country. While it has been impossible for them to inaugurate and carry forward large evangelistic campaigns, they have in one way or another come in touch with the great city movements, caught the fire, and their own way set on foot movements that have blessed their own communities. Indeed, we have failed to estimate the proper value of these large, central, evangelistic meetings. The souls directly saved do not begin to measure the scope of the work. Through the press and by individual contact and participation in the enthusiasm, other communities are stimulated and great blessing follows.

In this connection it seems proper to make special mention of the recent great pentecostal revival within our own bounds in the city of Paducah, Ky. More than a thousand people united with the First Baptist Church alone, as the result of a revival which lasted from November to March. It was a great meeting. Our beloved Brother Cheek, the pastor of the church, already weakened in health from the very outset, broke himself down in this great meeting, and God saw fit to take him home to rest. Viewed from one standpoint it was a sad culmination of such a useful life, but viewed from the proper standpoint it was a glorious ending of a devoted, consecrated ministry.

Baptists are pre-eminently the people to lead in this evangelistic movement which is only at present seen in part. Our church polity is such as to give us every advantage. The spirit and temperament of our people is another advantage.

In talking with a distinguished English minister after an extended tour in this country, he said to a member of this Committee, "I am now going back to England, and I want to say to you that the Baptists of America have the opportunity of their history." This was said by a man who is not a Baptist, but who has observed from every standpoint the situation among the churches of this country.

Southern Baptists more than any others have this opportunity. They are generally evangelistic. They believe in old-time religion. They take no stock in any other sort. The problems that occupy the minds of the brethren of other sections have not begun to agitate us much. If there comes along a man with a blue pencil and scissors attempting to destroy our Bible, or any part of it, whether much or little, he is at once made to feel that there are "no vacancies," and that he might as well move on to other quarters. Southern Baptists believe the Bible from Genesis to Revelation; they believe in its doctrines; they believe a sinner out of Christ is lost to an endless hell. Hence, they are evangelistic. They have never gotten far enough away from the religion of the fathers to fail to appreciate exhortation as well as exegesis.

But with all our opportunities as Southern Baptists there is a serious weakness. We have the evangelistic soil; we have the evangelistic spirit; but we need a better evangelistic organization. To be sure, this work is, and ought to be, under the direction of the churches, just as every other agency of the denomination is. It is our profound conviction that the supreme centers of evangelism are the churches.

But it is strange that Baptists, especially Southern Baptists, should so largely allow, by their own failure to provide otherwise, other denominations to conduct in their territory the great revivals of the past few years. Of course we all thank God for what has been done, and we stand ready to co-operate with every movement that looks in the direction of soul winning, but why is it that Baptists who have the best natural advantages in matters of evangelism in this country have not been more honored of God in that great revival campaigns of our section? It seems that there is but one answer to this question, and that is: The lack of proper organization for the distinct work of evangelism.

Our Northern brethren have realized this, and hence they are now organized. They have a general evangelist in the field with a number of State evangelists co-operating with him. They are conducting evangelistic campaigns in the cities and factory sections, and even in the country. They are also conducting evangelistic institutes for ministers, laymen, and singers, and schools for training in this line of work. They also provide evangelistic literature, tracts, and books of various kinds. All this is being done by the evangelistic department of our denomination North. We thank God that they have taken hold of this problem, and pray for them the richest blessing of heaven.

But why should Southern Baptists not be better organized? We need it worse than the North. We have a larger number of people scattered over a larger territory, and they are of such a temperament as that organization would be more helpful.

It is true that our Home Mission Board has been doing a great deal of evangelistic work through its missionaries. They have done more during the last few years than ever before. The missionaries are generally selected with the view of soul-winning. It is true also that our State Mission Boards are doing a great deal in this line. Many of them have splendid evangelists giving all of their time to this work.

We have had communication with fourteen State secretaries co-operating with the Southern Baptist Convention, and we have found that twelve of these State boards employ general or special evangelists whom they direct. The States that have tried the plan of employing special evangelists are enthusiastic over the results obtained.

But this kind of organization is not fully meeting the needs. What we need is organization that will more vigorously push evangelism throughout all the Southern country. We need a general evangelist, with just as many associates as he can get for a part or all of their time—men who can push the evangelistic work in all the vast neglected territory of our Southland, from our great cities and rapidly growing cotton factory towns to the country sections. We need evangelistic organization providing conventions and training schools for evangelists, pastors, laymen, and singers, keyed to the idea of evangelism. We need to train our people so that they can take their proper place in the world's evangelism, as well as take the world for Christ. As it now is, much of our great talent is going to waste, or is being trained and utilized by other people.

What shall be done? There are those who think we ought not to have any new agency through which this important work is to be done; others think that a new agency is demanded, and still others think that it is a work that should be committed to the Home Mission Board. It seems, therefore, that some distinct step forward in this direction ought to be taken by this Convention; that a more aggressive evangelism is demanded. Hence, we recommend:

First, That the Convention instruct its Home Mission Board to create the Department of Evangelism, and that a general evangelist, with as many associates as practicable, be employed.

Second, That the Home Mission Board be requested to adopt such measures and methods as may be found necessary to give effectiveness to this department of the work.

Third, That in view of this advanced work our people be requested to increase their contributions by at least $25,000 for its support, and that the Home Board be instructed to take the necessary steps to raise this amount in addition to the amount needed for other work.

LEN. G. BROUGHTON, Chairman,
W. W. HAMILTON
A. J. S. THOMAS,
GEO. W. TRUETT,
W. M. VINES.

APPENDIX D

Shall the Atlanta Board Be Instructed to Employ Evangelists and to Call for an Extra $25,000 for Their Support?
By B. H. Carroll

(Speech Before the Southern Baptist Convention at Chattanooga, Tenn., Monday, 4:30 P.M., May 14, 1906.)[1]

Brother President: If a blind man would see a phenomenon, its properties must be sufficiently phenomenal to visually impress even his sightless orbs. If a deaf man would hear a discussion, it must be one of such clearness and power as to make him at least feel the vibrations of the thunders he cannot hear.

This deaf man came to the mass-meeting yesterday afternoon to hear, and, if need be, to participate in such a discussion on the evangelist report pending before this Convention. But his surprise was painful to learn that while the boys were permitted to take a swim on this subject, they were not allowed to go near the water. They must content themselves with a dry polish. They might indeed amuse themselves with academic discussions of vague abstractions and generalities, but as it was Sunday, if they ventured to approach the practical, concrete work of our Lord, recommended in the report, then *esto procul profani*!

---

[1] *Baptist Standard*, May 31, 1906, 1–2.

If it had not been so pitiful it would have been amusing to see such men of affairs, such doers of God's word, such exponents of practical Christian work, as occupied this platform yesterday afternoon, constrained by convention interdict to steer the big ships of their speeches away from the direct course leading to a definite port, and to merely circle around and lose themselves in befogged and uncharted seas.

It certainly was a sight to see such mighty engineers instructed: "You may get up steam and whistle as loud and as long as you please, but you are stopped from sawing logs."

Anyone who knows the great commoner from my own State could see how restive and embarrassed he was by the extraordinary restriction imposed. And thus the great opportunity for deliberation on a definite report passed away—swift and returnless.

Brother President, the Sabbath was made for man, and not man for the Sabbath, and therefore the Son of Man is Lord also of the Sabbath Day. It is lawful to do good on the Sabbath day. If we scruple not every year from ten thousand pulpits to discuss every phase of the reports of our three great boards, and to take up collections for the respective departments of work entrusted to them, it could not have been very far out of the way to discuss this report Sunday afternoon in a mass-meeting.

The work was strictly religious, it was the Lord's work, and as holy as the day. On account of these scruples, however, we now, without due deliberation, must, in a few cramped minutes, dispose by vote, of one of the mightiest and most far-reaching measures ever submitted to this body. And yet certain supreme antecedent questions must be answered before we can reach an intelligent decision. These questions are:

1. What is an evangelist as distinguished from other preachers?
2. Is it a scriptural office and intended for permanent service in the kingdom of God?
3. Are there in the Scripture records unmistakable examples of evangelists, whose lives and labors illustrate the work of this office?
4. What specific parts of the New Testament treat of this office, and tell us of the men who filled it, and the work they did?

5. From these Scriptures what are the peculiar functions of this office, and what the qualifications of the men who fill it?

6. Are there in Baptist history experiments on this line to which we may confidently appeal for justification in entertaining the recommendations of this report?

These antecedent questions having been fairly answered, we will have the office itself outlined by clear scriptural definition. From the same holy book, we will have before us living examples which illustrate it. Then, also, from our own history will stand out before us actual experiments that demonstrate the feasibility and profit of employing such men.

Patrick Henry said: "I have no lamp by which my feet are guided but the lamp of experience." It becomes a Christian to say, rather: "I have no lamp by which my feet are guided but the lamp of God's Word." But if to the Word we add also the experiment, then may we Know that our theory of the Word has justified itself in the fact.

The conservative men of this Convention will not be disposed to adopt any rash or ill-advised experiment on the grounds of mysticism or mere sentiment. Baptists delight to feel under their feet the impregnable rock of the Holy Scriptures. As this is to me no new question, I may venture to answer, in some fashion, the antecedent questions propounded, which unanswered bar the way to intelligent decision. To the law then, and to the testimony.

Foremost of all the passages in God's Word I cite the pregnant paragraph in the fourth chapter of the letter of the Ephesians, extending from the fourth verse to the sixteenth, inclusive. Here are set forth the great unities: One Lord, one faith, one baptism, one body, one spirit, one work. For the preservation of these unities our Lord Himself, when He ascended into Heaven, gave gifts unto men. These gifts were distinct and varied. But all had the same general object in view, and all were necessary to the complete attainment of that object. Five distinct gifts are here mentioned, namely, apostles, prophets, evangelists, pastors and teachers. And if the first two, whose credentials and powers were extraordinary, must cease with the completion of the canon of the Scriptures, and with the accrediting of the church and the laying of the foundations once for all (see 1 Cor

12th, 13th, 14th chapters and Eph 2:20), certainly the other three must abide till the Master comes.

Apostles and prophets have fulfilled their mission, but evangelists, pastors, and teachers remain. These terms—apostles, prophets, evangelists, pastors, and teachers—are not rhetorical variations of the same idea. We are well able, from the Scriptures, to distinguish the evangelist from all the others. Evangelist and pastor, for example, mean not the same thing. A great evangelist may prove to be a poor pastor, and a great pastor may prove to be a poor evangelist. This is often seen. But it is scripturally true, and true in fact, that one man may be endowed with several gifts. Hence we sometimes find a great pastor, who is also a great evangelist when occasion calls him for the time being into that work.

In distinguishing we may drive down the first peg: The work of the pastor is local; the work of the evangelist is general. The pastor must mainly look after the one flock over which the Holy Ghost has made him bishop; the evangelist looks out over a larger field in which may be many churches and wide stretches of destitution without churches.

But the evangelist is not a free-lance, self-appointed to range at his own sweet will and for his own ends over boundless and unfenced pastures. He, too, as well as apostles and pastors, was set in the church (1 Cor 12:28). His work also must tend to preserve the holy unities. The mightiest excise of his power comes into play when for purposes of co-operation an effort is made to elicit, combine and wisely direct the energies and resources of many churches in great undertakings for the spread of the kingdom.

It would richly repay every member of this Convention to profoundly study this paragraph in the letter to the Ephesians. From it most clearly appear the objects of all the gifts: "And he gave some to be apostles, and some prophets, and some evangelists, and some pastors and teachers: for the perfecting of the saints, unto the work of ministering, unto the building up of the body of Christ, till we all attain unto the unity of the faith, and of the knowledge of the Son of God, unto a full-grown man, unto the measure of the stature of the fullness of Christ; that we may be no longer children, tossed to and fro and carried about with every wind of doctrine by the sleight of men, in craftiness, after the wiles of error, but speaking truth in love, may grow up in all things into him, who is the head, even

Christ, from whom all the body, fitly framed and knit together through that which every joint supplieth, according to the working in due measure of each several part, maketh the increase of the body unto the building up of itself in love."

Just here we may drive down another peg: The work of an evangelist is far more than merely holding protracted meetings. Soul-winning or soul-saving is a part indeed, but not all. See how much of it, in this passage, relates to the saint, to convert culture, to sound doctrine, to development of the church. But let us look next at scriptural examples. In Acts 21:8 we learn that Paul and his party were at Caesarea entertained in the home of Philip the Evangelist, who had been one of the seven Jerusalem deacons. The eighth chapter of Acts gives some account of his evangelical work in Samaria, in the desert towards Gaza and along the Mediterranean coastline up to Caesarea. The churches found there by Peter (Acts 9:23–43), and probably those found by Paul higher up this coast at Ptolemais and Tyre (Acts 21:3–7) were established by Philip. Samaria, therefore, the desert towards Egypt and all the eastern shore of the great sea, perpetuate the memory and fame of this mighty evangelist. Study the life of this truly great man. In Philip's case the soul-winning element predominates. But there is another illustrious example. Paul writes to Timothy (2 Tim 4:5): "Do the work of an evangelist." Here the context very clearly sets forth the nature of the work: "I charge thee in the sight of God, and of Christ Jesus, who shall judge the living and the dead, and by his appearing and his kingdom, preach the work, be urgent in season, out of season, reprove, rebuke, exhort with all long-suffering and teaching. For the time will come when they will not endure the sound doctrine; but, having itching ears, will heap to themselves teachers after their own lusts, and will turn away their ears from the truth, and turn aside unto fables." Compare this with these works of the first letter: "As I exhorted thee to tarry at Ephesus, when I was going into Macedonia, that thou mightest charge certain men not to teach a different doctrine, neither to give heed to fables and endless genealogies, which minister questionings rather than a dispensation of God which is in faith, so do I now," and "these things write I unto thee, hoping to come unto thee shortly; but if I tarry long, that thou mayest know how men ought to behave themselves in the house of God, which is the church

of the living God, the pillar and ground of the truth." From these passages
and their context, it will appear how much the evangelist had to do with
sound doctrine and church order. But his case is the more valuable from
the fact that Timothy was only one of many who, under Paul's directions,
were doing the work of an evangelist.

All that group of brilliant young men that constituted the staff of Paul
were evangelists, not pastors. What a galaxy of stars are here: Barnabas,
Mark, Luke, Silas, Timothy, Titus, Tichicus, Trophimus, Aristarchus, Eras-
tus, Epaphras, Gaius, Clement, Tertius, Jason, Sosipater, Justus, Crescens,
Epaphroditus, Achaicus, Stephanas, Fortunatus, Apollos, and many others,
were evangelists pure and simple. If matter went wrong at Ephesus he left
Timothy there to right them. For setting in order the affairs in Crete he left
Titus there.

The letters to Timothy and Titus were addressed to evangelists. Paul's
other letters bristle with references to evangelists and their work. His soul
ever leaps out to them. When away he yearns for their coming; when present his heart takes courage. Lonely in cold, polished Athens, he urges them
to rejoin him. Their coming to him at Corinth constrains him to speak out
more boldly. He writes: "At Troas I had no relief from my spirit, because
I found not Titus, my brother." And how he glories when Titus rejoins him
at Philippi with joyful tidings (2 Cor 7:13–14).

> Again we hear him: "I am glad of the coming of Stephanas and
> Fortunatus and Achaicus." And yet again: "Demas hath forsaken
> me, having loved this present world; Crescens has gone to Gala-
> tia; Titus unto Dalmatia; only Luke is with me; bring Mark to me;
> Erastus abode at Corinth; Trophimus have I left at Miletus sick."

Like a general surveying a hazardous battlefield or a widespread tacti-
cal campaign, his rapid messages send them here, there, and yonder. Here
a church is in disorder, there a mighty collection must be engineered, yonder a frightful heresy is spreading, and so he scattered them abroad to the
ends of the earth. Another time with lightning speed they are regathered
and massed in some great city, some Gibraltar of hell, some seat of Satan,
that can be conquered only by concentration and combination of power.

Ah, shall we never learn the economy and power of massing for the time being our forces and energies against some key position, some strategic point, where one victory means a thousand!

The secretary of our Home Board may dare to conduct the widespread and complicated campaign, entrusted to him, without evangelist coadjutors, but the apostle Paul would not so have dared.

Brethren, if you want a just conception of the office of an evangelist, study the story of Paul's companions as set forth in the Acts and the Epistles. That study will indeed emphasize the soul-winning feature of the evangelistic office, but, oh how much more than this will it disclose. Von Moltke might as well attempt to mobilize an army of a million men, transport them, feed them, clothe them, munition them, fight them without an efficient general staff as our Home Board can hope to fully elicit, combine and direct the mighty energies and forces of this Convention without evangelist coadjutors.

The necessity in our case is even greater, because we have no iron organization and must rely exclusively upon moral suasion and voluntary co-operation.

There remains of the antecedent questions only one: Are there in Baptist history experiments on this line that will justify our adoption of the recommendations of this report? In Texas, Brother president, this question is not debatable. It is res adjudicate. For three years I urged our State Board to employ mighty evangelists, whatever the cost. The appointment of the first one was only secured when I became personally responsible for his salary. Now we would not dream of conducting a great campaign without them. Out there we know what an evangelist is. An eccentric old gentleman of Georgia was accustomed to frequent the office of a great jurist. One day he said: "Judge, I've struck a hard word here in the paper. I don't know how to call it, nor what it means." "Spell it out," said the Judge. "Well, it's P-h-e (fe) n-o (no) m-c (me) n-a (nar) –Phe-no-me-na—now, what is that?" "You are one," said the judge. So if you ask, What is an evangelist, my reply is, The chairman of this evangelist committee—he is one.

(The speaker here refers to George W. Truett, who was not chairman of the committee.)

I may not becomingly refer to cases in your States, with which you are more familiar than I am. But I can cite cases in Texas. Every year, with us, we bottom our great enterprises upon the power of evangelism. The mighty streams of Texas contributions flow from rocks smitten by the rod of the evangelist. We have long since ceased to expect money from cold-steel agencies. Dry bones do not live till they are breathed upon by the omnific spirit. The mighty contributions from the persecuted and poverty-stricken Philippians did not come until "they first gave themselves to the Lord."

The sense of the responsibility of stewards, the consecration of self and all one has to the service of the Lord must precede intelligent, sufficient and loving contribution. When a man, sir, comes before the rich, not as a fawning beggar, but as an evangelist, instructed by the apostle of our Lord, "Put them on oath before God that are rich in this present world, that they be not high-minded, nor have their hope set on the uncertainty of riches, but on God, who giveth us richly all things to enjoy; that they do good, that they be rich in good works, that they be ready to sympathize, willing to contribute, laying up in store for themselves a good foundation against the time to come, that they may lay hold on the life which is life indeed"—when he stands there with streaming eyes and says, "I am nothing, count me as less than nothing, but O, rich man, I lay a Lazarus at thy gate; yea, in this care our own Lord Himself knocks at thy door of plenty, footsore, weary, cold, hungry, naked, shelterless"—then the rock rends and the fountain of contribution is unsealed, it leaps, it sparkles, it sings, it outflows.

It is worth a trip across a continent to attend one Texas evangelist meeting. Every year we have them. Our strongest men gather at them and co-labor and pray. Allow me to tell you of the Sky-Pilot of Madera Canyon. Far west in Texas, where the Sunset and Texas & Pacific Railways begin to converge toward junction at Sierra Blanca, there midway between the converging lines, in the Madera Mountains, in a narrow canyon, once the stronghold of the Comanche Indians, from which in my boyhood we vainly tried to drive them, there every year the cattlemen of the West gather from far and near. The tent of Salvation is stretched on the site of the wigwam, and "Jesus, Lover of My Soul," supplants the warwhoop. From Boston, from Chicago, from Oklahoma, Arizona, New Mexico, from Monterey and Chihuahua of Old Mexico, from points on the Texas & Pacific intermediate between Dallas and El Paso, from the stations on the Sunset between San Antonio and Sierra Blanca they come. Great trains of wagons and hacks and horses, from all the big ranches within a radius of 100 miles converge to the focus, lighting up the mountain sides with their campfires and breaking the eternal silence of nature or competing with the howls of coyotes by their songs making melody in the night.

Stockmen worth millions gather on the boulders with their cowboys and hold their prayer meetings. Oh, ye men of cities with stilted services, you should hear these prayers. And then the preaching, so direct, so tender, so full of faith. Behold one scene. A group of cowboys have ridden 200 miles to be present half a day. We meet them: "Have you come to be saved?" "Sure thing!" they reply. "But it must be done mighty quick; we start home at daylight." One service is sufficient. They hear, we pray, they are saved. That same night the whole camp gathers where we have dammed up the mountain stream; 1500 feet high on either hand the precipitous sides of the canyon overhang. The full moon, in the meridian at midnight, looks down and glasses itself in the baptismal waters which catch its sheen and ripple with smiles at its image. As ancient Israel responded to the blessings and curses of the law from Ebal to Gerizim, so our choir, distributed on the opposing mountain sides, throw back and forth to each other the paeans of salvation while we baptize them. And the mountain stream, in which trout yet leap and Indian maidens bathed not long ago, that stream becomes the monument, as its waters part, that carries up stairways of starlight and moonlight this story of hope to the disembodied saints in heaven. Oh, spirits of the just made perfect, ye shall not wait forever for glorification; there shall be a resurrection of the dead! Years after such a meeting you may secure contributions in thousands by a word.

We mass the forces and hold similar meetings in rich, blackland districts, long-frozen spiritually by the death-chilling spirit of Anti-nomianism and anti-missionism. In the glowing fervor of spiritual power, the frost-bound souls are thawed, and where once were suspicion and gangrene and do-nothingism, now are words of cheer and hands of help for the work of the Convention.

I was the honored guest of a rich man, who more than once had extended sympathy and help to the cause I represented. He is a great man of affairs. His mind, absorbed in mighty enterprises, he found little time for spiritual things. "My friend," said I, "if you ever thought well of me, and now would be food to yourself, drop all your business; get up a camping outfit; start tomorrow with your family and friends to the Palo Pinto camp meeting. Stay there to the final benediction. And if your soul is not overwhelmed with a blessing I will never prescribe for you again." He went. He stayed. He has not yet found places to store away all the rich blessing God showered upon him.

Brethren, is it sin to love this Southland more than other lands? From the haze of her great, smoky mountains to her tidewater districts on gulf and ocean, may not all of it be very dear to us without disparagement of other lands? It is a battle-scarred cemetery of memory and tears—a land of sorrows. Barred out from many former roads of ambition and promotion, cloud-covered with imminent future hazards, it is yet God's resurrection country, land of destiny and of glorious opportunity, habitat of sound doctrine and home of revivals; shall we not make it the world's vanguard of pure and undefiled religion, the firing line of world-wide evangelism?

If, indeed, like Judea of old, this land has a mission of religion that shall touch eternal shores, who of us would not "live and die for Dixie?"

In that direction points this report. I could wish indeed to recast some of its verbiage if time permitted recommitment. But may we not take it as it is? The root of the matter is in it. Following its index finger lies the highway of usefulness for the Atlanta board. The necessity for that board is a thousandfold greater now than when this Convention was organized in 1845. Carry out the provisions of that report wisely, and this board can raise a half million dollars annually as easily as this Convention could adopt a perfunctory and innocuous resolution. Let us give the report a rousing, unanimous endorsement. The bedrock of Scripture underlies it. Experience demonstrates its wisdom and feasibility. If the Home Board may employ any man, it may employ evangelists. Altogether, then, with a ring, let us support this measure. If I were the secretary of this board I would come before this body in humility and tears and say: "Brethren, give me evangelists. Deny not fins to things that must swim against the tide, nor wings to things that must fly against the wind."

(Note: This speech is dictated as recalled by memory. Some things said, or as they were said, have doubtless escaped me. In other things I have followed the notes of the speech, and so introduce some things not said or said somewhat differently. In many cases, it is a verbatim reproduction—in all things the substance. One great point was overlooked in the hurry of the speech, and this, as I have learned, called forth a solitary protest. If I knew the brother I would write to him. From reports I gather that he was troubled lest the independence of the churches would be infringed by this kind of evangelism. The explanation is very simple. Paul had apostolic authority to send an evangelist to a church with or without its consent. We have no such authority. The concurrence of the church is essential in our case. In our Texas work we never assume to inflict an evangelist on an unwilling church. The heart of our work is voluntary co-operation.)

Selected Bibliography

Southern Baptist History

Ammerman, Nancy Tatom. *Baptist Battles: Social Change and Religious Conflict in the Southern Baptist Convention*. New Brunswick, NJ: Rutgers University Press, 1990.

Baker, Robert A. *The Story of the Sunday School Board*. Nashville: Convention Press, 1966.

Barnes, W. W. *The Southern Baptist Convention 1845–1953: The First History of a Great Denomination*. Nashville: Broadman Press, 1954.

Boylan, Anne M. *Sunday School: The Formation of an American Institution 1790–1880*. New Haven, CT: Yale University Press, 1988.

Burroughs, P. E. *Fifty Fruitful Years 1891–1941: The Story of the Sunday School Board of the Southern Baptist Convention*. Nashville: Broadman Press, 1941.

Lawrence, J. B. *History of the Home Mission Board*. Nashville: Broadman Press, 1958.

McBeth, H. Leon. *The Baptist Heritage: Four Centuries of Baptist Witness*. Nashville: Broadman Press, 1987.

Scarborough, L. R. *A Modern School of the Prophets*. Nashville: Broadman Press, 1939.

Wilbanks, C. E. *What God Hath Wrought Through C. E. Matthews*. Atlanta: Home Mission Board and Southern Baptist Convention, 1957.

Southern Baptist Theology

Ashcraft, Morris. *Christian Faith and Beliefs*. Nashville: Broadman Press, 1984.

Autrey, C. E. *The Theology of Evangelism*. Nashville: Broadman Press, 1966.

Boyce, James P. *Abstract of Systematic Theology*. Philadelphia: Christian Gospel Foundation, 1887.

Bush, L. Russ, and Tom J. Nettles. *Baptists and the Bible*. Chicago: Moody Press, 1980.

Conner, Walter T. *Christian Doctrine*. Nashville: Broadman Press, 1937.

———. *The Gospel of Redemption*. Nashville: Broadman Press, 1945.

Dominy, Bert. *God's Work of Salvation*. Layman's Library of Christian Doctrine. Nashville: Broadman Press, 1986.

Draper, James T., Jr. *Authority: The Critical Issue for Southern Baptists*. Old Tappan, NJ: Fleming H. Revell Company, 1980.

George, Timothy, ed. *Baptist Theologians*. Nashville: Broadman Press, 1990.

Graves, J. R. *Old Landmarkism: What Is It?* Texarkana: Baptist Sunday School Committee, 1928.

Hamblin, Robert L., and William H. Stephens. *The Doctrine of Lordship*. Nashville: Convention Press, 1990.

Hobbs, Herschel H. *The Baptist Faith and Message*. Nashville: Convention Press, 1984.

———. *What Baptists Believe*. Nashville: Broadman Press, 1964.

Hogue, C. B. *The Doctrine of Salvation*. Nashville: Convention Press, 1978.

Humphreys, Fisher. *Thinking about God: An Introduction to Christian Theology*. New Orleans: Insight Press, 1974.

Moody, Dale. *The Word of Truth: A Summary of Christian Doctrine Based on Biblical Revelation*. Grand Rapids: Eerdmans, 1983.

Mullins, E.Y. *The Christian Religion in Its Doctrinal Expression*. Philadelphia: The Judson Press, 1959.

The Proceedings of the Conference on Biblical Inerrancy 1987. Nashville: Broadman Press, 1987.

Turner, J. Clyde. *These Things We Believe*. Nashville: Convention Press, 1956.

Southern Baptist Methods

Autrey, C. E. *Basic Evangelism*. Grand Rapids: Zondervan, 1979.

Barnette, J. N. *The Place of Sunday School in Evangelism*. Nashville: Convention Press, 1945.

Bisagno, John R. *The Power of Positive Evangelism: How to Hold a Revival*. Nashville: Broadman Press, 1968.

Burroughs, P. E. *How to Win to Christ*. Nashville: The Sunday School Board of the Southern Baptist Convention, 1934.

Cathey, Bill V. *A New Day in Church Revivals*. Nashville: Broadman Press, 1984.

Chaney, Charles L. *Church Planting at the End of the Twentieth Century*. Wheaton, IL: Tyndale House, 1984.

Criscoe, Arthur H., and Leonard Sanderson. *Decision Time: Commitment Counseling*. Nashville: The Sunday School Board of the Southern Baptist Convention, 1991.

Dobbins, Gaines S. *Evangelism According to Christ*. New York: Harper & Brothers, 1949.

Drummond, Lewis A. *Leading Your Church in Evangelism*. Nashville: Broadman Press, 1975.

Fish, Roy J. *Giving a Good Invitation*. Nashville: Broadman Press, 1974.

Flake, Arthur. *Building a Standard Sunday School*. Nashville: The Sunday School Board, 1934.

————. *The True Functions of the Sunday School*. Nashville: The Sunday School Board of the Southern Baptist Convention, 1936.

Frost, J. M. *The School of the Church*. New York: Fleming H. Revell Company, 1911.

Hadaway, C. Kirk, Francis M. DuBose, and Stuart A. Wright. *Home Cell Groups and House Churches*. Nashville: Broadman Press, 1987.

Hamilton, Thad. *Special Evangelistic Events*. Atlanta: Home Mission Board, 1991.

Hamilton, William Wistar. *Bible Evangelism*. Atlanta: Home Mission Board, 1921.

Hemphill, Ken, and R. Wayne Jones. *Growing an Evangelistic Sunday School*. Nashville: Broadman Press, 1989.

Hogue, C. B. *Love Leaves No Choice*. Waco, TX: Word Books, 1977.

Johnson, Ron, Joseph E. Hinkle, and Charles M. Lowry. *OIKOS: A Practical Approach to Family Evangelism*. Nashville: Broadman Press, 1982.

Kendall, R. T. *Stand Up and Be Counted: Call for Public Confession of Faith*. Grand Rapids: Zondervan, 1984.

Leavell, Roland Q. *Evangelism: Christ's Imperative Commission*. Nashville: Broadman Press, 1951.

————. *The Romance of Evangelism*. New York: Fleming H. Revell Company, 1952.

————. *Winning Others to Christ*. Nashville: The Sunday School Board of the Southern Baptist Convention Press, 1956.

Lewis, Larry L. *Organize to Evangelize: A Manual for Church Growth*. Nashville: Broadman Press, 1988.

Matthews, C. E. *A Church Revival*. Nashville: Broadman Press, 1955.

————. *Every Christian's Job*. Nashville: Convention Press, 1951.

————. *The Southern Baptist Program of Evangelism*. Rev. ed. Nashville: Convention Press, 1956.

McLarry, Newman R., ed. *Handbook on Evangelism*. Nashville: Convention Press, 1965.

Miles, Delos. *How Jesus Won Persons*. Nashville: Broadman Press, 1982.

————. *Introduction to Evangelism*. Nashville: Broadman Press, 1983.

Mullins, E. Y. *Talks on Soul Winning*. Nashville: The Sunday School Board of the Southern Baptist Convention, 1920.

Neighbour, Ralph W., Jr., and Cal Thomas. *Target-Group Evangelism*. Nashville: Broadman Press, 1975.

Ramsey, Howard, et al. *Continuing Witness Training: Pastor/Leader Manual*. Atlanta: Home Mission Board, 1982.

Revival Training Seminar Notebook. Atlanta: Home Mission Board, 1981.

Robinson, Darrell W. *Total Church Life*. Nashville: Broadman Press, 1985.

Rose, Larry L., and C. Kirk Hadaway. *The Urban Challenge*. Nashville: Broadman Press, 1982.

Sanderson, Leonard. *Personal Soul-Winning*. Nashville: Convention Press, 1958.

Sanderson, Leonard, and Ron Johnson. *Evangelism for All God's People*. Nashville: Broadman Press, 1952.

Scarborough, L. R. *With Christ After the Lost*. Rev. ed. Nashville: Broadman Press, 1990.

Schweer, G. William. *Personal Evangelism for Today*. Nashville: Broadman Press, 1984.

Sisemore, John T. *The Ministry of Visitation*. Nashville: Broadman Press, 1954.

Streett, R. Alan. *The Effective Invitation: A Practical Guide for the Pastor*. Old Tappan, NJ: Fleming H. Revell Company, 1984.

Wright, C. Thomas, M. Karin Robertson, and Barbara O. McGahey. *WIN School Teacher's Manual: A Lay Evangelism Strategy*. Atlanta: Home Mission Board, 1992.

Periodical and Journal Articles

Baptist History and Heritage: Bold Mission Thrusts in Baptist History 14, no. 1 (January 1979).

Baptist History and Heritage: Evangelism in Southern Baptist History 22, no. 1 (January 1987).

Baptist History and Heritage: Sunday Schools in Southern Baptist History 18, no. 1 (January 1983).

Clemmons, William B. "The Contribution of the Sunday School to Southern Baptist Churches." *Baptist History and Heritage: Sunday Schools in Southern Baptist History* 18, no. 1 (January 1983): 31-43.

Guy, Cal. "A Response: Evangelism and Missions." *Southwestern Journal of Theology* 28, no. 3 (Summer 1986): 29–32.

Johnson, Ron. "Where Are Southern Baptists with Evangelism?" *The Quarterly Review* 51, no. 1 (October–December 1990): 18–24.

Kelley, Chuck. "A Theological-Historical Look at Revivalism in the SBC." *Search* 20, no. 3 (Spring 1990): 29–37.

Parrot, Jack. "The Evangelism Question." *Search* 20, no. 3 (Spring 1990): 38–40.

Thompson, C. Lacy. "Who Are These People Called Southern Baptists?" *Baptist Message* 106, no. 28 (July 18, 1991): 1–7.

Unpublished Dissertations and Projects

Hamilton, Todd Condell. "William Wistar Hamilton: His Leadership Characteristics Compared with Leadership Principles Proposed by Tead, Titus, Ross, and Hendry." Ed.D. diss., New Orleans Baptist Theological Seminary, 1965.

Johnson, Ronald Wayne, "An Evaluation of the Home Mission Board Programs of Evangelism in Local Churches." D.Min. diss., The Southern Baptist Theological Seminary, 1988.

Jumper, George Robin. "An Investigation of the Concept of Committing to Christ as Lord in Conversion in Selected Southern Baptist Convention Gospel Presentations." Ph.D. diss., New Orleans Baptist Theological Seminary, 1990.

Kelley, Charles S., Jr. "An Investigation of the Changing Role of the Revival Meeting in the Southern Baptist Program of Evangelism, 1947–1980." Th.D. diss., New Orleans Baptist Theological Seminary, 1983.

Langlois, John N. "A Study of Roland Q. Leavell's Concept of Evangelism." Th.D. diss., New Orleans Baptist Theological Seminary, 1972.

Wilton, Donald John, "A Critical Investigation of Charles Everett Matthews' Concepts of Evangelism and an Assessment of His Impact upon the Southern Baptist Program of Evangelism." Th.D. diss., New Orleans Baptist Theological Seminary, 1986.

General Works

Bellah, Robert N., et al. *Habits of the Heart: Individualism and Commitment in American Life*. New York: Harper & Row, 1985.

Engel, James F. *Contemporary Christian Communications: Its Theory and Practice*. Nashville: Thomas Nelson, 1979.

Frankl, Razelle. *Televangelism: The Marketing of Popular Religion*. Carbondale: Southern Illinois University Press, 1987.

Name Index

Subject Index

Scripture Index

Genesis
1:31 *164*
3:1–7 *127*
3:8 *138*
3:8–9 *127*
3:12 *139*
3:15 *127*
3:17–19 *139*
12:1–3 *128*

Exodus
11:1–5 *129*
12:12–30 *129*

Deuteronomy
29:29 *126*

Joshua
24:15 *55*

1 Kings
18:21 *55*

2 Kings
23:1–3 *55*

Ezra
10:1–5 *55*
10:7–12 *55*

Psalms
19:1 *164*

Proverbs
14:12 *164*

Isaiah
53 *129*
53:6 *137*

Jonah
3:5 *55*

Matthew
4:19 *56, 129, 156*
5:13–14 *187*
5:29–30 *140*
6:33 *164*
7:21 *163*
9:35–38 *157*
9:37–38 *203*
10:16–20 *153*
12:30–32 *154*
12:46–50 *149*
24:14 *197*
25:41 *140*
25:46 *140*
28:18–20 *xv, 130, 171*

Mark
1:15 *164*
8:38 *62*
9:42–43 *140*
10:15 *218*
10:17–27 *149*
10:45 *150*
16:15 *130*

Luke
2:49 *150*
2:52 *148*
3:7–14 *55*
4:1 *148*

5:27–28 *56*
10:29–37 *145*
13:3 *162*
15 *130*
15:1–2 *149*
16:19–31 *140*
19:10 *127, 150*
24:44–49 *130*

John
1:1 *148, 163*
1:6–8 *130*
1:12 *130, 163*
1:14 *148, 163*
1:36 *129*
1:40–45 *129*
3:1–21 *149*
3:3 *142, 154, 163*
3:6 *154*
3:16 *151, 154, 161–64,
  209*
3:16–17 *163*
3:18 *162–63*
3:36 *140, 162*
4 *215*
4:7–30 *74*
4:35–38 *203*
5:24 *163*
8:1–11 *149*
10:10 *142, 163*
10:27–28 *144*
14:3 *163*
14:6 *163*
14:16 *152*
16:7–11 *153*
16:8 *154*
16:9–11 *154*